More
Bread
Machine
Magic

Also by the Authors

Bread Machine Magic

The Bread Machine Magic Book of Helpful Hints,
Revised and Updated

More Bread Machine Magic

More than 140 New Recipes
from the Authors of *Bread Machine Magic*
for Use in all Types and Sizes of Bread Machines

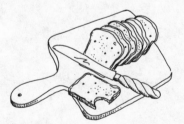

LINDA REHBERG · LOIS CONWAY
ILLUSTRATIONS BY DURELL GODFREY

ST. MARTIN'S GRIFFIN ⚞ *New York*

Design by Bonni Leon-Berman

Library of Congress Cataloging-in-Publication Data

Rehberg, Linda.
    More bread machine magic / Linda Rehberg, Lois Conway.—1st St. Martin's Griffin ed.
        p.   cm.
    Includes index.
    ISBN 0-312-16935-3
    1. Bread.   2. Automatic bread machines.   I. Conway, Lois.
II. Title.
TX769.R385   1997
641.8'15—dc21   97-20540
                                                                      CIP

10 9 8 7 6 5 4 3

This book is dedicated to our children . . .
Eric, Elliot, Michael,
and Shayna . . . with love.

Contents

Acknowledgments

Behind every well-tested cookbook is a bevy of discriminating taste testers. As usual, we've been blessed with many wonderful family members and friends who forfeited their diets for the cause. Thank you, family: Dennis and Jim, our great husbands, who know so much about baking breads and writing cookbooks now that they could probably write a few of their own; Lois's parents, Morris and Evelyn; her sister, Anita; the Conway children and grandchildren: Elliot and Sara, Eric, Michael, Stephanie, Garrett, Andrew, and Allyson; Linda's daughter, Shayna, and son-in-law, Ken; and her family: De De, Debbie, Shareen, Rick, Bill, Anne, and Christin. Thank you, kind-hearted friends: Gary and Rita Godshalk; Madelyn and Bob Robenhymer; Denise, Chris, and the operators at Chequers Beauty Salon, who always did a better job when they were tasting bread; Doug Wilks, who was often "paid" with a loaf; Jorge Felipe, who gratefully took so many test loaves off our hands; Artie Hernandez Nelson; Joan Stewart, who risked permanently ruining her taste for Italian panettone; Elaine Johnson, Mike Mosgrove, John Cruz, Linda Shackelford, Kathy Bearden, Karen Rockafellor, Connie Goff, Pam Elizaga, Sue Schoenleben, Sharon Kull, Nancy Caras, Tony Bechtold, Sue Wise, Andrea Littlejohn, Carol Roskos, Debbie Sather, Brenda Kuhn, Sandy Kelly, Eunice Heideman, Linda Clark, and the dedicated teachers of Bernardo Heights Middle School for all their helpful feedback. A special thanks to Delores Horn, who not only contributed recipes but did some valuable research for us, and to Julie Tyor, who provided such wonderful moral support.

We appreciate the readers of our first book for their gentle, and sometimes not-so-gentle, coaxing to write another *Bread Machine Magic*. It's been a long journey with too many side trips, but at last it's done.

Our very special thanks and online hugs {{}} to those wonderful friends we've met via the modem: Liz, an innovative cook who runs the Cooking Club on America Online, whose idea for a bread chat has evolved into an exciting meeting place for all bread machine bakers . . . thanks, Liz, for all your support; Linda Caldwell, her counterpart on Prodigy, who has breathed new life into "The Bread Board" with her gracious good humor and skillful handling of difficult situations. Her notes always wear a smile. Not to be overlooked . . . Kat and Elaine, you make the AOL Bread Chat the best place to be on Tuesday nights. Special warm hugs to Corgi,

Irene, Jill, Helen, Debby, Kim, and all the many people who visit the AOL Bread Chat and as audience members are the impetus to keep it going when there are too many machines and too little time. We thank Reggie and Jeff Dwork for their tireless work to bring bread machine baking to the world via the Internet with their Bread Digest list. Last, but never least, a warm, floury hug from both of us to Bev Janson, who has a generosity of spirit that knows no bounds. She's helped with the AOL Bread Chat, has contributed recipes and many suggestions to this book, and has become Lois's closest friend across the miles, even though they've never met.

We both wish to express our gratitude to the superb staff at the Great News Cooking School in Pacific Beach, California, as well. They are enthusiastic supporters and make teaching there a delight.

For a third time, we send our many thanks to Glenna Vance of Universal Foods, who continually shares her knowledge of not only bread but human nature. It's so comforting to have a friend like her who's always there when we need her.

We are also indebted to all those who contributed recipes and recipe ideas for this book: Judy Berney, Linda Caldwell, Marlene Casmaer, Camille Cox, Lynn Dominguez, Cecelia Fleming, Delores Horn, Bev Janson, Jerry Lovelady, Annie Miner, Eileen Shaughnessy, Molly Spradley, Kat Tarbet, and the kind folks at Pillsbury Company, Toastmaster, and King Arthur Flour. Each one is a classic! An extra thanks goes to George Hilley, who patiently maintained his half of our correspondence with great good humor.

We enjoyed working with Joy Chang, our enthusiastic and very patient editor, who suffered our being "a tad behind schedule" but continued to have faith in us. We miss her but our loss is Harvard's gain. Her assistant, Tara Schimming, answered our endless questions and still kept her sanity. Thanks, Tara! A very special thanks to our new editor, Marian Lizzi, who came in off the bench and saved the game. Thanks for going to bat for us, Marian!

We end with a most appreciative "thank you" to all the bread machine manufacturers for making it possible to test all these recipes. Getting to meet the people behind the scenes has given us a new appreciation and respect for the hard-working men and women who keep this industry alive.

Preface

We didn't have to think long and hard about a name for this book because our objective was to pick up where we left off four years ago when our first cookbook, *Bread Machine Magic,* was published. This is a cookbook very similar to our first one with an emphasis on good, fairly simple, well-tested recipes. There is one major difference, though . . . this book was written by two much more experienced bread bakers. We've filled the pages with new hints, new techniques, new ingredients, and new recipe sizes.

When we set out to write this cookbook, we made a pledge that we would only include recipes we were wild about and recipes that tested well with friends and family. Dozens of good-but-not-great recipes fell by the wayside. What remains is *More Bread Machine Magic.* We hope you will find many new "favorites" among these recipes. We encourage you to try ALL OF THEM! Several of the "superstar" recipes give no hint of their stellar status by name or description. We leave you the fun of finding them.

If you're a novice at bread machine baking, we want to welcome you to the world of bread baking made easy. Is it really as easy as tossing a few ingredients into a pan, pushing "Start," and walking away? Not quite, but once you learn the idiosyncrasies of your particular bread machine, a few basic facts, and how to judge your dough by a quick peek and a pinch, it will soon become second nature to you. We think you'll find the helpful hints in our first chapter enough to get you off to a very good start.

If you're a bread baker from way back in search of more tried-and-true recipes, we welcome you to these pages, also. You're probably familiar with the hints in our first chapter, but there may be one or two you've missed. Like us, you consider the dough cycle the "fun cycle." We have many dough-cycle recipes sprinkled throughout these chapters for you and a few that will challenge your bread baking skills. If you also love baking bread so much that you always have too many leftover loaves on hand—as we do—we've included many recipes that recycle those "stragglers" into brand-new taste sensations. Here's your chance to sample British bread soup, Italian bread salad, and tropical bread pudding.

As more and more people purchase the larger two-pound machines, they ask for a cookbook that includes recipes for their machines. We've responded to those requests in this cookbook. For the first time, we list recipes for *small* (1-pound / 2 cups of flour), *medium* (1½-pound / 3 cups of flour), and *large* (2-pound / 4 cups of flour) machines.

Most of all, we've endeavored to maintain our reputation for thoroughly tested, great-tasting recipes that bake up well in most machines. This book was a long time in the writing, but we had great fun testing! Now we extend the invitation to you . . . go have some fun with that marvelous machine of yours, push it to the limits, try things you've never attempted before. Let your creative impulses out. Experiment with our recipes and make them your own.

· Feeling whimsical? Bake a batch of dog bones for your trusty companion.

· You say you've never used the dough cycle before? Start easy with some dinner rolls or a pizza dough.

· Call a friend and bake bagels together.

· Bored with your normal routine? Start a sourdough starter and let it lead you into a whole new bread baking experience.

· Be adventurous. Try a bread from a foreign land.

· Spirits at low ebb? Give yourself a hug, then bake one of our chocolate breads.

· Kids bored? Call the children into the kitchen and turn them loose to bake pretzel bread or bread sticks, or whatever their little hands feel like fashioning. Bread baking can be a fabulous creative outlet for them and you may discover a future chef, artist, or architect in the making!

· Take coffee cakes or sweet rolls to share with coworkers or neighbors.

· Don't forget a sick friend or elderly relative. Sometimes a slice of warm, homemade bread can be heaven-sent.

You get the picture . . . put that bread machine of yours to good use. A sack of flour, a packet of yeast, a little of this and a little of that, and you're all set. Go have some fun and then share it with others!

Linda Rehberg and Lois Conway
February 3, 1997
San Diego, California
www.breadmachinemagic.com

I
Tips for Baking
the Perfect Loaf

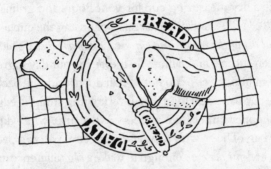

WE'D LIKE TO PUT IN A WORD about what qualifies as "the perfect loaf." Over the years, we've observed that many people consider their bread a success merely if it's tall . . . a "lid-thumper," as we call it. Let us tell you that we've had many a tall bread that was disappointing. They were full of air, the texture was coarse and crumbly, they lacked flavor, mouth appeal, and fell apart when sliced. So, height isn't everything! We say this so you won't feel as deflated as your bread if you bake up a loaf that doesn't reach the top of the pan. It can still taste superb! Treat yourself to a hearty, authentic European bread from a good bakery to see what we mean. Bottom line: When you're looking for the perfect loaf, consider taste and texture as well as height.

As far as bread baking hints and tips, we could fill a book with what we've learned over the past few years. In fact, we have. It's called *The Bread Machine Magic Book of Helpful Hints* and we went into great detail about every aspect of bread machine baking. We're pleased that many of the bread machine manufacturers use it as a handy reference book for their telephone operators. We hope you'll refer to it if you ever need a helping hand with your breads. Here we're just going to list a few crucial things we've found that contribute to good bread and will help steer you away from disasters and duds, plus a couple of new tricks we've learned since *The Bread Machine Magic Book of Helpful Hints* was published.

MEASURING

· Would you have guessed that proper measuring techniques and equipment would be first on the list of helpful hints? If you've ever baked bread by hand, you know you can be rather lackadaisical about measuring your ingredients. The same is *not* true when baking bread in a machine. It's very important to use accurate and proper measuring equipment and techniques. Sometimes as little as one tablespoon of liquid can make the difference between a great bread and a not-so-great one.

· Always use a dry measuring cup for your flours and grains. They normally come nested in ¼-, ⅓-, ½-, and 1-cup sizes. Avoid using the cup as a scooper. We'll repeat that: *Avoid using the measuring cup as a scooper!* This tip alone can make the difference between success and failure. To measure your dry ingredients properly, gently spoon them into the cup (do not pack it down with the back of the spoon or tap the side of the cup to settle it) and then level it with a straight-edged knife or spatula. Why be a spooner rather than a scooper? Because, when dipping down into your canister or bag of flour with the measuring cup, you can pack in at least one extra tablespoon of flour *per cup,* enough to make a big difference in your final product. When people call us complaining that all their breads are too short, heavy, or dense, this is the first question we always ask them: "Do you scoop up your flour with your measuring cup?" Bet you can guess what their answer is!

· Use a plastic or glass liquid measuring cup for your liquids, set the cup on a flat surface and check the measurement at eye level.

· If a recipe calls for both oil and honey or molasses, measure the oil first. The honey or molasses will then slide easily off the tablespoon.

OBSERVING THE DOUGH

· Another secret for success, and one we feel ranks right up there with proper measuring, is taking time to judge the dough. We call it the "peek-and-pinch test." This is a must the first time you bake a new bread or when the atmosphere is quite humid or very dry. You're looking for a dough that forms a smooth, pliable ball after about 10 minutes of kneading. It will be slightly tacky to the touch. It shouldn't be crumbly. It shouldn't be sticky. It shouldn't leave traces of dough in the bottom of the pan as the mixing blade rotates. And it shouldn't be so stiff that the bread machine sounds like it's straining to knead it or about to stall. There are always exceptions but we let you know which recipes will produce the atypical dough. Just read the "blurbs" at the start of the recipe. By the way, rye bread doughs will normally be on the wet side so you need to allow for a moister dough in all rye bread recipes.

We usually give the dough the "peek-and-pinch test" after several minutes of kneading to look and feel for moisture as well as pliability. Some doughs can look perfect but have no give to them. Doughs that are stiff will invariably bake up into short, dense loaves. Think sensuous! What you're looking for is a dough that is warm, soft, alive, and makes you want to pull it out of the machine and work with it for hours because it feels so wonderful.

· Early in the kneading cycle is when you have a chance to make adjustments to your bread dough. If it looks and feels dry or stiff, add liquid 1 tablespoon at a time until it softens. It usually only takes 1 or 2 tablespoons to correct it, so give the liquid a chance to be fully absorbed before adding more. On the other hand, if the dough is too wet or limp, add flour 1 tablespoon at a time. Again, in most cases, it only takes a little to correct the problem.

· We've also gotten in the habit of grabbing a rubber spatula when we check on the dough. Invariably, there are clumps of unmixed flour clinging to the sides or corners of the bread pan. We gently push them down into the mixture, avoiding any contact with the mixing blade.

CLIMATE AND TEMPERATURE OF INGREDIENTS

· The climate can have a great impact on your breads. When it's dry, your flour is "thirsty" and may require a tablespoon or more extra liquid. When it's rainy or humid, you may have to add a little more flour to counteract the extra moisture in the air and in your flour.

· Hot, sunny days can cause breads to rise too high or too quickly and then collapse. Choose the cooler morning or evening to bake, if possible, or use chilled ingredients.

· Cold winter months arrive and suddenly people think something's wrong with their bread machines. Doughs turn sluggish, breads bake up 1 or 2 inches shorter. There's nothing wrong. Just try to place your bread machine in a warm location; avoid putting it next to a cold exterior wall or window. Warm all cold ingredients.

· For the optimum loaf, most manufacturers recommend having dry ingredients at room temperature and liquids warmed to approximately 80°F. We find microwaving cold milk or buttermilk for 30 to 60 seconds will do the trick (depending on the wattage of your microwave and the amount of liquid). Eggs can be immersed in warm water for a minute or two to take off the chill.

INGREDIENTS

· The breads baked in the machine call for bread flour rather than all-purpose flour. Bread flour contains the highest amount of gluten, which gives the bread its structure and height. Look for a bread flour that contains 4 grams of protein per ¼ cup of flour. Check the nutritional analysis on the bag for this information.

· All-purpose (bleached or unbleached) flour is fine to use in the dough-cycle recipes.

· Whole wheat flour contains less gluten than bread flour. Breads that contain a large percentage of whole wheat flour tend to be smaller and denser in texture. Since whole wheat flour is ground from the complete wheat berry, it contains natural oils, so store it in the refrigerator or freezer to prevent it from becoming rancid.

· Vital wheat gluten is an additive that gives bread extra strength and increased height. It's especially useful when baking heavy whole grain breads that need a boost. We list it as an optional ingredient in several of our recipes.

· Avoid using tap water, especially if it is hard water. The best water to use is bottled spring water. It contains all the minerals the yeast needs for peak performance.

· Fat (butter, margarine, shortening, and oil) adds tenderness and flavor to bread as well as acts as a preservative to keep the bread from turning stale rapidly. If you eliminate fat you'll lose some of these qualities in your bread. Applesauce will replace some of the moisture and help preserve the freshness.

· Salt enhances the flavor of your bread and has an important role in regulating the yeast's activity. You can reduce the amount in the recipes, but you shouldn't eliminate it entirely.

· Sugar provides food for the yeast, makes the bread more moist and tender, and delays the staling process, which dries out bread. It also helps the crust to brown. If you reduce the amount of sugar too much, your breads will be rather anemic and dry. If you add too much sugar, the yeast has too much to eat and turns sluggish. Picture those little yeasties sacked out on the couch after a Thanksgiving Day feast . . . that's about how lethargic they become.

· Use only large eggs in these recipes. One large egg is equivalent to a scant ¼ cup liquid.

· We recommend Red Star active dry yeast. All our recipes were tested with it. It's okay to use other brands of yeast, but you may need to adjust the amounts. In most breads you can substitute ½ teaspoon instant or quick-acting yeast per cup of flour, except for breads with extra risings, such as our French Bread Extraordinaire.

TOXIC SPICES

· Here's a little fact you may not be aware of, which will explain why some of your cinnamon breads are low risers. Sweet brown spices such as cinnamon, nutmeg, cloves, and allspice contain a compound that is toxic to yeast. Limit their amount to a scant ½ teaspoon per cup of flour. If you prefer a stronger cinnamon or spice flavor, use it in a filling or a topping.

SUBSTITUTIONS

We list a great many ingredient substitutions in *The Bread Machine Magic Book of Helpful Hints,* but here are the most common ones:

· You can substitute water, rice milk, soy milk, or juices for regular milk.

· Milks can be used interchangeably: whole, low-fat, 1%, or skim.

· If you're out of milk, substitute water and add ¾ to 1 tablespoon nonfat dry milk or powdered soy milk for every ¼ cup of water used.

· Substitute Saco powdered buttermilk for fresh. Add 1 tablespoon powdered buttermilk to the dry ingredients for every ¼ cup buttermilk you are replacing.

· Replace the fat in a bread recipe with an equal amount of puréed fruit such as unsweetened applesauce or commercial products such as Wonderslim. Reduce the recipe's liquid by an equal amount. (*Helpful hint:* To keep a supply of unsweetened applesauce always on hand, freeze it by the tablespoon in an ice cube tray. Pop the applesauce cubes out of the tray when frozen and store in a zipper-type storage bag in the freezer for future use.)

· You can substitute a scant ¼ cup water, ¼ cup liquid egg substitute, or 2 egg whites for 1 whole egg. There is also a very good product called Egg Replacer that works well in breads (see Sources, page 259).

· To date, there are no salt substitutes that have the right properties for use in baking breads, but you can substitute a "lite" salt which contains both potassium chloride and sodium, such as Morton's Lite Salt.

RAISIN/NUT CYCLE

· Some machines pulverize dried fruits and nuts if they're added at the beginning with the rest of the ingredients, so it's important to use the Raisin/Nut cycle to keep that from happening. We've found that pulverized raisins add too much extra sweetness to the loaf and prevent it from rising well.

· When the machine beeps that it's time to add the dried fruits or nuts, observe the dough first. If it seems a little dry or stiff, adding 1 tablespoon water at that point will help incorporate the extra ingredients.

· No Raisin/Nut cycle? Not to worry. If your machine doesn't pulverize dried fruits and nuts, you can add them in the beginning with the rest of the ingredients or during the rest period between the first and second kneading cycle. If your machine does mash them into nonexistence, consult the cycle timing chart in your manual, set a timer, and add them 5 minutes before the end of the second kneading cycle.

· You can also flour your raisins in advance and store them in the refrigerator to use when needed.

DOUGH ON THE TIMER SETTING

· Most machines don't allow you to use the timer for the dough cycle (which we think is a shame). There is a way to do it, however, as long as you're certain you'll be home in time. Rather than selecting the dough cycle, choose the Standard Bake cycle and set your timer for the bread to be completed 1½ hours after the time you need the dough (see Note). For example, if you want to make pizza some evening and would like the dough ready by 5:00 P.M., select the Standard Bake cycle, set the timer for the bread to be done at 6:30, and when the dough nears the end of its final rise, remove it from the bread pan before it begins to bake (turn off your bread machine, of course). (Note: Consult your manual. Some machines do not have a cool-down cycle and you'd want to set the timer for approximately 1 hour past the time you actually need the dough.)

· Is this setting the Delayed Bake timer for such and such a time too confusing when all you want is pizza dough ready by 5:00 Friday night? Here's another option: Just make your pizza dough 1, 2, even 3 days ahead of time, place it in an oiled bag in the refrigerator, and take it out when you arrive home Friday evening. Simple!

DINNER ROLLS AND SWEET ROLLS

· If you have a favorite bread recipe and would like to convert it into dinner rolls or sweet rolls, simply reduce the liquid by ⅛ cup and use one of our dinner or sweet roll recipes as a guideline.

TIPS FOR HIGH ALTITUDE BAKERS

· Reduce the amount of yeast by about one-third.
· Increase the salt by 25 percent.
· Add ½ to 1 tablespoon gluten per cup of flour.
· If the above solutions don't work on a particular loaf, try baking it on the Rapid Bake cycle.

JIFFY BREAD

· Here's a good one from our online friends Bev Janson and Linda Caldwell: Line up 5 or 6 zipper-type storage bags on the counter. Mark each with the name of your favorite bread and the amount of water and yeast required for that recipe. Fill each bag with the rest of the ingredients, seal, and place in the refrigerator or freezer. When you need a bread, allow the bag of ingredients to come to room temperature, toss the contents into your bread machine, add the water and yeast called for in the recipe, and you have bread in a jiffy! Yes, it's okay to add wet ingredients such as oil and honey to the bag . . . just bury them in the middle of the flour.

BREAD MACHINE MIXES

· Of course, we're partial to breads made from scratch, but at the same time, we feel there's a place for the mixes as well. For one thing, they're almost fool-proof, so they're a great way for the first-time bread machine baker to gain a little confidence. If you start out with a few successes, you're much more likely to get hooked on the fun and tolerate the occasional failures. When people come to us with concerns that their machines might be broken, the first thing we suggest is that they try a mix. That usually proves that all is well with their beloved bread machines. The bread machine mixes are also ideal for the Delayed Bake cycle. There's nothing that will spoil if it sits at room temperature for several hours. Best of all, there are now gluten-free bread machine mixes on the market for people who were forced to pay exorbitant prices for their special breads in the market (see Sources, page 259). So don't overlook those mixes on your grocery store shelves. Many are quite good.

A Tip for French Bread Bakers

· In our opinion, the very best French bread—the kind with the thin crust that crackles when you remove it from the oven—can only be obtained by using a clay or stoneware pot such as La Cloche. If you're serious about baking great French bread, this is a must! They're sold in gourmet cooking stores or see our Sources section (page 249). We also recommend our recipe for French Bread Extraordinaire (pages 19–20).

Tips for Whole Grain Bread Lovers

· For the best possible whole grain breads, you need to use freshly ground whole grain flours. Some health food stores carry it. Make sure it's only a day or two old for it can turn rancid quickly. If you're unable to find it there, check with a local bakery. If you're lucky, they will sell you some. Be sure and store whole grain flours in the refrigerator or freezer to prevent rancidity.

· Once you discover the superiority of freshly ground flour, you should consider purchasing a grain mill if you do a great deal of bread baking. Look for one that's easy to clean and not too noisy. (See Sources, page 249.) The KitchenAid mixers have a grinding attachment that we've heard works well, too.

Slicing and Serving the Bread

· If you plan to bake bread quite often, it's worth it to invest in a good bread knife. We prefer the serrated type. For slicing large quantities of bread, we use an electric knife. There are also fancy knives with guides to ensure even slices every time and slicing guides that hold the bread and do the same. We've listed a few in our Sources section (see page 249).

SERRATED KNIFE

Storage

· You can store bread, roll, or pizza dough in a lightly oiled zipper-type storage bag in the refrigerator for 2 to 3 days. Allow it to come to room temperature before shaping.

· Breads low in fat or breads that contain eggs will turn stale much sooner than other breads. It's best to eat them the same day or freeze them. Breads that are high in sugar or breads that contain honey, molasses, fruits, or vegetables will stay moist longer than other breads.

· We've found that storing bread in adjustable plastic bread boxes keeps it fresh longer than anything else we've tried. If you don't have those handy bread boxes, placing your bread in a sealed plastic bag works well, too. For longer storage, we recommend slicing the loaf, placing it in sealed freezer bags, and freezing it for up to a month. DO NOT STORE BREAD IN THE REFRIGERATOR. It will begin to dry out immediately.

· We give sources for the plastic bread boxes as well as storage bags and attractive gift bags in our Sources section (see page 259).

TROUBLESHOOTING

Common causes for short, dense loaves:

· The flour was scooped, not spooned into the measuring cup.
· The dough was too dry.
· Hard tap water was used. For best results use spring water or add 1 teaspoon vinegar or lemon juice to the water.
· Too many heavy extras such as raisins and nuts were added.
· All-purpose rather than bread flour was used.
· Cold weather, cold room, or machine against an exterior wall, window, or under an air conditioner.
· It was a whole grain recipe with little or no bread flour.
· The recipe was too high in fat and/or sugar. Limit these ingredients to 2 tablespoons per cup of flour.

Common causes for sunken loaves:

· The dough was too wet.
· The salt was omitted.
· The bread was baked at a high altitude.
· The bread rose too long. Try a Rapid Bake cycle.
· There wasn't enough gluten in the bread to hold its shape.
· Too much yeast.

Common causes for loaves that mushroom over the top of the pan:

· The dough was too wet.
· The recipe was too large for the pan.
· Too much yeast.
· An unusually hot day.

If you notice your dough is about to hit the top of the lid and it hasn't begun to bake yet, you can deflate it by poking it several times with a toothpick. It may not bake up into the most attractive loaf, but you'll save yourself much grief later on trying to scrub up after an overflow.

CYBERSPACE BREAD BAKING

· We urge you to join the high-tech bakers online either through services such as America Online or via an Internet server. There are so many wonderful bread bakers in cyberspace who are willing to lend a hand and share experiences. Check out our Web site at: www.breadmachinemagic.com for more information on our bread machine chats. We'd be lost without our online baking friends and we are always ready to welcome "newbies."

· There are many good Web sites and newsgroups for bread bakers on the Internet. There's also a very reputable online "newsletter" called the Bread Digest that we recommend. See our Sources section (page 259) for information on how to subscribe.

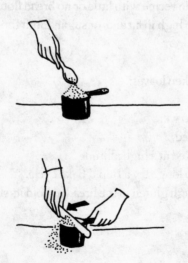

1½ teaspoons = ½ tablespoon
3 teaspoons = 1 tablespoon
4 tablespoons = ¼ cup
5⅓ tablespoons = ⅓ cup
16 tablespoons = 1 cup

⅛ cup = 2 tablespoons
⅜ cup = ¼ cup + 2 tablespoons
⅝ cup = ½ cup + 2 tablespoons
⅞ cup = ¾ + 2 tablespoons
1⅛ cup = 1 cup + 2 tablespoons
1 cup all-purpose flour = 130 grams = 4.59 ounces
1 cup bread flour = 135 grams = 4.76 ounces
1 cup whole wheat flour = 128 grams = 4.51 ounces
4 ounces grated cheese = 1 cup
1 stick butter = 8 tablespoons = ½ cup = ¼ pound
1 large egg = scant ¼ cup liquid

"Some people cast their bread upon the water and expect it to be returned to them toasted and buttered."

2
A Few Important Words about Our Recipes

THERE ARE SO MANY DIFFERENT MAKES and models of bread machines these days, with new versions appearing all the time, it's impossible to test recipes on every single one of them. Instead, we chose ten of the most popular bread machines—ones that we felt were a good representation but also differed from each other. In addition, we randomly tested our recipes on numerous other machines. If there were one or two machines that produced a dud, we let you know about it.

Our recipes are listed as "small," "medium," and "large." The small is the 1-pound loaf that contains approximately 2 cups flour. The medium is the 1½-pound loaf that uses about 3 cups flour. The large is the 2-pound loaf that calls for approximately 4 cups flour. One very important note about the large (2-pound) recipes: Not every "2-pound machine" had a bread pan large enough to accommodate a 2-pound recipe calling for 4 cups of flour. Wow, you should have seen some of our overflows! We suggest you measure the capacity of your pan if you own a 2-pound bread machine. In our testing, we found the pan had to hold at least 13 cups of water to be workable. (Note: Some horizontal pans work well even though they don't have quite that large a capacity. We didn't have the same overflow problems with them as we did with the vertical pans.) If you have a 2-pound machine with a bread pan that holds anything less than 13 cups of water, we suggest you *always* start with the medium-size recipe first. If it's a high-riser, you'll know not to tempt the fates by trying the large size. In fact, no matter what the capacity of your bread pan is, we strongly suggest that as a good, cautionary rule of thumb, ALWAYS START WITH THE MEDIUM-SIZE LOAF FIRST, RATHER THAN THE LARGE.

In many of our recipes, we recommend using a large baking sheet. We're particularly fond of the heavy 13×18-inch rimmed pans that are carried by the large warehouse clubs and restaurant supply stores. Here's another tip for you: If you want to make life simpler for yourself, cut a piece of Teflon pan liner to fit your pan and you'll never have to grease another baking sheet again!

You'll notice in several of our recipes we list vital wheat gluten as an optional ingredient. Because results can sometimes vary greatly from one machine to the next, we listed this optional ingredient when the bread just needed a little more "oooomph" in some bread machines but not all. We suggest trying the recipe first without the gluten. If it doesn't rise high enough or needs more body, cross out the word "optional," so you'll know next time to add the gluten.

Most of our recipes specify bread flour. It's important to use the higher-rising bread flour in the bread machine recipes. However, we use all-purpose flour for our coffee cakes, rolls, and most other dough recipes. We simply prefer the softer texture it gives those products. Feel free to substitute bread flour if you like.

Several of our recipes call for eggs. Use large-size eggs only.

We recommend Red Star active dry yeast in our recipes. We prefer the results it gives and we also enjoy the money saved by buying it in bulk at warehouse club stores. You can use a different yeast, but you may need to adjust the amount to compensate for the change.

We have listed ingredients in the order we feel they should be added to the machine, liquids first. If your bread machine manual recommends adding the yeast first, then simply start from the bottom of our ingredient list and work up.

To create "generic" recipes suited for all machines, we have given a range of liquids. As we state in each recipe, start with the least amount, observe the dough, and add the extra liquid 1 tablespoon at a time, if necessary. In time, you'll find that your particular machine uses the minimum or the maximum amount most of the time and you can automatically add that amount each time. It's still a good idea to peek at the dough and pinch it at least once during kneading anyway. The weather can always play tricks on you.

We don't give a range of liquid for our dough recipes because they need to be a little drier to hold their shape during baking. However, it's still a good idea to check the dough during the kneading cycle. Machines vary greatly in the consistency of the dough they produce. If the dough appears too limp, add flour a tablespoon at a time. If it's too dry and your machine is straining to mix it, add liquid a tablespoon at a time. The reason we do list a range of liquids in our sourdough recipes is because sourdough starters can be very thin like a cream soup or of medium consistency like a pancake batter or very thick like a muffin mix. The thinner your starter, the less liquid you're likely to need and vice versa.

We give a variety of baking cycle options at the end of most recipes. In case your machine doesn't have the recommended cycle, you can choose an alternate one from the list of optional cycles. Also, if a recipe doesn't bake up well in your machine, it's possible that trying it on a different cycle will improve your results. For instance, if the Standard Bake cycle on your machine is less than 3 hours from start to finish, heavier breads may not bake up quite as high. Switching to the longer Whole Wheat cycle will probably do the trick. Conversely, if your lighter loaves have a tendency to overflow the pan quite often or collapse, switch to a shorter cycle, i.e., from Whole Wheat to Standard Bake or from Standard Bake to Rapid Bake.

Don't overlook the "blurbs" at the beginning of each recipe. We often use them to emphasize an important step or ingredient.

If you find yourself skipping to the wrong-size recipe as you're adding ingredients to the bread pan, we've found that placing a large sticky note over the other two recipes solves the problem.

We have included a nutritional analysis at the end of each recipe to be used as a general guideline. The information was calculated on an average 1½-pound loaf containing fourteen ½-inch slices of bread.

Lastly, there are over 140 new recipes in this book and many of them have creative suggestions attached, giving you countless new variations to try as well. To aid you in locating a recipe quickly we have placed them in alphabetical order within each chapter.

"A toast to bread for without bread
there would be no toast."

3
White
Breads

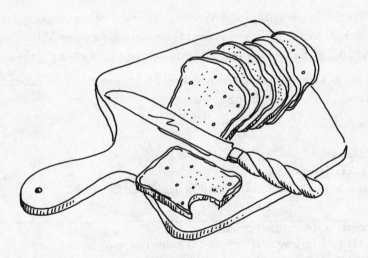

Antique White Bread

This is bread like Grandma used to bake. Cut it into thick slices while still warm and grab some while you can. A loaf of this bread certainly won't last long enough to become an antique!

	SMALL LOAF	MEDIUM LOAF	LARGE LOAF
WATER	⅝ to ¾ cup	1 to 1⅛ cups	1⅜ to 1½ cups
OIL	2 tablespoons	3 tablespoons	¼ cup
SALT	¾ teaspoon	1 teaspoon	1½ teaspoons
SUGAR	2 tablespoons	3 tablespoons	¼ cup
BREAD FLOUR	2 cups	3 cups	4 cups
RED STAR BRAND ACTIVE DRY YEAST	1½ teaspoons	1½ teaspoons	2 teaspoons

I. Place all ingredients in bread pan, using the least amount of liquid listed in the recipe. Select Medium Crust setting and press Start.

2. Observe the dough as it kneads. After 5 to 10 minutes, if it appears dry and stiff or if your machine sounds as if it's straining to knead it, add more liquid 1 tablespoon at a time until dough forms a smooth, pliable ball that is slightly tacky to the touch.

3. After the baking cycle ends, remove bread from pan, place on cake rack, and allow to cool 1 hour before slicing.

CRUST: Medium
BAKE CYCLE: Standard
OPTIONAL BAKE CYCLES: Sweet Bread/Delayed Timer/Rapid Bake

NUTRITIONAL INFORMATION PER SLICE
Calories 134/Fat 3.2 grams/Carbohydrates 23.1 grams/Protein 2.9 grams/Fiber .8 grams/Sodium 153 milligrams/Cholesterol 0 milligrams

French Bread Extraordinaire!

*T*his *recipe is an encore presentation from our second book,* The Bread Machine Magic Book of Helpful Hints. *This method, though time-consuming, produces an exceptional loaf of French bread, much like the ones baked in the boulangeries of Paris. The extra risings fully develop the bread's flavor. The finished loaf will have a crisp crust and very moist, chewy interior.* Bon appétit!

	SMALL LOAF	MEDIUM LOAF	LARGE LOAF
WATER	⅞ to 1 cup	1⅛ to 1¼ cups	1½ to 1⅝ cups
SALT	1 teaspoon	1½ teaspoons	2 teaspoons
UNBLEACHED WHITE FLOUR	2⅓ cups	3½ cups	4⅔ cups
RED STAR BRAND ACTIVE DRY YEAST	2 teaspoons	2 teaspoons	2½ teaspoons

1. Place dough ingredients in bread pan, select Dough setting, and press Start.

2. When the dough cycle ends, the machine will beep. Set a timer and allow the dough to rise 1 more hour. Open the machine, punch down the dough, set the timer again, and let dough rise another hour in the machine. Turn off bread machine, remove bread pan, and turn out dough onto a lightly floured countertop or cutting board. Form into a smooth, round ball, then flatten it with your hands.

3. Place a clean kitchen towel (not terry cloth) in a round wicker basket that's at least twice the size of the dough. Dust the towel liberally with flour. Place the round dough in the center of the basket. Place basket in a warm place and let dough rise, uncovered, about 45 minutes, until doubled in size.

4. Gently turn dough out of basket upside down onto a greased baking sheet. With a very sharp knife held almost parallel to the loaf, carefully slash the top of the dough at sharp angles in a # pattern.

5. Preheat oven to 450°F. Carefully place a small pan on the floor or bottom shelf of the oven. Add at least 1 cup boiling water to the pan. Place dough in oven and bake for 20 minutes. Remove from oven and place on cake rack to cool 1 hour before slicing. To preserve the crisp crust, do not store in plastic wrap or bag. Bread can be loosely covered or left out for up to 2 days before it dries out completely.

VARIATION: If you want to make French breads with crusts so thin and crispy they crackle when you remove them from the oven, try baking this bread in a La Cloche clay cooker. They're sold in both round and oblong shapes in gourmet cooking stores, or check the Sources section (page 249) for suppliers.

1. Omit steps 3 through 5. Liberally cover base of La Cloche with cornmeal. Place the rounded dough onto the base and flatten slightly.

2. Slash the dough as indicated in step 4. Cover it with a clean towel (again, not terry cloth), then place it in a warm oven to rise until doubled in size, about 30 to 45 minutes.

3. While the dough is rising, soak the lid of La Cloche upside down in a sink of water. (Cushion the handle with a dishcloth or sponge.) (See Note.)

4. For a dark crust, preheat the oven to 450°F. Place the wet lid over the dough; bake for 30 minutes. Remove the lid and bake for another 10 to 15 minutes, until dark brown.

5. For a lighter crust, preheat the oven to 450°F. Place the wet lid over the dough; bake for 15 minutes. Reduce the heat to 400°F and bake for another 15 minutes. Remove the lid and bake for 8 to 10 minutes, until golden-brown.

NOTE: The manufacturer of La Cloche, Sassafras Enterprises, does not recommend soaking the lid before baking because the absorption factor of stoneware is less than 1 percent. We call for soaking the lid in our recipe because we tested it both ways and preferred the crust of the bread baked with the soaked lid. A third option is to skip the soaking step but spritz the inside of the lid with a little water just before placing it over the dough.

BAKE CYCLE: Dough

NUTRITIONAL INFORMATION PER SLICE
Calories 115/Fat .3 grams/Carbohydrates 23.9 grams/Protein 3.4 grams/Fiber .9 grams/
Sodium 230 milligrams/Cholesterol 0 milligrams

Italian Bread

This bread turns out picture-perfect in some but not all machines. It's too good to discard, so we hope most bakers will have the picture-perfect results. If you find it on the pale side, switch to a Dark Crust setting.

	SMALL LOAF	MEDIUM LOAF	LARGE LOAF
WATER	¾ to ⅞ cup	1⅛ to 1¼ cups	1⅜ to 1½ cups
OLIVE OIL	1 tablespoon	1½ tablespoons	2 tablespoons
SALT	¾ teaspoon	1 teaspoon	1½ teaspoons
BREAD FLOUR	2 cups	3 cups	4 cups
VITAL WHEAT GLUTEN (OPTIONAL)	2 tablespoons	3 tablespoons	4 tablespoons
RED STAR BRAND ACTIVE DRY YEAST	1½ teaspoons	1½ teaspoons	2 teaspoons

I. Place all ingredients in bread pan, using the least amount of liquid listed in the recipe. Select Medium Crust setting, the French Bread cycle, and press Start.

2. Observe the dough as it kneads. After 5 to 10 minutes, if it appears dry and stiff or if your machine sounds as if it's straining to knead it, add more liquid 1 tablespoon at a time until dough forms a smooth, soft, pliable ball that is slightly tacky to the touch.

3. After the baking cycle ends, remove bread from pan, place on cake rack, and allow to cool 1 hour before slicing.

CRUST: Medium
BAKE CYCLE: French Bread
OPTIONAL BAKE CYCLES: Standard/Delayed Timer/Rapid Bake

NUTRITIONAL INFORMATION PER SLICE
Calories 111/Fat 1.7 grams/Carbohydrates 21 grams/Protein 3.6 grams/Fiber .8 grams/Sodium 153 milligrams/Cholesterol 0 milligrams

Ken's Light White Bread

*L*inda and her husband, Dennis, welcome their new son, Ken Ward, into the family by naming this very healthy bread after him. May he live long and prosper!

	SMALL LOAF	MEDIUM LOAF	LARGE LOAF
WATER	¾ to ⅞ cup	1 to 1⅛ cups	1½ to 1⅝ cups
UNSWEETENED APPLESAUCE	1½ tablespoons	2 tablespoons	3 tablespoons
SUGAR	1 tablespoon	1½ tablespoons	2 tablespoons
SALT	1 teaspoon	1½ teaspoons	2 teaspoons
BREAD FLOUR	2 cups	3 cups	4 cups
NONFAT DRY MILK POWDER	2 teaspoons	1 tablespoon	4 teaspoons
RED STAR BRAND ACTIVE DRY YEAST	1½ teaspoons	1½ teaspoons	2 teaspoons

1. Place all ingredients in bread pan, using the least amount of liquid listed in the recipe. Select Medium Crust setting and press Start.

2. Observe the dough as it kneads. After 5 to 10 minutes, if it appears dry and stiff or if your machine sounds as if it's straining to knead it, add more liquid 1 tablespoon at a time until dough forms a smooth, soft, pliable ball that is slightly tacky to the touch.

3. After the baking cycle ends, remove bread from pan, place on cake rack, and allow to cool 1 hour before slicing.

CRUST: Medium
BAKE CYCLE: Standard
OPTIONAL BAKE CYCLES: Whole Wheat/French Bread/Delayed Timer/Rapid Bake

---

NUTRITIONAL INFORMATION PER SLICE
Calories 123/Fat .3 grams/Carbohydrates 26 grams/Protein 3.5 grams/Fiber 1 gram/Sodium 269 milligrams/Cholesterol .1 milligrams

---

Miss Muffet Bread

Curds and whey never tasted so good! Find yourself a tuffet and enjoy this taste treat, but beware of nasty old spiders! (This bread varied greatly from one machine to the next, probably because of the range of moisture content in different brands of cottage cheese. It's one you'll need to watch during kneading.)

	SMALL LOAF	MEDIUM LOAF	LARGE LOAF
MILK	³⁄₈ to ½ cup	¾ to ⅞ cup	1 to 1⅛ cups
LOW-FAT COTTAGE CHEESE	½ cup	¾ cup	1 cup
BUTTER OR MARGARINE	1 tablespoon	1½ tablespoons	2 tablespoons
SUGAR	1½ tablespoons	3 tablespoons	3 tablespoons
POWDERED WHEY (OPTIONAL)	1 teaspoon	1½ teaspoons	2 teaspoons
SALT	1 teaspoon	1½ teaspoons	2 teaspoons
BREAD FLOUR	2 cups	3 cups	4 cups
RED STAR BRAND ACTIVE DRY YEAST	1½ teaspoons	1½ teaspoons	2 teaspoons

I. Place all ingredients in bread pan, using the least amount of liquid listed in the recipe. Select Light Crust setting and press Start.

2. Observe the dough as it kneads. After 5 to 10 minutes, if it appears dry and stiff or if your machine sounds as if it's straining to knead it, add more liquid 1 tablespoon at a time until dough forms a smooth, soft, pliable ball that is slightly tacky to the touch.

3. After the baking cycle ends, remove bread from pan, place on cake rack, and allow to cool 1 hour before slicing.

CRUST: Light
BAKE CYCLE: Standard
OPTIONAL BAKE CYCLES: Sweet Bread/Rapid Bake

NUTRITIONAL INFORMATION PER SLICE
Calories 131/Fat 1.5 grams/Carbohydrates 24.1 grams/Protein 4.8 grams/Fiber .8 grams/Sodium 300 milligrams/Cholesterol 1.1 milligrams

---

Mom's White Bread

This pale, crisp-crusted white bread is reminiscent of the loaves Linda's mother would bake on occasion. If you prefer a darker crust, add 1 to 2 tablespoons instant nonfat milk powder or bake on the Dark Crust setting.

	SMALL LOAF	MEDIUM LOAF	LARGE LOAF
WATER	¾ to ⅞ cup	1⅛ to 1¼ cups	1⅜ to 1½ cups
SHORTENING	2 teaspoons	1 tablespoon	4 teaspoons
SALT	¾ teaspoon	1 teaspoon	1½ teaspoons
SUGAR	1 tablespoon	1½ tablespoons	2 tablespoons
BREAD FLOUR	2 cups	3⅓ cups	4 cups
RED STAR BRAND ACTIVE DRY YEAST	1½ teaspoons	1½ teaspoons	2 teaspoons

1. Place all ingredients in bread pan, using the least amount of liquid listed in the recipe. Select Medium Crust setting and press Start.

2. Observe the dough as it kneads. After 5 to 10 minutes, if it appears dry and stiff or if your machine sounds as if it's straining to knead it, add more liquid 1 tablespoon at a time until dough forms a smooth, soft, pliable ball that is slightly tacky to the touch.

3. After the baking cycle ends, remove bread from pan, place on cake rack, and allow to cool 1 hour before slicing.

CRUST: Medium
BAKE CYCLE: Standard
OPTIONAL BAKE CYCLES: Whole Wheat/French Bread/Delayed Timer/Rapid Bake

---

NUTRITIONAL INFORMATION PER SLICE
Calories 121/Fat 1.2 grams/Carbohydrates 23.8 grams/Protein 3.1 grams/Fiber .9 grams/Sodium 153 milligrams/Cholesterol 0 milligrams

---

Semolina Bread

*T*his is a crusty, chewy white bread unlike any other. For a real treat, try it in a sandwich with thick slices of provolone cheese, home-grown tomatoes, fresh basil, salt, pepper, and a drizzle of garlic-flavored olive oil. Magnifico!

	SMALL LOAF	MEDIUM LOAF	LARGE LOAF
WATER	7/8 to 1 cup	1¼ to 1⅜ cups	1½ to 1⅝ cups
OLIVE OIL	2 teaspoons	1 tablespoon	1½ tablespoons
SUGAR	2 teaspoons	1 tablespoon	1½ tablespoons
SALT	1 teaspoon	1½ teaspoons	2 teaspoons
BREAD FLOUR	1 cup	1½ cups	2 cups
SEMOLINA FLOUR	1 cup	1½ cups	2 cups
RED STAR BRAND ACTIVE DRY YEAST	1 teaspoon	1½ teaspoons	2 teaspoons

1. Place all ingredients in bread pan, using the least amount of liquid listed in the recipe. Select Medium Crust setting and press Start.

2. Observe the dough as it kneads. After 5 to 10 minutes, if it appears dry and stiff or if your machine sounds as if it's straining to knead it, add more liquid 1 tablespoon at a time until dough forms a smooth, soft, pliable ball that is slightly tacky to the touch.

3. After the baking cycle ends, remove bread from pan, place on cake rack, and allow to cool 1 hour before slicing.

CRUST: Medium
BAKE CYCLE: Standard
OPTIONAL BAKE CYCLES: Whole Wheat/French Bread/Delayed Timer/Rapid Bake

NUTRITIONAL INFORMATION PER SLICE
Calories 126/Fat 1.3 grams/Carbohydrates 24.2 grams/Protein 3.8 grams/Fiber 1.1 grams/Sodium 229 milligrams/Cholesterol 0 milligrams

Speedy Spud Bread

*T*his potato bread takes advantage of the microwave and your machine's Rapid Bake cycle to turn out a very delicious bread in the shortest time possible. It helps to have a small food scale to weigh the potatoes for accuracy.

	SMALL LOAF	MEDIUM LOAF	LARGE LOAF
POTATO	1 small (6 oz.)	1 medium (9 oz.)	1 large (12 oz.)
WATER	¾ to ⅞ cup	1⅛ to 1¼ cups	1⅜ to 1½ cups
OLIVE OIL	1½ tablespoons	2 tablespoons	3 tablespoons
SUGAR	1 tablespoon	1½ tablespoons	2 tablespoons
SALT	1 teaspoon	1½ teaspoons	2 teaspoons
BREAD FLOUR	2 cups	3 cups	4½ cups
RED STAR BRAND ACTIVE DRY YEAST	1 teaspoon	1½ teaspoons	2 teaspoons

1. Scrub potato, pat dry, and pierce with a fork. Microwave on HIGH until soft, approximately 6 to 8 minutes. Cut potato in half, scoop out the insides, and place in bread pan.

2. Place rest of ingredients in bread pan, using the least amount of liquid listed in the recipe. Select Medium Crust setting and Rapid Bake cycle. Press Start.

3. Observe the dough as it kneads. After 5 to 10 minutes, if it appears dry and stiff or if your machine sounds as if it's straining to knead it, add more liquid 1 tablespoon at a time until dough forms a smooth, soft, pliable ball that is slightly tacky to the touch.

4. After the baking cycle ends, remove bread from pan, place on cake rack, and allow to cool 1 hour before slicing.

CRUST: Medium
BAKE CYCLE: Rapid Bake
OPTIONAL BAKE CYCLES: Standard/Delayed Timer

NUTRITIONAL INFORMATION PER SLICE
Calories 140/Fat 2.2 grams/Carbohydrates 26.4 grams/Protein 3.3 grams/Fiber 1.2 grams/Sodium 231 milligrams/Cholesterol 0 milligrams

---

Tuscan Bread

Centuries ago when the Duke of Tuscany declared a tax on salt, bakers stopped using it. To this day the traditional Tuscan loaf is free of salt and delicious as ever. It tends to be on the pale side in most machines, so you'll probably need to bake this one on a Dark Crust setting.

	SMALL LOAF	MEDIUM LOAF	LARGE LOAF
WATER	¾ to ⅞ cup	1⅛ to 1¼ cups	1½ to 1⅝ cups
OLIVE OIL	1½ tablespoons	2 tablespoons	3 tablespoons
SUGAR	2 teaspoons	1 tablespoon	4 teaspoons
BREAD FLOUR	2 cups	3 cups	4 cups
RED STAR BRAND ACTIVE DRY YEAST	1½ teaspoons	1½ teaspoons	2 teaspoons

1. Place all ingredients in bread pan, using the least amount of liquid listed in the recipe. Select Dark Crust setting and French Bread cycle. Press Start.

2. Observe the dough as it kneads. After 5 to 10 minutes, if it appears dry and stiff or if your machine sounds as if it's straining to knead it, add more liquid 1 tablespoon at a time until dough forms a smooth, soft, pliable ball that is slightly tacky to the touch.

3. After the baking cycle ends, remove bread from pan, place on cake rack, and allow to cool 1 hour before slicing.

CRUST: Dark
BAKE CYCLE: French
OPTIONAL BAKE CYCLES: Standard/Delayed Timer/Rapid Bake

NUTRITIONAL INFORMATION PER SLICE
Calories 199/Fat 2.2 grams/Carbohydrates 21.3 grams/Protein 2.9 grams/Fiber .8 grams/Sodium .7 milligrams/Cholesterol 0 milligrams

4

Whole Grain Breads

Bauernbrot

We love the hearty flavor and texture of European breads and this Austrian peasant bread is one of our favorites. If you're unfamiliar with the Dough cycle, this is a good one for you beginners. It's easy to shape and a treat to eat. Use leftover bread for turkey or ham sandwiches.

	SMALL LOAF	MEDIUM LOAF	LARGE LOAF
WATER	¾ cup	1⅛ cups	1½ cups
MOLASSES	1 tablespoon	1½ tablespoons	2 tablespoons
SALT	½ teaspoon	¾ teaspoon	1 teaspoon
BREAD FLOUR	1½ cups	2¼ cups	3 cups
BUCKWHEAT FLOUR	½ cup	¾ cup	1 cup
VITAL WHEAT GLUTEN	2 tablespoons	3 tablespoons	4 tablespoons
CARAWAY SEEDS	1 teaspoon	1½ teaspoons	2 teaspoons
RED STAR BRAND ACTIVE DRY YEAST	2 teaspoons	2½ teaspoons	3 teaspoons

1. Place ingredients in bread pan, select Dough setting, and press Start.

2. When the dough has risen long enough, the machine will beep. Turn off bread machine, remove bread pan, and turn out dough onto a lightly floured countertop or cutting board. Lightly grease a large baking sheet.

3. Shape dough into 1 large or 2 small round loaves. Places on greased baking sheet.

4. Cover and let rise in a warm oven 45 to 60 minutes, until doubled in size. (Hint: To warm oven slightly, turn oven on Warm setting for 1 minute, then turn it off, and place covered dough in oven to rise. Remove pan from oven before preheating.)

5. Preheat oven to 350°F. Bake for 40 to 45 minutes.

6. Remove from oven and cool on rack.

Small recipe yields 1 large or 2 small round loaves
Medium recipe yields 1 large or 2 small round loaves
Large recipe yields 1 large or 2 small round loaves

BAKE CYCLE: Dough

NUTRITIONAL INFORMATION PER SLICE
Calories 126/Fat 1.4 grams/Carbohydrates 24.8 grams/Protein 4.8 grams/Fiber 2.5 grams/Sodium 116 milligrams/Cholesterol 0 milligrams

Bev's Killer Rye Bread

Though we only know her via the modem, Bev Janson has become a wonderful friend to both of us. She's always sending us great new bread recipes to try and Lois would be lost without Bev's help when Lois hosts the America Online Bread Chat. Here's one of Bev's most popular creations. If you're a rye bread fan, we know you'll love it.

	SMALL LOAF	MEDIUM LOAF	LARGE LOAF
WATER	¾ to ⅞ cup	1⅜ to 1½ cups	1½ to 1⅝ cups
BUTTER OR MARGARINE	2 teaspoons	1 tablespoon	4 teaspoons
BROWN SUGAR	¼ cup	⅓ cup	½ cup
SALT	1 teaspoon	1½ teaspoons	2 teaspoons
BREAD FLOUR	1½ cups	2¼ cups	3 cups
RYE FLOUR	½ cup	¾ cup	1 cup
VITAL WHEAT GLUTEN	2 tablespoons	3 tablespoons	4 tablespoons
GRATED ORANGE RIND	2 tablespoons	3 tablespoons	4 tablespoons
RAISINS	½ cup	⅔ cup	1 cup
RED STAR BRAND ACTIVE DRY YEAST	1½ teaspoons	2 teaspoons	2½ teaspoons
CARAWAY SEEDS	1 tablespoon	1½ tablespoons	2 tablespoons

1. Place all ingredients in bread pan, using the least amount of liquid listed in the recipe. Select Light Crust setting and Whole Wheat cycle. Press Start.

2. Observe the dough as it kneads. After 5 to 10 minutes, if it appears dry and stiff or if your machine sounds as if it's straining to knead it, add more liquid 1 tablespoon at a time until dough forms a smooth, soft, pliable ball that is slightly tacky to the touch.

3. After the baking cycle ends, remove bread from pan, place on cake rack, and allow to cool 1 hour before slicing.

CRUST: Light
BAKE CYCLE: Whole Wheat
OPTIONAL BAKE CYCLES: Standard/Sweet Bread/Raisin/Nut/Delayed Timer

NUTRITIONAL INFORMATION PER SLICE
Calories 144/Fat 1.1 grams/Carbohydrates 30.7 grams/Protein 3.4 grams/Fiber 2.1 grams/Sodium 13.8 milligrams/Cholesterol 0 milligrams

Buttermilk Wheat Bread

We urge you to bake this bread for people who don't think they like whole wheat breads, then watch the expression on their faces when they bite into a slice. This is a wonderfully flavored introduction to the world of whole wheat bread.

	SMALL LOAF	MEDIUM LOAF	LARGE LOAF
BUTTERMILK	1 to 1⅛ cups	1⅜ to 1½ cups	1⅝ to 1¾ cups
OIL	1 tablespoon	1½ tablespoons	2 tablespoons
HONEY	2 tablespoons	3 tablespoons	¼ cup
SALT	1 teaspoon	1½ teaspoons	2 teaspoons
BREAD FLOUR	1⅓ cups	2 cups	2⅔ cups
WHOLE WHEAT FLOUR	⅔ cup	1 cup	1⅓ cups
RED STAR BRAND ACTIVE DRY YEAST	1½ teaspoons	2 teaspoons	2½ teaspoons

1. Place all ingredients in bread pan, using the least amount of liquid listed in the recipe. Select Medium Crust setting and press Start.

2. Observe the dough as it kneads. After 5 to 10 minutes, if it appears dry and stiff or if your machine sounds as if it's straining to knead it, add more liquid 1 tablespoon at a time until dough forms a smooth, soft, pliable ball that is slightly tacky to the touch.

3. After the baking cycle ends, remove bread from pan, place on cake rack, and allow to cool 1 hour before slicing.

CRUST: Medium
BAKE CYCLE: Standard
OPTIONAL BAKE CYCLES: Whole Wheat/Sweet Bread/Rapid Bake

NUTRITIONAL INFORMATION PER SLICE
Calories 124/Fat 1.8 grams/Carbohydrates 24 grams/Protein 3.4 grams/Fiber 1.7 grams/Sodium 237 milligrams/Cholesterol .2 milligram

---

Crazy Mixed-Up Grain Bread

Just read the ingredients in this bread and you'll know why people enjoy it so much. Try it and you'll see that healthy bread can be delicious.

	SMALL LOAF	MEDIUM LOAF	LARGE LOAF
WATER	1 to 1⅛ cups	1¼ to 1⅜ cups	1½ to 1⅝ cups
OIL	1½ tablespoons	2 tablespoons	3 tablespoons
HONEY	1½ tablespoons	2 tablespoons	3 tablespoons
SALT	½ teaspoon	¾ teaspoon	1 teaspoon
BREAD FLOUR	1⅓ cups	2 cups	2⅔ cups
WHOLE WHEAT FLOUR	⅓ cup	½ cup	⅔ cup
VITAL WHEAT GLUTEN (OPTIONAL)	2 tablespoons	3 tablespoons	4 tablespoons
OLD-FASHIONED OATS	3 tablespoons	¼ cup	6 tablespoons
WHEAT BRAN	3 tablespoons	¼ cup	6 tablespoons
BULGUR	3 tablespoons	¼ cup	6 tablespoons
SUNFLOWER SEEDS	3 tablespoons	¼ cup	6 tablespoons
RED STAR BRAND ACTIVE DRY YEAST	1½ teaspoons	2 teaspoons	2½ teaspoons

1. Place all ingredients in bread pan, using the least amount of liquid listed in the recipe. Select Medium Crust and Whole Wheat cycle. Press Start.

2. Observe the dough as it kneads. After 5 to 10 minutes, if it appears dry and stiff or if your machine sounds as if it's straining to knead it, add more liquid 1 tablespoon at a time until dough forms a smooth, soft, pliable ball that is slightly tacky to the touch.

3. After the baking cycle ends, remove bread from pan, place on cake rack, and allow to cool 1 hour before slicing.

CRUST: Medium
BAKE CYCLE: Whole Wheat
OPTIONAL BAKE CYCLES: Standard/Delayed Timer/Rapid Bake

NUTRITIONAL INFORMATION PER SLICE
Calories 120/Fat 3.5 grams/Carbohydrates 19.8 grams/Protein 3.3 grams/Fiber 2.4 grams/Sodium 116 milligrams/Cholesterol 0 milligrams

---

Crunchy Granola Bread

This is a flavorful, healthy bread which baked up better on the Whole Wheat cycle in some machines, while others needed some added vital wheat gluten. Try it for the first time on the Whole Wheat cycle without the gluten. Place the ingredients in the bread pan in the order listed. This allows the granola to soften a little while you add the rest of the ingredients.

	SMALL LOAF	MEDIUM LOAF	LARGE LOAF
GRANOLA	¼ cup	⅓ cup	½ cup
BUTTERMILK	⅞ to 1 cup	1⅜ to 1½ cups	1⅝ to 1¾ cups
OIL	1½ tablespoons	2 tablespoons	3 tablespoons
HONEY	2 tablespoons	3 tablespoons	¼ cup
SALT	1 teaspoon	1½ teaspoons	2 teaspoons
BREAD FLOUR	1½ cups	2 cups	3 cups
WHOLE WHEAT FLOUR	½ cup	1 cup	1 cup
CORNMEAL	2 tablespoons	3 tablespoons	¼ cup
VITAL WHEAT GLUTEN (OPTIONAL)	1½ tablespoons	2 tablespoons	3 tablespoons
RAW, UNSALTED SUNFLOWER SEEDS	3 tablespoons	¼ cup	⅓ cup
GRATED ORANGE PEEL (OPTIONAL)	of ½ small orange	of ½ medium orange	of 1 small orange
RED STAR BRAND ACTIVE DRY YEAST	1½ teaspoons	2 teaspoons	2½ teaspoons
RAISINS	3 tablespoons	¼ cup	⅓ cup

1. Place all ingredients except raisins in bread pan, using the least amount of liquid listed in the recipe. Select Light Crust setting and Raisin/Nut cycle. Press Start.

2. Observe the dough as it kneads. After 5 to 10 minutes, if it appears dry and stiff or if your machine sounds as if it's straining to knead it, add more liquid 1 tablespoon at a time until dough forms a smooth, soft, soft, pliable ball that is slightly tacky to the touch.

3. At the beep, add the raisins.

4. After the baking cycle ends, remove bread from pan, place on cake rack, and allow to cool 1 hour before slicing.

CRUST: Light
BAKE CYCLE: Raisin/Nut
OPTIONAL BAKE CYCLES: Standard/Sweet Bread

NUTRITIONAL INFORMATION PER SLICE
Calories 175/Fat 4.5 grams/Carbohydrates 29.8 grams/Protein 4.9 grams/Fiber 2.5 grams/Sodium 251 milligrams/Cholesterol .7 milligrams

---

Elegant Oatmeal Bread

*T*his is an easy way to eat your oatmeal in the morning. We like to set this one on the Delayed Bake cycle and wake to the smell of it baking. If you have any leftovers, it's also wonderful for sandwiches.

	SMALL LOAF	MEDIUM LOAF	LARGE LOAF
OLD-FASHIONED OATS	½ cup	⅔ cup	1 cup
WATER	¾ to ⅞ cup	1⅛ to 1¼ cups	1⅜ to 1½ cups
BUTTER OR MARGARINE	1 tablespoon	1½ tablespoons	2 tablespoons
HONEY	2 tablespoons	3 tablespoons	¼ cup
SALT	1 teaspoon	1¼ teaspoons	2 teaspoons
BREAD FLOUR	2 cups	2½ cups	3 cups
RED STAR BRAND ACTIVE DRY YEAST	1½ teaspoons	2 teaspoons	2½ teaspoons

I. Place all ingredients in bread pan, using the least amount of liquid listed in the recipe. Select Medium Crust setting and press Start.

2. Observe the dough as it kneads. After 5 to 10 minutes, if it appears dry and stiff or if your machine sounds as if it's straining to knead it, add more liquid 1 tablespoon at a time until dough forms a smooth, soft, pliable ball that is slightly tacky to the touch.

3. After the baking cycle ends, remove bread from pan, place on cake rack, and allow to cool 1 hour before slicing.

CRUST: Medium
BAKE CYCLE: Standard
OPTIONAL BAKE CYCLES: Whole Wheat/Sweet Bread/Delayed Timer/Rapid Bake

NUTRITIONAL INFORMATION PER SLICE
Calories 120/Fat 1.4 grams/Carbohydrates 23.4 grams/Protein 3.2 grams/Fiber 1.2 grams/Sodium 244 milligrams/Cholesterol 0 milligrams

Fifty-Fifty Whole Wheat Bread

Here's a bread that's perfect for those who know they "should" be eating whole wheat but are reluctant to climb on the bandwagon. Even Lois, who doesn't care for most whole wheat breads, loves this one.

	SMALL LOAF	MEDIUM LOAF	LARGE LOAF
WATER	⅝ to ¾ cup	⅞ to 1 cup	1 to 1⅛ cups
EGG	1	1	2
SHORTENING	3 tablespoons	¼ cup	6 tablespoons
SUGAR	2 tablespoons	3 tablespoons	¼ cup
SALT	¾ teaspoon	1 teaspoon	1½ teaspoons
WHOLE WHEAT FLOUR	1 cup	1½ cups	2 cups
BREAD FLOUR	1 cup	1½ cups	2 cups
RED STAR BRAND ACTIVE DRY YEAST	1½ teaspoons	2 teaspoons	2½ teaspoons

1. Place all ingredients in bread pan, using the least amount of liquid listed in the recipe. Select Whole Wheat cycle and Medium Crust setting. Press Start.

2. Observe the dough as it kneads. After 5 to 10 minutes, if it appears dry and stiff or if your machine sounds as if it's straining to knead it, add more liquid 1 tablespoon at a time until dough forms a smooth, soft, pliable ball that is slightly tacky to the touch.

3. After the baking cycle ends, remove bread from pan, place on cake rack, and allow to cool 1 hour before slicing.

CRUST: Medium
BAKE CYCLE: Whole Wheat
OPTIONAL BAKE CYCLES: Standard/Sweet Bread/Rapid Bake

NUTRITIONAL INFORMATION PER SLICE
Calories 141/Fat 4.4 grams/Carbohydrates 22.3 grams/Protein 3.7 grams/Fiber 2.1 grams/Sodium 158 milligrams/Cholesterol 15.2 milligrams

George's White Wheat Bread

*O*ne of the benefits of writing bread machine cookbooks is the new people we meet over the phone or via the mail. George Hilley from Reston, Virginia, is a prime example. He called us out of the blue one day, we had a lovely long chat, and he said he was going to send us his favorite whole wheat bread recipe. When we tried it ourselves, we agreed . . . this one is a keeper. If you have difficulty finding the white whole wheat flour, you can order it from King Arthur (see Sources, page 259) or substitute regular whole wheat flour.

	SMALL LOAF	MEDIUM LOAF	LARGE LOAF
QUAKER MULTI-GRAIN CEREAL - OR OLD-FASHIONED OATS	¼ cup	⅓ cup	½ cup
BUTTERMILK	1 to 1⅛ cups	1⅜ to 1½ cups	1⅞ to 2 cups
UNSALTED BUTTER	1 tablespoon	1½ tablespoons	2 tablespoons
WILDFLOWER HONEY (OR ANY SIMILAR DARK HONEY)	1½ tablespoons	2 tablespoons	3 tablespoons
SALT	1 teaspoon	1½ teaspoons	2 teaspoons
WHITE WHOLE WHEAT FLOUR	1¼ cups	1¾ cups	2½ cups
BREAD FLOUR	¾ cup	1¼ cups	1½ cups
VITAL WHEAT GLUTEN (OPTIONAL)	1½ tablespoons	2 tablespoons	3 tablespoons
RED STAR BRAND ACTIVE DRY YEAST	1½ teaspoons	2 teaspoons	2½ teaspoons

1. Place all ingredients in bread pan, using the least amount of liquid listed in the recipe. Select Medium Crust setting and Whole Wheat cycle. Press Start.

2. Observe the dough as it kneads. After 5 to 10 minutes, if it appears dry and stiff or if your machine sounds as if it's straining to knead it, add more liquid 1 tablespoon at a time until dough forms a smooth, soft, pliable ball that is slightly tacky to the touch.

3. After the baking cycle ends, remove bread from pan, place on cake rack, and allow to cool 1 hour before slicing.

CRUST: Medium
BAKE CYCLE: Whole Wheat
OPTIONAL BAKE CYCLES: Standard/Rapid Bake

NUTRITIONAL INFORMATION PER SLICE
Calories 128/Fat 1.9 grams/Carbohydrates 24.1 grams/Protein 4.4 grams/Fiber 2.5 grams/Sodium 253 milligrams/Cholesterol 4.1 milligrams

Judy's Fluffy Cracked Wheat Bread

We are indebted to Judy Berney for this wonderful recipe. This is a bread that consistently bakes up with a perfectly rounded top. It also tastes as good as it looks. Don't start adding ingredients to your bread pan until you read the first step. You need to allow 30 minutes for the cracked wheat to soften in the water first.

	SMALL LOAF	MEDIUM LOAF	LARGE LOAF
CRACKED WHEAT	3 tablespoons	¼ cup	6 tablespoons
WATER	¾ to ⅞ cup	1 to 1⅛ cups	1⅜ to 1½ cups
OLIVE OIL	3 tablespoons	¼ cup	6 tablespoons
SUGAR	2 tablespoons	3 tablespoons	¼ cup
SALT	¾ teaspoon	1 teaspoon	1½ teaspoons
BREAD FLOUR	1⅓ cups	2 cups	2⅔ cups
WHOLE WHEAT FLOUR	⅔ cup	1 cup	1⅓ cups
VITAL WHEAT GLUTEN (OPTIONAL)	2 teaspoons	1 tablespoon	4 teaspoons
RED STAR BRAND ACTIVE DRY YEAST	1½ teaspoons	2 teaspoons	2½ teaspoons

1. Place the cracked wheat and the water in the bread pan, using the least amount of water listed in the recipe. Allow 30 minutes to soften the cracked wheat before adding anything else.

2. Add the rest of the ingredients, select Light Crust setting and Whole Wheat cycle. Press Start.

3. Observe the dough as it kneads. After 5 to 10 minutes, if it appears dry and stiff or if your machine sounds as if it's straining to knead it, add more liquid 1 tablespoon at a time until dough forms a smooth, soft, pliable ball that is slightly tacky to the touch.

4. After the baking cycle ends, remove bread from pan, place on cake rack, and allow to cool 1 hour before slicing.

VARIATION: Place all ingredients in bread pan in order and set Delayed Bake timer for a 1-hour delay. You won't need to presoak the grain.

CRUST: Light
BAKE CYCLE: Whole Wheat
OPTIONAL BAKE CYCLES: Standard/Sweet Bread/Delayed Timer/Rapid Bake

---

NUTRITIONAL INFORMATION PER SLICE
Calories 177/Fat 3.3 grams/Carbohydrates 32 grams/Protein 4.5 grams/Fiber 2.2 grams/Sodium 158 milligrams/Cholesterol 46 milligrams

---

Kamut Bread

Kamut is an ancient grain that is high in protein but low in gluten. If you've seen kamut flour in the stores and were curious enough to buy some, here's a recipe that will put it to good use. You'll be surprised how flavorful this strange-sounding bread is. If you can't find kamut flour at your local health store or grocery, try one of the suppliers in our Sources section (see page 259).

	SMALL LOAF	MEDIUM LOAF	LARGE LOAF
BUTTERMILK	⅞ to 1 cup	1¼ to 1⅜ cups	1½ to 1⅝ cups
OIL	2 tablespoons	3 tablespoons	¼ cup
HONEY	2 tablespoons	3 tablespoons	¼ cup
SALT	½ teaspoon	1 teaspoon	1½ teaspoons
BREAD FLOUR	1 cup	1½ cups	2 cups
WHOLE WHEAT FLOUR	⅔ cup	1 cup	1⅓ cups
KAMUT FLOUR	⅔ cup	1 cup	1⅓ cups
VITAL WHEAT GLUTEN	2 tablespoons	3 tablespoons	¼ cup
RED STAR BRAND ACTIVE DRY YEAST	1½ teaspoons	2 teaspoons	2½ teaspoons

1. Place all ingredients in bread pan, using the least amount of liquid listed in the recipe. Select Medium Crust setting and Whole Wheat cycle. Press Start.

2. Observe the dough as it kneads. After 5 to 10 minutes, if it appears dry and stiff or if your machine sounds as if it's straining to knead it, add more liquid 1 tablespoon at a time until dough forms a smooth, soft, pliable ball that is slightly tacky to the touch.

3. After the baking cycle ends, remove bread from pan, place on cake rack, and allow to cool 1 hour before slicing.

CRUST: Medium
BAKE CYCLE: Whole Wheat
OPTIONAL BAKE CYCLES: Standard/Rapid Bake

NUTRITIONAL INFORMATION PER SLICE
Calories 163/Fat 3.6 grams/Carbohydrates 28.3 grams/Protein 5.4 grams/Fiber 2.7 grams/Sodium 177 milligrams/Cholesterol .8 milligrams

Light Oatmeal Bread

*I*sn't it great when something that's good for you also tastes delicious! Here's a fla-vorful bread for guilt-free nibbling. On most machines, this loaf baked up best on the Rapid Bake cycle (anything less than 3 hours). If that's not the case with yours, then switch to the Regular Bake cycle.

	SMALL LOAF	MEDIUM LOAF	LARGE LOAF
OLD-FASHIONED ROLLED OATS	½ cup	¾ cup	1 cup
WATER	⅞ to 1 cup	1¼ to 1⅜ cups	1½ to 1⅝ cups
UNSWEETENED APPLESAUCE	1½ tablespoons	2 tablespoons	3 tablespoons
BROWN SUGAR	1½ tablespoons	2 tablespoons	3 tablespoons
SALT	1 teaspoon	1 teaspoon	2 teaspoons
BREAD FLOUR	1¾ cups	2¾ cups	3½ cups
RED STAR BRAND ACTIVE DRY YEAST	1½ teaspoons	2 teaspoons	2½ teaspoons

1. Place all ingredients in bread pan, using the least amount of liquid listed in the recipe. Select Medium Crust setting and Rapid Bake cycle. Press Start.

2. Observe the dough as it kneads. After 5 to 10 minutes, if it appears dry and stiff or if your machine sounds as if it's straining to knead it, add more liquid 1 tablespoon at a time until dough forms a smooth, soft, pliable ball that is slightly tacky to the touch.

3. After the baking cycle ends, remove bread from pan, place on cake rack, and allow to cool 1 hour before slicing.

CRUST: Medium
BAKE CYCLE: Rapid Bake
OPTIONAL BAKE CYCLES: Standard/Sweet Bread/Delayed Timer

NUTRITIONAL INFORMATION PER SLICE
Calories 115/Fat .4 grams/Carbohydrates 23.8 grams/Protein 3.3 grams/Fiber 1.3 grams/Sodium 154 milligrams/Cholesterol 0 milligrams

---

Light Whole Wheat Bread

Not every machine produces a good one hundred percent whole wheat bread. This recipe worked in most of them. If it doesn't fare well in yours, you can substitute some bread flour for part of the whole wheat flour to give the desired boost.

	SMALL LOAF	MEDIUM LOAF	LARGE LOAF
WATER	⅞ to 1 cup	1 to 1⅛ cups	1⅜ to 1½ cups
UNSWEETENED APPLESAUCE	1½ tablespoons	2 tablespoons	3 tablespoons
HONEY	2 tablespoons	3 tablespoons	¼ cup
SALT	½ teaspoon	½ teaspoon	1 teaspoon
WHOLE WHEAT FLOUR	2 cups	3 cups	4 cups
VITAL WHEAT GLUTEN	2 tablespoons	3 tablespoons	4 tablespoons
RED STAR BRAND ACTIVE DRY YEAST	1½ teaspoons	1½ teaspoons	2 teaspoons

I. Place all ingredients in bread pan, using the least amount of liquid listed in the recipe. Select Medium Crust setting and Whole Wheat cycle. Press Start.

2. Observe the dough as it kneads. After 5 to 10 minutes, if it appears dry and stiff or if your machine sounds as if it's straining to knead it, add more liquid 1 tablespoon at a time until dough forms a smooth, soft, pliable ball that is slightly tacky to the touch.

3. After the baking cycle ends, remove bread from pan, place on cake rack, and allow to cool 1 hour before slicing.

CRUST: Medium
BAKE CYCLE: Whole Wheat
OPTIONAL BAKE CYCLES: Standard/Sweet Bread/Delayed Timer/Rapid Bake

---

NUTRITIONAL INFORMATION PER SLICE
Calories 102/Fat .5 grams/Carbohydrates 22.4 grams/Protein 3.6 grams/Fiber 3.3 grams/Sodium 77.8 milligrams/Cholesterol 0 milligrams

---

Pumpernickel Raisin Bread

A*ll the different flavors meld together well in this bread. It suggests a cold win-ter night, a cozy fire, and mugs of hot cider.*

	SMALL LOAF	MEDIUM LOAF	LARGE LOAF
WATER	⅞ to 1 cup	1⅜ to 1½ cups	1⅝ to 1¾ cups
OIL	1 tablespoon	1½ tablespoons	2 tablespoons
MOLASSES	3 tablespoons	⅓ cup	6 tablespoons
SALT	1 teaspoon	1½ teaspoons	2 teaspoons
BREAD FLOUR	⅔ cup	1½ cups	1⅓ cups
RYE FLOUR	⅔ cup	1 cup	1⅓ cups
WHOLE WHEAT FLOUR	⅔ cup	1 cup	1⅓ cups
COCOA POWDER	2 tablespoons	3 tablespoons	¼ cup
VITAL WHEAT GLUTEN (OPTIONAL)	1½ teaspoons	2 tablespoons	3 tablespoons
CARAWAY SEEDS	2 teaspoons	1 tablespoon	4 teaspoons
RED STAR BRAND ACTIVE DRY YEAST	2 teaspoons	2 teaspoons	2½ teaspoons
RAISINS	⅓ cup	½ cup	⅔ cup

1. Place all ingredients except raisins in bread pan, using the least amount of liquid listed in the recipe. Select Light Crust setting and Raisin/Nut cycle. Press Start.

2. Observe the dough as it kneads. After 5 to 10 minutes, if it appears dry and stiff or if your machine sounds as if it's straining to knead it, add more liquid 1 tablespoon at a time until dough forms a smooth, soft, pliable ball that is slightly tacky to the touch.

3. At the beep, add raisins.

4. After the baking cycle ends, remove bread from pan, place on cake rack, and allow to cool 1 hour before slicing.

CRUST: Light
BAKE CYCLE: Raisin/Nut
OPTIONAL BAKE CYCLES: Standard/Whole Wheat/Sweet Bread/Delayed Timer

---

NUTRITIONAL INFORMATION PER SLICE
Calories 153/Fat 2.2 grams/Carbohydrates 30.8 grams/Protein 3.8 grams/Fiber 3.4 grams/Sodium 231 milligrams/Cholesterol 0 milligrams

---

Scandinavian Rye Bread

We're very fond of the combination of rye flour, orange, and anise that Scandinavian breads offer. If you haven't tried it before, we urge you to do so with this hearty, dark bread.

	SMALL LOAF	MEDIUM LOAF	LARGE LOAF
WATER	½ cup	⅞ cup	1⅛ cups
OIL	1 tablespoon	1½ tablespoons	2 tablespoons
DARK KARO SYRUP	¼ cup	⅓ cup	½ cup
SALT	¼ teaspoon	½ teaspoon	½ teaspoon
ALL-PURPOSE FLOUR	1½ cups	2⅓ cups	3 cups
RYE FLOUR	½ cup	⅔ cup	1 cup
GRATED ORANGE RIND	1 teaspoon	1½ teaspoons	2 teaspoons
ANISE SEED	½ teaspoon	¾ teaspoon	1 teaspoon
CARDAMOM	½ teaspoon	¾ teaspoon	1 teaspoon
RED STAR BRAND ACTIVE DRY YEAST	1½ teaspoons	2 teaspoons	2½ teaspoons

1. Place dough ingredients in bread pan and select Dough setting. Press Start.

2. When the dough has risen long enough, the machine will beep. Turn off bread machine, remove bread pan, and turn out dough onto a lightly floured countertop or cutting board.

3. Grease a large baking sheet. Gently shape dough into a smooth ball. Flatten slightly and place on prepared baking sheet. With a sharp knife, slash the loaf with an X or # on the top.

4. Cover and let rise in a warm oven 45 to 60 minutes until doubled in size. (Hint: To warm oven slightly, turn oven on Warm setting for 1 minute, then turn it off, and place covered dough in oven to rise. Remove pan from oven before preheating.)

5. Preheat oven to 350° F. Bake for 40 to 45 minutes.

6. Remove from oven, place on cake rack, and allow to cool 1 hour before slicing.

BAKE CYCLE: Dough

NUTRITIONAL INFORMATION PER SLICE
Calories 128/Fat 1.8 grams/Carbohydrates 25 grams/Protein 2.7 grams/Fiber 1.4 grams/Sodium 81.7 milligrams/Cholesterol 0 milligrams

Shayna's Honey Wheat Berry Bread

*T*his wholesome, fat-free loaf is a bread muncher's delight. It's loaded with nu-
trients and has a wonderful chewy texture. No wonder Shayna has all that en-
ergy to bike the hills of Portland, row on the Willamette River, and hike the
Olympic Peninsula.

	SMALL LOAF	MEDIUM LOAF	LARGE LOAF
COOKED WHEAT BERRIES (RECIPE FOLLOWS)	½ cup	⅔ cup	1 cup
WATER	1 to 1⅛ cups	1¼ to 1⅜ cups	1½ to 1⅝ cups
HONEY	1½ tablespoons	2 tablespoons	3 tablespoons
SALT	¾ teaspoon	1 teaspoon	1½ teaspoons
BREAD FLOUR	1⅓ cups	2 cups	2⅓ cups
WHOLE WHEAT FLOUR	1 cup	1½ cups	2 cups
VITAL WHEAT GLUTEN (OPTIONAL)	2 tablespoons	3 tablespoons	4 tablespoons
RED STAR BRAND ACTIVE DRY YEAST	2 teaspoons	2 teaspoons	2½ teaspoons

1. Place all ingredients in bread pan, using the least amount of liquid listed in the
recipe. Select Medium Crust setting and press Start.

2. Observe the dough as it kneads. After 5 to 10 minutes, if it appears dry and stiff or
if your machine sounds as if it's straining to knead it, add more liquid 1 tablespoon at
a time until dough forms a smooth, soft, pliable ball that is slightly tacky to the
touch.

3. After the baking cycle ends, remove bread from pan, place on cake rack, and
allow to cool 1 hour before slicing.

Cooked Wheat Berries

	SMALL	MEDIUM	LARGE
WHEAT BERRIES	¼ cup	⅓ cup	½ cup
WATER	½ cup	⅔ cup	1 cup

I. Place wheat berries and water in a small saucepan and bring to a boil over high heat. Cover, reduce heat to low, and cook for about 30 minutes, until all the water is absorbed.

CRUST: Medium

BAKE CYCLE: Standard

OPTIONAL BAKE CYCLES: Whole Wheat/Delayed Timer/Rapid Bake

NUTRITIONAL INFORMATION PER SLICE
Calories 129/Fat .5 grams/Carbohydrates 27.2 grams/Protein 4.7 grams/Fiber 2.4 grams/Sodium 154 milligrams/Cholesterol 0 milligrams

---

Sweet Wheat Bread

O *ne of the most popular breads in our second book,* The Bread Machine Magic Book of Helpful Hints, *is the Sweet Milk Bread. This is the whole wheat version of that recipe.*

	SMALL LOAF	MEDIUM LOAF	LARGE LOAF
WATER	⅝ to ¾ cup	1 to 1⅛ cups	1 to 1⅛ cups
SWEETENED CONDENSED MILK	⅜ cup	½ cup	¾ cup
SALT	1 teaspoon	1 teaspoon	1½ teaspoons
BUTTER OR MARGARINE	1 tablespoon	1 tablespoon	1½ tablespoons
BREAD FLOUR	1 cup	1½ cups	2 cups
WHOLE WHEAT FLOUR	1 cup	1½ cups	2 cups
WHEAT GERM	1 tablespoon	1½ tablespoons	2 tablespoons
RED STAR BRAND ACTIVE DRY YEAST	1½ teaspoons	2 teaspoons	2½ teaspoons

1. Place all ingredients in bread pan, using the least amount of liquid listed in the recipe. Select Light Crust setting and press Start.

2. Observe the dough as it kneads. After 5 to 10 minutes, if it appears dry and stiff or if your machine sounds as if it's straining to knead it, add more liquid 1 tablespoon at a time until dough forms a smooth, soft, pliable ball that is slightly tacky to the touch.

3. After the baking cycle ends, remove bread from pan, place on cake rack, and allow to cool 1 hour before slicing.

CRUST: Light
BAKE CYCLE: Standard
OPTIONAL BAKE CYCLES: Whole Wheat/Sweet Bread/Rapid Bake

NUTRITIONAL INFORMATION PER SLICE
Calories 137/Fat 2 grams/Carbohydrates 25.9 grams/Protein 4.4 grams/Fiber 2.2 grams/Sodium 177 milligrams/Cholesterol 3.7 milligrams

---

5
Sourdoughs

SOURDOUGH STARTER

Basic Sourdough Starter

If you'd like to try your hand at making your own sourdough starter, this is an easy and nearly foolproof recipe. Use only fresh, good-quality yogurt with live, active cultures. (We recommend Dannon, Mountain High, or Altadena.)

SKIM (NONFAT) MILK MILK	1 cup
PLAIN YOGURT (WITH LIVE, ACTIVE CULTURES)	3 tablespoons
BREAD FLOUR	1 cup

1. Heat milk to 90° to 100°F.

2. Stir in yogurt.

3. Pour mixture into a clean 1½-quart glass or ceramic crock, jar, or bowl. Cover with a nonmetallic lid; set in a warm place (70° to 90°F) for 24 hours. (On warm days you can place the starter in a sunny window or on the counter in a warm kitchen. On cooler days, place it in a gas oven with a pilot light, an electric oven with the light left on, on top of the water heater, or on a heating pad set on low.)

4. After 24 hours, the milk will thicken and form curds. At this point, gradually stir in bread flour until well blended. Cover with lid and set in a warm place again until mixture ferments and bubbles and a clear liquid forms on top, about 2 to 5 days. Stir daily.

5. Starter is now ready to use. Stir, cover loosely, and refrigerate.

IF AT ANY POINT IN THE PROCESS THE STARTER TURNS PINK, ORANGE, BLACK, OR FUZZY, THROW IT OUT AND START OVER.

MAINTAINING YOUR STARTER

1. Every time you use some of the starter you must replace it with equal amounts of milk and flour. For instance, if you use 1 cup of starter, return 1 cup of milk and 1 cup of bread flour to the jar. Allow starter to stand in a warm place for 3 to 12 hours until it bubbles again. Stir, cover loosely, and refrigerate. (Note: We prefer a thick starter and quite often use ⅔ cup milk and 1 cup of flour to maintain it.)

2. Starters maintain their vitality and sourness best if used at least weekly. If neglected for several weeks, your starter can be perked back up by feeding it equal amounts of milk and flour (1 cup of each) and leaving it in a warm spot until it starts bubbling again. (As long as you're giving it some TLC, take a moment to freshen up its container as well. Pour the starter into a clean bowl, feed it, and wash out its container, rinsing well if you're using soap. Once it shows signs of life again, pour it back into its original container, cover loosely, and refrigerate.)

SOURDOUGH FACTS

· Use only wooden utensils and glass or ceramic containers. The acid in the starter will corrode metal.

· Do not keep sourdough starters in tightly sealed containers. Gases that form must be allowed to escape. If they can't escape, expect a real explosion!

· The yellowish or grayish-beige liquid that rises to the top is the "hooch." Simply stir it back into the starter before use.

· Fluorides and chlorine in tap water can impair or kill sourdough's effectiveness. Use bottled spring water instead.

VARIATIONS:

Water Starter Substitute 1 cup bottled water for the milk in the basic recipe. When feeding or replenishing the starter, use flour and bottled water.

Whole Wheat Starter Substitute 1 cup whole wheat flour for the bread flour in the basic recipe. When feeding or replenishing the starter, use whole wheat flour and milk or water.

Rye Starter Substitute 1 cup rye flour for the bread flour in the basic recipe. When feeding or replenishing the starter, use rye flour and milk or water.

Beer Starter Substitute 1 cup flat beer for the milk in the basic recipe. When feeding or replenishing the starter, use flour and flat beer.

Potato Starter Peel and cube one large baking potato (10 to 12 ounces). Place in small saucepan with 2 cups water. Boil gently until very tender. Do not drain. Mash potato and water together with potato masher. Measure out 1 cup. Add to warm milk in the basic recipe and continue as directed, adding yogurt and flour. After each use, replenish with equal parts of flour and either bottled water or potato cooking water. (Also, adding 1 plain mashed potato [6 to 8 ounces] to the starter occasionally will maintain the rich potato flavor of the starter.)

Sourdough starters can be frozen for 3 months and then thawed overnight in the refrigerator. Dehydrating your starter is a nifty way of preserving a treasured sourdough starter for an even longer period of time (about twice as long). Consider doing it as a backup. If you dehydrate some of your favorite starter and your original gets tossed out by mistake or goes south for some reason, all is not lost. Dehydration is also a great way to "package up" your starter and share it with friends all over the country!

Here's all there is to it: Spoon enough starter on foam-type paper plates or wax-paper—lined trays to coat the entire surface with a thin layer of starter. A thin coating will dry completely in approximately 24 hours. Once dry it will lift off the plate easily. Place the dried starter in a food processor, blender, coffee grinder, or grain mill and process briefly until coarsely ground. It should be stored in a glass jar or plastic bag someplace cool (the freezer is okay).

When you are ready to rehydrate your dried starter, place ½ cup warm water 90° to 100°F in a 1½-quart glass or ceramic container. Add ¼ cup of the ground starter and then ¼ cup of flour. Stir well with a wooden spoon. Place container in a warm location (between 75° and 95°F) and within several hours your starter should show signs of life with surface bubbles. At that point, add another ½ cup warm water and ½ cup more flour, stir, and allow the starter to feed overnight at room temperature before you use it or loosely cover it and put it in the refrigerator for later use. Any unused dehydrated starter can be re-stored in a cool location.

NOTE: This does not work in a electric dehydrator with heated air. We've tried it. It's too warm for the fragile starter.

Ciabatta

Ciabatta *means "slipper" in Italian. This oval-shaped, slightly flat bread is a favorite of Linda's. In fact, she considers it our best bread ever! Though it's a little tricky to handle because the dough is so sticky, patience and practice will prevail. We give a range of flour so you can customize your loaf. The less flour, the flatter the bread. You'll know you've gotten it right when you slice into the bread and expose a very light, porous interior with several large holes. The crust is thin and crisp, the center is chewy, and the taste is divine. Does it get any better than this?*

	SMALL LOAF	MEDIUM LOAF	LARGE LOAF
WATER	1 cup	1¼ cups	1⅝ cups
SOURDOUGH STARTER	⅓ cup	½ cup	⅔ cup
SALT	¾ teaspoon	1 teaspoon	1½ teaspoons
BREAD FLOUR	2⅛ to 2¼ cups	3 to 3¼ cups	4 to 4¼ cups
NONFAT DRY MILK POWDER	1 teaspoon	1½ teaspoons	2 teaspoons
RED STAR BRAND ACTIVE DRY YEAST	1½ teaspoons	2 teaspoons	2½ teaspoons

1. Place dough ingredients in bread pan, select Dough setting, and press Start.

2. When the dough has risen long enough, the machine will beep. Turn off bread machine, remove bread pan, and turn out dough onto a heavily floured countertop or cutting board. This is a very wet, sticky dough. Sprinkle some flour on top of dough as well.

3. Grease a large baking sheet.

FOR THE SMALL RECIPE

With a sharp knife, divide dough into 2 pieces. Handling the dough as little as possible, use a spatula or dough scraper to shape the 2 loaves into rough 4×8-inch ovals.

FOR THE MEDIUM RECIPE

With a sharp knife, divide dough into 2 pieces. Handling the dough as little as possible, use a spatula or dough scraper to shape the 2 loaves into rough 4×10-inch ovals.

With a sharp knife, divide dough into 3 pieces. Handling the dough as little as possible, use a spatula or dough scraper to shape the 3 loaves into rough 4×10-inch ovals.

4. Transfer loaves with spatula to prepared baking sheet.

5. Cover and let rise in a warm oven 30 to 45 minutes until almost doubled in size. (Hint: To warm oven slightly, turn oven on Warm setting for 1 minute, then turn it off, and place covered dough in oven to rise. Remove pan from oven before preheating.)

6. Preheat oven to 425°F. Bake for 25 to 30 minutes until dark brown.

7. Remove from oven and cool on a rack 1 hour before slicing.

Small and medium recipes yield 2 loaves
Large recipe yields 3 loaves

BAKE CYCLE: Dough

NUTRITIONAL INFORMATION PER SLICE
Calories 109/Fat .3 grams/Carbohydrates 22.4 grams/Protein 3.3 grams/Fiber .9 grams/Sodium 156 milligrams/Cholesterol .2 milligrams

---

Molly's Sourdough Bread

This recipe came to us fourth-hand. We call it Molly's Bread, but it was given to Molly Spradley by Jean Martin, whose dad adapted it for his bread machine from an old recipe of his. Whatever the route it took, we're delighted to have it. Finally, a sourdough recipe that works well in all machines! Thank you, Molly, Jean, and Jean's dad.

	SMALL LOAF	MEDIUM LOAF	LARGE LOAF
SOURDOUGH STARTER	⅔ cup	1 cup	1⅓ cups
WATER	⅜ to ½ cup	½ to ⅝ cup	¾ to ⅞ cup
OIL	2 teaspoons	1 tablespoon	4 teaspoons
SUGAR	1 tablespoon	1½ tablespoons	2 tablespoons
SALT	½ teaspoon	¾ teaspoon	1 teaspoon
BREAD FLOUR	2 cups	3 cups	4 cups
VITAL WHEAT GLUTEN	1 teaspoon	1 teaspoon	2 teaspoons
RED STAR BRAND ACTIVE DRY YEAST	1½ teaspoons	1½ teaspoons	2 teaspoons

1. Place all ingredients in bread pan, using the least amount of liquid listed in the recipe. Select Medium Crust setting and press Start.

2. Observe the dough as it kneads. After 5 to 10 minutes, if it appears dry and stiff or if your machine sounds as if it's straining to knead it, add more liquid 1 tablespoon at a time until dough forms a smooth, soft, pliable ball that is slightly tacky to the touch.

3. After the baking cycle ends, remove bread from pan, place on cake rack, and allow to cool 1 hour before slicing.

CREATIVE SUGGESTION: Jean's dad in Arcade, New York, likes to toss in two snack-size boxes of raisins at the Raisin/Nut cycle beep.

CRUST: Medium
BAKE CYCLE: Standard
OPTIONAL BAKE CYCLES: French Bread/Delayed Timer/Rapid Bake

NUTRITIONAL INFORMATION PER SLICE
Calories 133/Fat 1.4 grams/Carbohydrates 25.7 grams/Protein 3.7 grams/Fiber .9 grams/Sodium 119 milligrams/Cholesterol .4 milligrams

---

Onion Caraway Sourdough Loaf

Here's a bread worthy of being served to any sourdough enthusiast. The combined tart and tangy ingredients were made for each other. Since sourdough starters vary in consistency, adjust the water to suit. If yours is quite thick, you may need to add the extra water during kneading. If it's very thin, start with the least amount of water called for in the recipe.

DOUGH

	SMALL LOAF	MEDIUM LOAF	LARGE LOAF
WATER	¼ to ⅜ cup	½ to ⅝ cup	¾ to ⅞ cup
SOURDOUGH STARTER	¾ cup	1 cup	1½ cups
SUGAR	1 teaspoon	1½ teaspoons	2 teaspoons
SALT	1 teaspoon	1½ teaspoons	2 teaspoons
BREAD FLOUR	2 cups	3 cups	4 cups
RED STAR BRAND ACTIVE DRY YEAST	1½ teaspoons	2 teaspoons	2½ teaspoons

1. Place dough ingredients in bread pan, select Dough setting, and press Start.

2. In a nonstick skillet over medium heat, sauté sliced onions in butter until brown, about 15 minutes, stirring frequently. Stir in caraway seeds, remove from heat, and let cool.

3. When the dough has risen long enough, the machine will beep. Turn off bread machine, remove bread pan, and turn out dough onto a lightly floured countertop or cutting board. Grease a large baking sheet.

FILLING

	SMALL LOAF	MEDIUM LOAF	LARGE LOAF
BUTTER OR MARGARINE	1 tablespoon	1½ tablespoons	2 tablespoons
ONIONS, THINLY SLICED	1 large	2 medium	2 large
CARAWAY SEEDS	1½ teaspoons	2 teaspoons	1 tablespoon

For the Small Loaf

Roll dough into a 9×14-inch rectangle. Spread sautéed onion mixture on top.

For the Medium Loaf

Roll dough into a 9×18-inch rectangle. Spread sautéed onion mixture on top.

For the Large Loaf

Divide the dough in half. Roll each into 9×14-inch rectangles. Spread half of the sautéed onion mixture on top of each.

4. Starting with long edge, roll up into a log and pinch edges to seal.

5. Place on prepared baking sheet, bend into a crescent shape, cover, and let rise in a warm oven 30 to 45 minutes until doubled in size. (Hint: To warm oven slightly, turn oven on Warm for 1 minute, then turn it off, and place covered dough in oven to rise. Remove pan from oven before preheating.)

6. Preheat oven to 400°F. Place loaf in oven and mist with water from a plant mister. Bake for 30 to 35 minutes, misting once after 5 minutes and a second time after 10 minutes.

7. Remove from oven and cool on a wire rack.

Creative Suggestions:

1. This would also make an excellent spiral bread. See the recipe for Pesto Spiral Bread on pages 157–58 for complete directions.

2. This recipe would also be good with a little chopped, crispy bacon in the filling.

Small and Medium recipes yield 1 loaf
Large recipe yields 2 loaves

BAKE CYCLE: Dough

NUTRITIONAL INFORMATION PER SLICE
Calories 132/Fat 1.4 grams/Carbohydrates 25.5 grams/Protein 3.8 grams/Fiber 1.1 grams/Sodium 249 milligrams/Cholesterol .4 milligrams

---

SOUR DOUGH
MISTER

Sourdough Potato Bread

A few notes to share on this high riser: If you're thinking about making a large loaf, try the medium size first. In 2-pound machines with small bread pans, this lively dough wants to climb right out of the pan. Unlike other recipes, the water in this one is an optional ingredient. We found most machines didn't need it. Lastly, regular sourdough starter will serve just as well if you don't have a potato sourdough starter available.

	SMALL LOAF	MEDIUM LOAF	LARGE LOAF
POTATO SOURDOUGH STARTER	¾ cup	1 cup	1¼ cups
OIL	1½ tablespoons	2 tablespoons	3 tablespoons
EGG	1	1	2
PLAIN MASHED POTATOES	½ cup	¾ cup	1 cup
SUGAR	1½ tablespoons	2 tablespoons	3 tablespoons
SALT	¾ teaspoon	1 teaspoon	1½ teaspoons
BREAD FLOUR	2 cups	3 cups	4 cups
RED STAR BRAND ACTIVE DRY YEAST	1 teaspoon	1½ teaspoons	2 teaspoons
WATER (OPTIONAL)	1 to 2 tablespoons	1 to 3 tablespoons	2 to 4 tablespoons

1. Place all ingredients in bread pan, omitting the water to start. Select Medium Crust setting and press Start.

2. Observe the dough as it kneads. After 5 to 10 minutes, if it appears dry and stiff or if your machine sounds as if it's straining to knead it, add water 1 tablespoon at a time until dough forms a smooth, soft, pliable ball that is slightly tacky to the touch.

3. After the baking cycle ends, remove bread from pan, place on cake rack, and allow to cool 1 hour before slicing.

CRUST: Medium
BAKE CYCLE: Standard
OPTIONAL BAKE CYCLES: French/Rapid Bake

NUTRITIONAL INFORMATION PER SLICE
Calories 136/Fat 2.6 grams/Carbohydrates 24.2 grams/Protein 3.5 grams/Fiber .9 grams/Sodium 158 milligrams/Cholesterol 15.2 milligrams

---

Sourdough Rye Bread

*S*ourdough starter and rye flour seem to be ingredients just meant for each other. No rye sourdough starter on hand? No problem. You can use your regular starter instead.

	SMALL LOAF	MEDIUM LOAF	LARGE LOAF
WATER	$3/8$ to $1/2$ cup	$1/2$ to $5/8$ cup	$3/4$ to $7/8$ cup
RYE SOURDOUGH STARTER	$3/4$ cup	1 cup	$1\frac{1}{2}$ cups
OIL	$1\frac{1}{2}$ tablespoons	2 tablespoons	3 tablespoons
SUGAR	$1\frac{1}{2}$ teaspoons	2 teaspoons	3 teaspoons
SALT	1 teaspoon	$1\frac{1}{2}$ teaspoons	2 teaspoons
BREAD FLOUR	$1\frac{1}{2}$ cups	$2\frac{1}{3}$ cups	3 cups
RYE FLOUR	$1/2$ cup	$2/3$ cup	1 cup
RED STAR BRAND ACTIVE DRY YEAST	$1\frac{1}{2}$ teaspoons	2 teaspoons	2 teaspoons

1. Place ingredients in bread pan, select Dough setting, and press Start.

2. When the dough has risen long enough, the machine will beep. Turn off bread machine, remove bread pan, and turn out dough onto a lightly floured countertop or cutting board.

FOR THE SMALL RECIPE
Shape dough into one 10-inch oblong loaf or 1 large round loaf or one 24-inch-long baguette or 6 French rolls.

FOR THE MEDIUM RECIPE
Shape dough into one 12-inch oblong loaf or 1 large round loaf or two 18-inch-long baguettes or 9 French rolls.

FOR THE LARGE RECIPE
Shape dough into two 10-inch oblong loaves or 2 large round loaves or two 24-inch-long baguettes or 12 French rolls.

3. Place loaf (loaves) on a baking sheet that is well greased or sprinkled with corn-meal. With a sharp knife or razor blade, slash the rolls or baguettes straight down

the center about ½-inch deep. On the oblong loaf, make three diagonal slashes. On the round loaf, slash an X or # on top.

4. Cover and let rise in a warm oven 30 to 45 minutes until doubled in size. (Hint: To warm oven slightly, turn oven on Warm setting for 1 minute, then turn it off, and place covered dough in oven to rise. Remove pan from oven before preheating.)

5. Preheat oven to 375°F. Place loaves in oven and mist with water from a plant mister. Bake for 35 to 40 minutes, misting once after 5 minutes and a second time after 10 minutes.

6. Remove from oven and cool on wire racks.

Small recipe yields 1 loaf, 1 baguette, or 6 rolls
Medium recipe yields 1 loaf, 2 baguettes, or 9 rolls
Large recipe yields 2 loaves, 2 baguettes, or 12 rolls

BAKE CYCLE: Dough

NUTRITIONAL INFORMATION PER SLICE
Calories 96/Fat 2.3 grams/Carbohydrates 16.1 grams/Protein 2.4 grams/Fiber 1.6 grams/
Sodium 233 milligrams/Cholesterol .4 milligrams

DOUGH SCRAPER

Tomato Parmesan Sourdough Bread

irvana for sourdough lovers with a taste for something extra, this bread is a sophisticated addition to any bread basket.

	SMALL LOAF	MEDIUM LOAF	LARGE LOAF
WATER	¼ to ⅜ cup	½ to ⅝ cup	¾ to ⅞ cup
SOURDOUGH STARTER	¾ cup	1 cup	1½ cups
SUGAR	1 teaspoon	1½ teaspoons	2 teaspoons
SALT	1 teaspoon	1½ teaspoons	2 teaspoons
BREAD FLOUR	2 cups	3 cups	4 cups
FRESHLY GRATED PARMESAN CHEESE	⅓ cup	½ cup	⅔ cup
CLOVES GARLIC, MINCED	2	3	4
SUN-DRIED TOMATOES, SNIPPED	3 tablespoons	¼ cup	6 tablespoons
RED STAR BRAND ACTIVE DRY YEAST	1½ teaspoons	2 teaspoons	2½ teaspoons

1. Place ingredients in bread pan, select Dough setting, and press Start.

2. When the dough has risen long enough, the machine will beep. Turn off bread machine, remove bread pan, and turn out dough onto a lightly floured countertop or cutting board.

FOR THE SMALL RECIPE

Shape dough into one 10-inch oblong loaf or 1 round loaf or one 24-inch thin baguette or 6 French rolls.

FOR THE MEDIUM RECIPE

Shape dough into one 12-inch oblong loaf or 1 round loaf or two 18-inch thin baguettes or 9 French rolls.

FOR THE LARGE RECIPE

Shape dough into two 10-inch oblong loaves or 2 large round loaves or two 24-inch thin baguettes or 12 French rolls.

3. Place loaf (loaves) on a baking sheet that is well greased or sprinkled with cornmeal. With a sharp knife or razor blade, slash the rolls or baguettes straight down

the center about ½-inch deep. On the oblong loaf, make three diagonal slashes. On the round loaf, slash an X or # on top.

4. Cover and let rise in a warm oven 30 to 45 minutes until doubled in size. (Hint: To warm oven slightly, turn oven on Warm setting for 1 minute, then turn it off, and place covered dough in oven to rise. Remove pan from oven before preheating.)

5. Preheat oven to 400°F. Place loaves in oven and mist with water from a plant mister. Bake for 20 to 25 minutes, misting once after 5 minutes and a second time after 10 minutes.

6. Remove from oven and cool on wire racks. To preserve the crisp crust, do not store in plastic wrap or bags. Bread can be loosely covered or left out for up to 2 days before it dries out completely.

Small recipe yields 1 loaf, 1 baguette, or 6 rolls
Medium recipe yields 1 loaf, 2 baguettes, or 9 rolls
Large recipe yields 2 loaves, 2 baguettes, or 12 rolls

BAKE CYCLE: Dough

NUTRITIONAL INFORMATION PER ROLL
Calories 136/Fat 1.3 grams/Carbohydrates 25.5 grams/Protein 5 grams/Fiber 1.1 grams/ Sodium 288 milligrams/Cholesterol 2.6 milligrams

---

Whole Wheat Sourdough Bread

*S*ourdough fans will stand up and cheer when they taste this one. It's delicious. So get that whole wheat starter going tonight. (If you don't have time to make a whole wheat starter, you can use your regular sourdough starter.)

	SMALL LOAF	MEDIUM LOAF	LARGE LOAF
WHOLE WHEAT STARTER	⅔ cup	1 cup	1⅓ cups
MILK	⅝ to ¾ cup	⅞ to 1 cup	1¼ to 1⅜ cups
BUTTER OR MARGARINE	1½ tablespoons	2 tablespoons	3 tablespoons
SUGAR	2 tablespoons	3 tablespoons	¼ cup
SALT	1 teaspoon	1½ teaspoons	2 teaspoons
BREAD FLOUR	1⅓ cups	2 cups	2⅔ cups
WHOLE WHEAT FLOUR	⅔ cup	1 cup	1⅓ cups
WHEAT BRAN	⅓ cup	½ cup	⅔ cup
RED STAR BRAND ACTIVE DRY YEAST	1 teaspoon	1½ teaspoons	2 teaspoons

I. Place all ingredients in bread pan, using the least amount of liquid listed in the recipe. Select Medium Crust setting and Whole Wheat cycle. Press Start.

2. Observe the dough as it kneads. After 5 to 10 minutes, if it appears dry and stiff or if your machine sounds as if it's straining to knead it, add more liquid 1 tablespoon at a time until dough forms a smooth, soft, pliable ball that is slightly tacky to the touch.

3. After the baking cycle ends, remove bread from pan, place on cake rack, and allow to cool 1 hour before slicing.

CRUST: Medium
BAKE CYCLE: Whole Wheat
OPTIONAL BAKE CYCLES: Standard/French Bread/Rapid Bake

NUTRITIONAL INFORMATION PER SLICE
Calories 145/Fat 2 grams/Carbohydrates 28.2 grams/Protein 4.8 grams/Fiber 2.7 grams/Sodium 262 milligrams/Cholesterol 1 milligram

6

Sweet Breads

Boston Brown Bread

This yeast-free bread can only be baked in machines with a cake/quick bread cycle. Once you try it, you'll find it hard to believe this rich, moist bread has no fat in the recipe. Serve it warm with homemade baked beans or cold for breakfast with a dollop of flavored cream cheese.

	MEDIUM LOAF
BUTTERMILK	2 cups
MOLASSES	1 cup
WHOLE WHEAT FLOUR	1 cup
RYE FLOUR	1 cup
CORNMEAL	1 cup
SALT	1 teaspoon
BAKING SODA	2 teaspoons
RAISINS (OPTIONAL)	1 cup

1. Place all ingredients in bread pan, select Cake/Quick Bread setting, and press Start.

2. Make sure the batter is well mixed before baking begins. It's so thick, you may need to give it a stir or two with a spatula.

3. When the bread starts baking, set a timer for 60 minutes. After 60 minutes of baking, test the bread for doneness with a long wooden or bamboo skewer. If the skewer comes out clean and the bread is firm, shut off the machine and remove the bread. (We've learned the hard way that some machines have an overly long baking cycle for cakes and quick breads, so it's best to check them early.)

4. Place the bread on a cake rack and allow it to cool before slicing.

CREATIVE SUGGESTION: If you choose to use raisins, you can soak them in rum or vanilla overnight for added flavor.

Serves 10 to 12

BAKE CYCLE: Cake/Quick Bread

NUTRITIONAL INFORMATION PER SLICE
Calories 186/Fat .8 grams/Carbohydrates 42 grams/Protein 4.2 grams/Fiber 3.5 grams/Sodium 312 milligrams/Cholesterol 1.3 milligrams

---

Cammy's Greek Bread

We owe a big "thank you" to Linda's longtime friend, Camille Cox, for this scrumptious bread. It's an adaptation of a favorite recipe given many, many years ago. This bread always draws rave reviews when shared with friends. Don't pass it up. It's also a bread that defies the rules because the dough looks more like a batter than a bread dough in some machines. Have faith, it will bake up just fine.

	SMALL LOAF	MEDIUM LOAF	LARGE LOAF
MILK	½ to ⅝ cup	⅞ to 1 cup	1 to 1⅛ cups
EGG	1	1	2
SHORTENING	3 tablespoons	¼ cup	6 tablespoons
HONEY	3 tablespoons	¼ cup	6 tablespoons
VANILLA	2 teaspoons	1 tablespoon	4 teaspoons
BREAD FLOUR	2 cups	3 cups	4 cups
RED STAR BRAND ACTIVE DRY YEAST	1 teaspoon	1½ teaspoons	2 teaspoons

1. Place all ingredients in bread pan, using the least amount of liquid listed in the recipe. Select Light Crust setting and Sweet Bread cycle. Press Start.

2. After the baking cycle ends, remove bread from pan, place on cake rack, and allow to cool 1 hour before slicing.

CRUST: Light
BAKE CYCLE: Sweet Bread
OPTIONAL BAKE CYCLES: Standard/Whole Wheat/Rapid Bake

NUTRITIONAL INFORMATION PER SLICE
Calories 161/Fat 4.4 grams/Carbohydrates 26.2 grams/Protein 3.8 grams/Fiber .8 grams/Sodium 13 milligrams/Cholesterol 15.8 milligrams

Chock-O-Nut Bread

People find it hard to believe this bread comes out of a machine. You'll have to try it yourself to see what we mean.

	SMALL LOAF	MEDIUM LOAF	LARGE LOAF
MILK	⅝ to ¾ cup	1 to 1⅛ cups	1½ to 1⅝ cups
OIL	2 tablespoons	3 tablespoons	¼ cup
CHOCOLATE SYRUP	3 tablespoons	¼ cup	6 tablespoons
SUGAR	1 tablespoon	1½ tablespoons	2 tablespoons
SALT	¼ teaspoon	¼ teaspoon	½ teaspoon
BREAD FLOUR	2 cups	3 cups	4 cups
COCOA POWDER	1 tablespoon	1½ tablespoons	2 tablespoons
RED STAR BRAND ACTIVE DRY YEAST	1½ teaspoons	2 teaspoons	2½ teaspoons
CHOPPED WALNUTS OR PECANS	⅓ cup	½ cup	⅔ cup
CHOCOLATE CHIPS	⅓ cup	½ cup	⅔ cup

I. Place all ingredients except the nuts and chocolate chips in bread pan, using the least amount of liquid listed in the recipe. Select Light Crust setting and Raisin/Nut cycle. Press Start.

2. Observe the dough as it kneads. After 5 to 10 minutes, if it appears dry and stiff or if your machine sounds as if it's straining to knead it, add more liquid 1 tablespoon at a time until dough forms a smooth, soft, pliable ball that is slightly tacky to the touch.

3. At the beep, add the nuts and chocolate chips.

4. After the baking cycle ends, remove bread from pan, place on cake rack, and allow to cool 1 hour before slicing.

CRUST: Light
BAKE CYCLE: Raisin/Nut
OPTIONAL BAKE CYCLES: Standard/Whole Wheat/Sweet Bread

NUTRITIONAL INFORMATION PER SLICE
Calories 209/Fat 8.4 grams/Carbohydrates 30.3 grams/Protein 4.6 grams/Fiber 1.6 grams/Sodium 53 milligrams/Cholesterol .7 milligrams

---

Cinnamon Raisin Bread

This breakfast favorite is easy to assemble. Remember, though, if you add too much cinnamon you can hamper the yeast activity.

	SMALL LOAF	MEDIUM LOAF	LARGE LOAF
BUTTERMILK	1 to 1⅛ cups	1⅜ to 1½ cups	1⅝ to 1¾ cups
OIL	2 teaspoons	1 tablespoon	4 teaspoons
SUGAR	2 tablespoons	¼ cup	6 tablespoons
SALT	1 teaspoon	1 teaspoon	1½ teaspoons
BREAD FLOUR	2 cups	3 cups	4 cups
CINNAMON	¾ teaspoon	1 teaspoon	1½ teaspoons
RED STAR BRAND ACTIVE DRY YEAST	1½ teaspoons	2 teaspoons	2½ teaspoons
RAISINS	½ cup	⅔ cup	1 cup

1. Place all ingredients in bread pan except the raisins, using the least amount of liquid listed in the recipe. Select Medium Crust setting and Raisin/Nut cycle. Press Start.

2. Observe the dough as it kneads. After 5 to 10 minutes, if it appears dry and stiff or if your machine sounds as if it's straining to knead it, add more liquid 1 tablespoon at a time until dough forms a smooth, soft, pliable ball that is slightly tacky to the touch.

3. At the beep, add raisins.

4. After the baking cycle ends, remove bread from pan, place on cake rack, and allow to cool 1 hour before slicing.

CRUST: Medium
BAKE CYCLE: Raisin/Nut
OPTIONAL BAKE CYCLES: Standard/Whole Wheat/Sweet Bread

NUTRITIONAL INFORMATION PER SLICE
Calories 150/Fat 1.5 grams/Carbohydrates 30.4 grams/Protein 3.9 grams/Fiber 1.3 grams/Sodium 180 milligrams/Cholesterol .9 milligrams

---

Coco-Loco Bread

Grab your sandals, your suntan lotion, a loaf of this tropical bread, and hit the beach! Be sure to use very ripe bananas. They provide the needed moisture that greener bananas lack.

	SMALL LOAF	MEDIUM LOAF	LARGE LOAF
SLICED VERY RIPE BANANA	1 cup	1½ cups	2 cups
BUTTERMILK (OPTIONAL)	⅛ cup	¼ to ⅜ cup	⅛ to ¼ cup
EGG	1	1	2
COCONUT EXTRACT	¾ teaspoon	1 teaspoon	1½ teaspoons
OIL	2 tablespoons	3 tablespoons	¼ cup
HONEY	1½ tablespoons	2 tablespoons	3 tablespoons
SALT	½ teaspoon	¾ teaspoon	1 teaspoon
BREAD FLOUR	2¼ cups	3⅓ cups	4½ cups
RED STAR BRAND ACTIVE DRY YEAST	1½ teaspoons	2 teaspoons	2½ teaspoons
CRUSHED PINEAPPLE, WELL DRAINED	¼ cup	⅓ cup	½ cup
FLAKED COCONUT	¼ cup	⅓ cup	½ cup
SNIPPED DATES	¼ cup	⅓ cup	½ cup
CHOPPED WALNUTS	¼ cup	⅓ cup	½ cup

1. Place all ingredients in bread pan except the pineapple, coconut, dates, and walnuts, using the least amount of liquid listed in the recipe. Select Light Crust setting and the Raisin/Nut cycle. Press Start.

2. Observe the dough as it kneads. After 5 to 10 minutes, if it appears dry and stiff or if your machine sounds as if it's straining to knead it, add more liquid 1 tablespoon at a time until dough forms a smooth, soft, pliable ball that is slightly tacky to the touch.

3. At the beep add the remaining ingredients.

4. After the baking cycle ends, remove bread from pan, place on cake rack, and allow to cool 1 hour before slicing.

CRUST: Light
BAKE CYCLE: Raisin/Nut
OPTIONAL BAKE CYCLES: Standard/Whole Wheat/Sweet Bread

NUTRITIONAL INFORMATION PER SLICE
Calories 203/Fat 5.9 grams/Carbohydrates 33.9 grams/Protein 4.1 grams/Fiber 2 grams/Sodium 128 milligrams/Cholesterol 15.4 milligrams

---

Dad's Rice Pudding Bread

*L*inda has fond memories of her dad at the dinner table pouring milk over left-over rice and sprinkling cinnamon and sugar on top. His version of rice pudding was the inspiration for this bread. Watch the dough ball, as it will vary each time you make this bread. If you use freshly cooked rice, you will have less need to add extra liquid.

	SMALL LOAF	MEDIUM LOAF	LARGE LOAF
MILK	⅜ to ½ cup	⅞ to 1 cup	1⅜ to 1½ cups
EGG	1	1	2
BUTTER OR MARGARINE	2 tablespoons	3 tablespoons	4 tablespoons
COOKED, COOLED RICE	⅔ cup	1 cup	1⅓ cups
SALT	1½ teaspoons	2 teaspoons	3 teaspoons
SUGAR	2 tablespoons	3 tablespoons	¼ cup
BREAD FLOUR	2 cups	3½ cups	4½ cups
CINNAMON	1½ teaspoons	2 teaspoons	1 tablespoon
RED STAR BRAND ACTIVE DRY YEAST	1½ teaspoons	1½ teaspoons	2 teaspoons
RAISINS	⅓ cup	½ cup	⅔ cup

1. Place all ingredients except raisins in bread pan, using the least amount of liquid listed in the recipe. Select Light Crust setting and Raisin/Nut cycle. Press Start.

2. Observe the dough as it kneads. After 5 to 10 minutes, if it appears dry and stiff or if your machine sounds as if it's straining to knead it, add more liquid 1 tablespoon at a time until dough forms a smooth, soft, pliable ball that is slightly tacky to the touch.

3. At the beep, add the raisins.

4. After the baking cycle ends, remove bread from pan, place on cake rack, and allow to cool 1 hour before slicing.

CRUST: Light
BAKE CYCLE: Raisin/Nut
OPTIONAL BAKE CYCLES: Standard/Whole Wheat/Sweet Bread

NUTRITIONAL INFORMATION PER SLICE
Calories 195/Fat 3.4 grams/Carbohydrates 36.1 grams/Protein 5 grams/Fiber 1.4 grams/Sodium 349 milligrams/Cholesterol 16 milligrams

---

Delores's Raisin Walnut Bread

*D*elores Horn is a friend of Lois's and a wonderful cook and baker in her own right. She has two bread machines and is constantly creating new breads. She shared this one with us and it has become our favorite morning toast. We found a light setting was needed on most machines.

	SMALL LOAF	MEDIUM LOAF	LARGE LOAF
WATER	⅞ to 1 cup	1¼ to 1⅜ cups	1⅜ to 1½ cups
WALNUT OIL	1½ tablespoons	2 tablespoons	3 tablespoons
HONEY	1½ tablespoons	2 tablespoons	3 tablespoons
SALT	¾ teaspoon	1 teaspoon	1½ teaspoons
WHOLE WHEAT FLOUR	1 cup	1½ cups	2 cups
BREAD FLOUR	1 cup	1½ cups	2 cups
VITAL WHEAT GLUTEN (OPTIONAL)	1 tablespoon	2 tablespoons	3 tablespoons
NONFAT DRY MILK	1 tablespoon	1½ tablespoons	2 tablespoons
GROUND CARDAMOM	¼ teaspoon	½ teaspoon	½ teaspoon
GRATED LEMON PEEL	¼ teaspoon	½ teaspoon	¾ teaspoon
RED STAR BRAND ACTIVE DRY YEAST	1½ teaspoons	2 teaspoons	2½ teaspoons
RAISINS	¼ cup	⅓ cup	½ cup
COARSELY CHOPPED WALNUTS	¼ cup	⅓ cup	½ cup

1. Place all ingredients, except raisins and walnuts, in bread pan, using the least amount of liquid listed in the recipe. Select Light Crust setting and Raisin/Nut cycle. Press Start.

2. Observe the dough as it kneads. After 5 to 10 minutes, if it appears dry and stiff or if your machine sounds as if it's straining to knead it, add more liquid 1 tablespoon at a time until dough forms a smooth, soft, pliable ball that is slightly tacky to the touch.

3. At the beep, add raisins and walnuts.

4. After the baking cycle ends, remove bread from pan, place on cake rack, and allow to cool 1 hour before slicing.

CRUST: Light
BAKE CYCLE: Raisin/Nut
OPTIONAL BAKE CYCLES: Standard/Whole Wheat/Sweet Bread/Delayed Timer

---

NUTRITIONAL INFORMATION PER SLICE
Calories 152/Fat 4 grams/Carbohydrates 26 grams/Protein 4.4 grams/Fiber 2.5 grams/Sodium 157 milligrams/Cholesterol .1 milligrams

---

Irish Soda Bread

This is an "old country bread" that is chock full of currants and caraway seeds and has a delicious creamy texture.

	SMALL LOAF	MEDIUM LOAF	LARGE LOAF
BUTTERMILK	⁵⁄₈ to ¾ cup	1 to 1⅛ cups	1⅛ to 1¼ cups
EGG	1	1	2
HONEY	3 tablespoons	¼ cup	6 tablespoons
BUTTER OR MARGARINE	2 tablespoons	3 tablespoons	4 tablespoons
SALT	1 teaspoon	1 teaspoon	1½ teaspoons
BREAD FLOUR	2 cups	3⅓ cups	4⅓ cups
CARAWAY SEEDS	2 teaspoons	1 tablespoon	4 teaspoons
BAKING SODA	¾ teaspoon	1 teaspoon	1½ teaspoons
RED STAR BRAND ACTIVE DRY YEAST	2 teaspoons	2 teaspoons	2½ teaspoons
CURRANTS	¼ cup	⅓ cup	½ cup

1. Place all ingredients except currants in bread pan, using the least amount of liquid listed in the recipe. Select Light Crust setting and Raisin/Nut cycle. Press Start.

2. Observe the dough as it kneads. After 5 to 10 minutes, if it appears dry and stiff or if your machine sounds as if it's straining to knead it, add more liquid 1 tablespoon at a time until dough forms a smooth, soft, pliable ball that is slightly tacky to the touch.

3. At the beep, add the currants.

4. After the baking cycle ends, remove bread from pan, place on cake rack, and allow to cool 1 hour before slicing.

CRUST: Light
BAKE CYCLE: Raisin/Nut
OPTIONAL BAKE CYCLES: Standard/Sweet Bread/Rapid Bake

NUTRITIONAL INFORMATION PER SLICE
Calories 171/Fat 2.7 grams/Carbohydrates 32.3 grams/Protein 4.5 grams/Fiber 1.2 grams/Sodium 267 milligrams/Cholesterol 15.9 milligrams

Jam and Oats Bread

*T*his bread cries out for real homemade jam or good-quality store-bought preserves—fruit-sweetened or sugar-free spreads just don't work. Cut it in thick
slabs before it cools completely to fully appreciate this loaf.

	SMALL LOAF	MEDIUM LOAF	LARGE LOAF
OLD-FASHIONED OATS	½ cup	⅔ cup	1 cup
MILK	¾ to ⅞ cup	1⅛ to 1¼ cups	1¾ to 1⅞ cups
BUTTER OR MARGARINE	1 tablespoon	1½ tablespoons	2 tablespoons
YOUR FAVORITE JAM OR PRESERVES	⅓ cup	½ cup	⅔ cup
SALT	1 teaspoon	1½ teaspoons	2 teaspoons
BREAD FLOUR	2 cups	3 cups	4 cups
RED STAR BRAND ACTIVE DRY YEAST	1½ teaspoons	1½ teaspoons	2 teaspoons

I. Place all ingredients in bread pan, using the least amount of liquid listed in the
recipe. Select Light Crust setting and press Start.

2. Observe the dough as it kneads. After 5 to 10 minutes, if it appears dry and stiff or
if your machine sounds as if it's straining to knead it, add more liquid 1 tablespoon at
a time until dough forms a smooth, soft, pliable ball that is slightly tacky to the
touch.

3. After the baking cycle ends, remove the bread from pan, place on cake rack, and
allow to cool 1 hour before slicing.

CRUST: Light
BAKE CYCLE: Standard
OPTIONAL BAKE CYCLES: Whole Wheat/Sweet Bread/Rapid Bake

NUTRITIONAL INFORMATION PER SLICE
Calories 160/Fat 1.6 grams/Carbohydrates 31.9 grams/Protein 4.2 grams/Fiber 1.3
grams/Sodium 255 milligrams/Cholesterol .8 milligrams

Kat's Blueberry Bread

Kat Tarbet is Lois's co-host on the America Online Bread Chat and is also a fine cook and baker. We love this "blueberry cheesecake bread" but should warn you that it baked up too soft in several machines. When we altered the recipe to correct that problem, we lost the essence of this bread. So if yours is a "softie" you may have to accept it with its flaws or cut back on the amount of cream cheese. If you can't find dried blueberries, substitute any dried fruit.

	SMALL LOAF	MEDIUM LOAF	LARGE LOAF
WATER	⅝ to ¾ cup	⅞ to 1 cup	1⅛ to 1¼ cups
CREAM CHEESE, SOFTENED	3 ounces	4 ounces	6 ounces
BUTTER OR MARGARINE	1 tablespoon	2 tablespoons	2 tablespoons
SUGAR	2½ tablespoons	3½ tablespoons	¼ cup
SALT	1 teaspoon	1¼ teaspoons	2 teaspoons
BREAD FLOUR	2½ cups	3¼ cups	4½ cups
GRATED LEMON PEEL	½ teaspoon	1 teaspoon	1½ teaspoons
CARDAMOM	1 teaspoon	1½ teaspoons	2 teaspoons
NONFAT DRY MILK	1 tablespoon	2 tablespoons	2 tablespoons
RED STAR BRAND ACTIVE DRY YEAST	1½ teaspoons	2 teaspoons	2½ teaspoons
DRIED BLUEBERRIES	⅓ cup	½ cup	⅔ cup

1. Place all ingredients except dried blueberries in bread pan, using the least amount of liquid listed in the recipe. Select Light Crust setting and Raisin/Nut cycle. Press Start.

2. Observe the dough as it kneads. After 5 to 10 minutes, if it appears dry and stiff or if your machine sounds as if it's straining to knead it, add more liquid 1 tablespoon at a time until dough forms a smooth, soft, pliable ball that is slightly tacky to the touch.

3. At the beep, add the dried blueberries.

4. After the baking cycle ends, remove bread from pan, place on cake rack, and allow to cool 1 hour before slicing.

CREATIVE SUGGESTION: Substitute any dried fruit for the blueberries. Use grated orange peel instead of grated lemon peel.

CRUST: Light
BAKE CYCLE: Raisin/Nut
OPTIONAL BAKE CYCLES: Standard/Whole Wheat/Sweet Bread/Delayed Timer

---

NUTRITIONAL INFORMATION PER SLICE
Calories 165/Fat 4.8 grams/Carbohydrates 26.4 grams/Protein 3.9 grams/Fiber 1.3 grams/Sodium 239 milligrams/Cholesterol 9 milligrams

---

Lois's Banana Poppy Seed Bread

A favorite among our tasters, this is one Lois always turns to for her banana "fix." It's important to note that you must use very ripe bananas to get the proper moisture. Also, because it takes a while for the bananas to release all their moisture, don't be too quick to add liquid to the dough if it appears dry at first.

	SMALL LOAF	MEDIUM LOAF	LARGE LOAF
SLICED VERY RIPE BANANA	1 cup	1½ cups	2 cups
BUTTERMILK	⅜ to ½ cup	⅝ to ¾ cup	⅝ to ¾ cup
ALMOND EXTRACT	1 teaspoon	1½ teaspoons	2 teaspoons
OIL	2 tablespoons	3 tablespoons	¼ cup
HONEY	1½ tablespoons	2 tablespoons	3 tablespoons
SALT	½ teaspoon	1 teaspoon	1 teaspoon
BREAD FLOUR	1⅓ cups	2 cups	2⅔ cups
WHOLE WHEAT FLOUR	⅔ cup	1 cup	1⅓ cups
POPPY SEEDS	1½ tablespoons	2 tablespoons	3 tablespoons
RED STAR BRAND ACTIVE DRY YEAST	1½ teaspoons	2 teaspoons	2½ teaspoons

1. Place all ingredients in bread pan, using the least amount of liquid listed in the recipe. Select Light Crust setting and press Start.

2. Observe the dough as it kneads. After 5 to 10 minutes, if it appears dry and stiff or if your machine sounds as if it's straining to knead it, add more liquid 1 tablespoon at a time until dough forms a smooth, soft, pliable ball that is slightly tacky to the touch.

3. After the baking cycle ends, remove bread from pan, place on cake rack, and allow to cool 1 hour before slicing.

CRUST: Light
BAKE CYCLE: Standard
OPTIONAL BAKE CYCLES: Whole Wheat/Sweet Bread/Rapid Bake

NUTRITIONAL INFORMATION PER SLICE
Calories 149/Fat 3.4 grams/Carbohydrates 26.6 grams/Protein 3.6 grams/Fiber 2 grams/Sodium 165 milligrams/Cholesterol .4 milligrams

Nanny's Irish Bread

This bread was inspired by the grandmother of Linda's friend Eileen Shaughnessy. "Nanny," as she was affectionately called by her 40+ grandchildren, hailed from County Meath, Ireland, where the yeast-free version of this sweet bread was a staple.

	SMALL LOAF	MEDIUM LOAF	LARGE LOAF
EGG	1	1	2
VANILLA	½ teaspoon	¾ teaspoon	1 teaspoon
SOUR CREAM	1 cup	1½ cups	2 cups
SUGAR	½ cup	¾ cup	1 cup
BREAD FLOUR	2½ cups	3¾ cups	5 cups
BAKING SODA	¾ teaspoon	1 teaspoon	1½ teaspoons
RED STAR BRAND ACTIVE DRY YEAST	1½ teaspoons	2 teaspoons	2½ teaspoons
RAISINS	½ cup	¾ cup	1 cup

1. Place all ingredients except raisins in bread pan, select Light Crust setting and Raisin/Nut cycle. Press Start.

2. At the beep, add raisins.

3. After the baking cycle ends, remove bread from pan, place on cake rack, and allow to cool 1 hour before slicing.

CRUST: Light
BAKE CYCLE: Raisin/Nut
OPTIONAL BAKE CYCLES: Standard/Whole Wheat/Sweet Bread

NUTRITIONAL INFORMATION PER SLICE
Calories 244/Fat 5.5 grams/Carbohydrates 44.1 grams/Protein 4.9 grams/Fiber 1.5 grams/Sodium 90.2 milligrams/Cholesterol 15.2 milligrams

---

New England Maple Syrup Bread

*W*hat, no pancakes? You won't need them with this rich breakfast bread. There won't be any sleepyheads left when they get a whiff of this one baking. (It needed gluten in some machines to get a higher rise.)

	SMALL LOAF	MEDIUM LOAF	LARGE LOAF
WATER	⅜ to ½ cup	¾ to ⅞ cup	½ to ⅝ cup
OIL	1 tablespoon	1½ tablespoons	2 tablespoons
MAPLE SYRUP	3 tablespoons	¼ cup	6 tablespoons
SOUR CREAM	¼ cup	6 tablespoons	½ cup
EGG	1	1	2
SALT	1 teaspoon	1½ teaspoons	2 teaspoons
BROWN SUGAR	1 tablespoon	1½ tablespoons	2 tablespoons
WHOLE WHEAT FLOUR	1 cup	1½ cups	2 cups
BREAD FLOUR	1 cup	1½ cups	2 cups
VITAL WHEAT GLUTEN (OPTIONAL)	2 tablespoons	3 tablespoons	4 tablespoons
GROUND CINNAMON	¾ teaspoon	1 teaspoon	1½ teaspoons
GROUND CLOVES	¼ teaspoon	½ teaspoon	¾ teaspoon
RED STAR BRAND ACTIVE DRY YEAST	1½ teaspoons	2 teaspoons	2½ teaspoons

1. Place all ingredients in bread pan, using the least amount of liquid listed in the recipe. Select Whole Wheat cycle and Light Crust setting. Press Start.

2. Observe the dough as it kneads. After 5 to 10 minutes, if it appears dry and stiff or if your machine sounds as if it's straining to knead it, add more liquid 1 tablespoon at a time until dough forms a smooth, soft, pliable ball that is slightly tacky to the touch.

3. After the baking cycle ends, remove bread from pan, place on cake rack, and allow to cool 1 hour before slicing.

CRUST: Light
BAKE CYCLE: Whole Wheat
OPTIONAL BAKE CYCLES: Standard/Sweet Bread

NUTRITIONAL INFORMATION PER SLICE
Calories 145/Fat 3.5 grams/Carbohydrates 25.2 grams/Protein 3.9 grams/Fiber 2.1 grams/Sodium 239 milligrams/Cholesterol 17.9 milligrams

Pecan Bread

*T*ry *this bread with one of the butters or spreads in the last chapter. The first that comes to mind is the wonderful Praline Butter. Hmmmm . . . pecans on top of pecans. Too much of a good thing? We think not. Don't omit Step 1 in the directions. Toasting the pecans brings out so much more of their flavor.*

	SMALL LOAF	MEDIUM LOAF	LARGE LOAF
OIL	2 tablespoons	3 tablespoons	¼ cup
CHOPPED PECANS	⅔ cup	¾ cup	1⅓ cups
MILK	⅜ to ½ cup	⅝ to ¾ cup	1 cup
WATER	⅜ cup	½ cup	⅜ to ½ cup
DARK KARO SYRUP	2 tablespoons	3 tablespoons	¼ cup
SALT	1 teaspoon	1½ teaspoons	2 teaspoons
BREAD FLOUR	2 cups	3 cups	4 cups
RED STAR BRAND ACTIVE DRY YEAST	1½ teaspoons	1½ teaspoons	2 teaspoons

1. In a small skillet over medium heat, toast the pecans in oil until lightly browned, about 5 minutes. Remove pan from heat and allow pecans to cool to room temperature. Or, spread pecans in a single layer on a baking sheet and toast in a preheated 350°F oven. Bake for 10 to 15 minutes or until nuts are very hot and have a definite aroma. Stir often to prevent burning. You will *not* need the oil if you use this method.

2. Place all ingredients, including the pecans and oil, in bread pan, using the least amount of liquid listed in the recipe. Select Medium Crust setting and press Start.

3. Observe the dough as it kneads. After 5 to 10 minutes, if it appears dry and stiff or if your machine sounds as if it's straining to knead it, add more liquid 1 tablespoon at a time until dough forms a smooth, soft, pliable ball that is slightly tacky to the touch.

4. After the baking cycle ends, remove bread from pan, place on cake rack, and allow to cool 1 hour before slicing.

CRUST: Medium
BAKE CYCLE: Standard
OPTIONAL BAKE CYCLES: Sweet Bread/Raisin/Nut

NUTRITIONAL INFORMATION PER SLICE
Calories 180/Fat 7.6 grams/Carbohydrates 24.5 grams/Protein 3.7 grams/Fiber 1.2 grams/Sodium 235 milligrams/Cholesterol .45 milligrams

Portuguese Sweet Bread

I n addition to being good just plain, this is a great "leftover" bread. We've enjoyed it in bread pudding, as French Toast, and as crumbs, sprinkled over baked desserts. See if you don't agree.

	SMALL LOAF	MEDIUM LOAF	LARGE LOAF
WATER	3/8 to 1/2 cup	5/8 to 3/4 cup	3/4 to 7/8 cup
EGG	1	2	3
BUTTER OR MARGARINE	3 tablespoons	4 tablespoons	6 tablespoons
SUGAR	1/4 cup	1/3 cup	1/2 cup
SALT	3/4 teaspoon	1 1/2 teaspoons	1 1/2 teaspoons
BREAD FLOUR	2 cups	3 1/4 cups	4 1/4 cups
NONFAT DRY MILK POWDER	1 1/2 tablespoons	2 tablespoons	3 tablespoons
RED STAR BRAND ACTIVE DRY YEAST	2 teaspoons	2 teaspoons	2 1/2 teaspoons

I. Place all ingredients in bread pan, using the least amount of liquid listed in the recipe. Select Light Crust setting and Sweet Bread cycle. Press Start.

2. Observe the dough as it kneads. After 5 to 10 minutes, if it appears dry and stiff or if your machine sounds as if it's straining to knead it, add more liquid 1 tablespoon at a time until dough forms a smooth, soft, pliable ball that is slightly tacky to the touch.

3. After the baking cycle ends, remove bread from pan, place on cake rack, and allow to cool 1 hour before slicing.

CRUST: Light
BAKE CYCLE: Sweet Bread
OPTIONAL BAKE CYCLES: Standard/Whole Wheat/Rapid Bake

NUTRITIONAL INFORMATION PER SLICE
Calories 158/Fat 3.5 grams/Carbohydrates 26.8 grams/Protein 4.3 grams/Fiber .9 grams/
Sodium 281 milligrams/Cholesterol 30.5 milligrams

Rum Raisin Almond Bread

H*ere's bread that's both chewy and crunchy. Our taste testers give it a big thumbs-up.*

	SMALL LOAF	MEDIUM LOAF	LARGE LOAF
RAISINS	½ cup	⅔ cup	1 cup
RUM	3 tablespoons	¼ cup	6 tablespoons
MILK	⅜ to ½ cup	1 to 1⅛ cups	¾ to ⅞ cup
OIL	3 tablespoons	¼ cup	6 tablespoons
EGG	1	1	2
ALMOND EXTRACT	1 teaspoon	1½ teaspoons	2 teaspoons
SALT	1 teaspoon	1½ teaspoons	2 teaspoons
BROWN SUGAR	3 tablespoons	¼ cup	6 tablespoons
BREAD FLOUR	2¼ cups	3 cups	4½ cups
VITAL WHEAT GLUTEN (OPTIONAL)	1 tablespoon	2 tablespoons	3 tablespoons
GRATED LEMON RIND	of ½	of 1 small	of 1 medium
RED STAR BRAND ACTIVE DRY YEAST	1½ teaspoons	2 teaspoons	2½ teaspoons
SLIVERED ALMONDS	½ cup	⅔ cup	1 cup
WATER	2 teaspoons	1 tablespoon	1½ tablespoons

1. In a small bowl, soak the raisins in the rum for 15 to 20 minutes. Drain the raisins, reserving the rum. Place the rum in a measuring cup; add milk to measure ⅜ cup (small), 1 cup (medium), or ¾ cup (large).

2. Place all ingredients, except raisins, almonds, and water, in bread pan, using the least amount of liquid listed in the recipe. Select Light Crust and Raisin/Nut setting. Press Start.

3. Observe the dough as it kneads. After 5 to 10 minutes, if it appears dry and stiff or if your machine sounds as if it's straining to knead it, add more liquid 1 tablespoon at a time until dough forms a smooth, soft, pliable ball that is slightly tacky to the touch.

4. At the beep, add the raisins, almonds, and the extra water.

5. After the baking cycle ends, remove bread from pan, place on cake rack, and allow to cool 1 hour before slicing.

CRUST: Light
BAKE CYCLE: Raisin/Nut
OPTIONAL BAKE CYCLES: Standard/Sweet Bread

NUTRITIONAL INFORMATION PER SLICE
Calories 235/Fat 8 grams/Carbohydrates 33.7 grams/Protein 5.6 grams/Fiber 2 grams/Sodium 243 milligrams/Cholesterol 15.8 milligrams

Stephanie and Garrett's Chocolate Chips and Peanut Butter Bits Bread

I t's hard to tell who enjoys this bread more . . . toddlers or oldsters. Go ahead, bake up a loaf and allow yourself to feel young at heart again.

	SMALL LOAF	MEDIUM LOAF	LARGE LOAF
MILK	⅝ to ¾ cup	1 to 1⅛ cups	1⅛ to 1¼ cups
EGG	1	1	2
VANILLA	¼ teaspoon	½ teaspoon	½ teaspoon
OIL	1 tablespoon	1½ tablespoons	2 tablespoons
SUGAR	1½ tablespoons	2 tablespoons	3 tablespoons
SALT	¾ teaspoon	1 teaspoon	1½ teaspoons
BREAD FLOUR	2 cups	3 cups	4 cups
UNSWEETENED COCOA POWDER	3 tablespoons	¼ cup	6 tablespoons
RED STAR BRAND ACTIVE DRY YEAST	1 teaspoon	1½ teaspoons	2 teaspoons
PEANUT BUTTER CHIPS	¼ cup	⅓ cup	½ cup
CHOCOLATE CHIPS	¼ cup	⅓ cup	½ cup

1. Place all ingredients except peanut butter chips and chocolate chips in bread pan, using the least amount of liquid listed in the recipe. Select Light Crust setting and Raisin/Nut cycle. Press Start.

2. Observe the dough as it kneads. After 5 to 10 minutes, if it appears dry and stiff or if your machine sounds as if it's straining to knead it, add more liquid 1 tablespoon at a time until dough forms a smooth, soft, pliable ball that is slightly tacky to the touch.

3. At the beep, add the peanut butter chips and chocolate chips.

4. After the baking cycle, remove bread from pan, place on cake rack, and allow to cool 1 hour before slicing.

CRUST: Light
BAKE CYCLE: Raisin/Nut
OPTIONAL BAKE CYCLES: Standard/Whole Wheat/Sweet Bread/Rapid Bake

---

NUTRITIONAL INFORMATION PER SLICE
Calories 176/Fat 5.2 grams/Carbohydrates 28 grams/Protein 4.9 grams/Fiber 1.5 grams/Sodium 176 milligrams/Cholesterol 16.3 milligrams

7
Savory
Breads

Au Gratin Bread

*I*f you want to call everyone to dinner without making a sound, put this potato
bread in your machine and have it set to bake at dinnertime. They'll come run-
ning! This bread delivers in taste what it promises in aroma. Since moisture levels in
potatoes vary, you may need to adjust the liquid in this recipe. Do take the time to
watch the dough ball during kneading as we suggest in Step 2.

	SMALL LOAF	MEDIUM LOAF	LARGE LOAF
HEAVY CREAM	¼ to ⅜ cup	⅝ to ¾ cup	⅞ to 1 cup
POTATO WATER (THE WATER IN WHICH THE POTATO WAS COOKED)	¼ cup	½ cup	⅜ cup
PLAIN MASHED POTATO (AT ROOM TEMPERATURE)	¼ cup	⅓ cup	½ cup
BUTTER OR MARGARINE	1 tablespoon	1½ tablespoons	2 tablespoons
SALT	1 teaspoon	1½ teaspoons	2 teaspoons
SUGAR	1 tablespoon	1½ tablespoons	2 tablespoons
BREAD FLOUR	2 cups	3 cups	4 cups
EXTRA SHARP CHEDDAR CHEESE, DICED	½ cup (2 ounces)	¾ cup (3 ounces)	1 cup (4 ounces)
CHOPPED ONION	3 tablespoons	¼ cup	6 tablespoons
RED STAR BRAND ACTIVE DRY YEAST	1½ teaspoons	1½ teaspoons	2 teaspoons

1. Place all ingredients in bread pan, using the least amount of liquid listed in the
recipe. Select Medium Crust setting and press Start.

2. Observe the dough as it kneads. After 5 to 10 minutes, if it appears dry and stiff
or if your machine sounds as if it's straining to knead it, add more liquid 1 tablespoon
at a time until dough forms a smooth, soft, pliable ball that is slightly tacky to the touch.

3. After the baking cycle ends, remove bread from pan, place on cake rack, and
allow to cool 1 hour before slicing.

CRUST: Medium
BAKE CYCLE: Standard
OPTIONAL BAKE CYCLES: Whole Wheat/Sweet Bread/Rapid Bake

NUTRITIONAL INFORMATION PER SLICE
Calories 177/Fat 7.1 grams/Carbohydrates 23.2 grams/Protein 4.7 grams/Fiber .9 grams/Sodium 287 milligrams/Cholesterol 21 milligrams

Bacon, Egg, and Cheese Bread

We call this "breakfast in a bread pan."

	SMALL LOAF	MEDIUM LOAF	LARGE LOAF
BACON	4 slices	6 slices	8 slices
WATER	⅝ to ¾ cup	¾ to ⅞ cup	1 to 1⅛ cups
EGG	1	1	2
RESERVED BACON DRIPPINGS	2 teaspoons	1 tablespoon	4 teaspoons
SUGAR	1 tablespoon	1½ tablespoons	2 tablespoons
SALT	¾ teaspoon	1 teaspoon	1½ teaspoons
BREAD FLOUR	2 cups	3 cups	4 cups
GRATED SHARP CHEDDAR CHEESE	¾ cup (3 ounces)	1 cup (4 ounces)	1½ cups (6 ounces)
RED STAR BRAND ACTIVE DRY YEAST	1½ teaspoons	2 teaspoons	2½ teaspoons

I. In a skillet, cook bacon until crisp. Remove from pan, drain or pat with paper towels, and reserve the drippings. Crumble the bacon.

2. Place all ingredients in bread pan, using the least amount of liquid listed in the recipe. Select Light Crust setting and press Start.

3. Observe the dough as it kneads. After 5 to 10 minutes, if it appears dry and stiff or if your machine sounds as if it's straining to knead it, add more liquid 1 tablespoon at a time until dough forms a smooth, soft, pliable ball that is slightly tacky to the touch.

4. After the baking cycle ends, remove bread from pan, place on cake rack, and allow to cool 1 hour before slicing.

CRUST: Light
BAKE CYCLE: Standard
OPTIONAL BAKE CYCLES: Whole Wheat/Sweet Bread/Raisin/Nut/Rapid Bake

NUTRITIONAL INFORMATION PER SLICE
Calories 166/Fat 5.6 grams/Carbohydrates 22 grams/Protein 6.2 grams/Fiber .8 grams/Sodium 261 milligrams/Cholesterol 28 milligrams

Cecelia's Onion Cheese Bread

To toast or not to toast, that is the question. Whether 'tis best warm from the machine or thickly sliced and toasted, we just can't decide. How do you vote? Kudos to Linda's friend Cecelia Fleming for coming up with the idea for this taste sensation.

	SMALL LOAF	MEDIUM LOAF	LARGE LOAF
WATER	⅜ to ½ cup	½ to ⅝ cup	⅝ to ¾ cup
PROCESSED CHEESE SPREAD, SUCH AS CHEEZ WHIZ	⅔ cup	1 cup	1⅓ cups
SUGAR	1½ tablespoons	2 tablespoons	3 tablespoons
BREAD FLOUR	2 cups	3 cups	4 cups
MINCED FRESH ONION	3 tablespoons	¼ cup	6 tablespoons
RED STAR BRAND ACTIVE DRY YEAST	1½ teaspoons	2 teaspoons	2½ teaspoons
MELTED BUTTER OR MARGARINE	1 tablespoon	1½ tablespoons	2 tablespoons
DEHYDRATED CHOPPED ONION	3 tablespoons	¼ cup	6 tablespoons

1. Place all ingredients in bread pan, except melted butter and dehydrated onion, using the least amount of liquid listed in the recipe. Select Light Crust setting and press Start.

2. Observe the dough as it kneads. After 5 to 10 minutes, if it appears dry and stiff or if your machine sounds as if it's straining to knead it, add more liquid 1 tablespoon at a time until dough forms a smooth, soft, pliable ball that is slightly tacky to the touch.

3. After the last punch down, before the dough rises for the final time, quickly remove the ball of dough from the pan, brush with melted butter, and roll it in the dehydrated onions to coat. Immediately place the dough back into the pan for the final rise and bake. (Hint: Most manuals list the cycle times so you can calculate when to remove the dough. It's approximately 2 hours before the bread finishes baking. Also, be sure and close the lid when you take the dough out, to keep the warm air from escaping.)

4. After the baking cycle ends, remove bread from pan, place on cake rack, and allow to cool 1 hour before slicing.

VARIATION: If you miscalculate or forget to remove the dough on time, all is not lost. You can remove the dough anytime during the last rising cycle, shape it into a loaf, coat it with the butter and onion, and place it in a bread pan(s). Turn off the bread machine, of course. (For the small loaf, use a greased 8×4-inch pan; for the medium use a greased 9×5-inch pan; for the large loaf use two greased 8×4-inch pans.) Cover and let the bread rise until doubled in size, then bake in a 350°F oven for 50 minutes until golden-brown.

CRUST: Light
BAKE CYCLE: Standard
OPTIONAL BAKE CYCLES: Whole Wheat/Sweet Bread/Rapid Bake

NUTRITIONAL INFORMATION PER SLICE
Calories 184/Fat 6.7 grams/Carbohydrates 24.5 grams/Protein 6.2 grams/Fiber 1 gram/Sodium 233 milligrams/Cholesterol 10.3 milligrams

---

Goat Cheese and Cilantro Bread

The name says it all—this is a gourmet bread that combines the flavors so popular on dining tables today. We've added garlic, but you can let your imagination run wild and add any other seasonings you like. Lois likes to throw in some Herbes de Provence occasionally.

	SMALL LOAF	MEDIUM LOAF	LARGE LOAF
WATER	5/8 to 3/4 cup	1 1/8 to 1 1/4 cups	1 1/4 to 1 3/8 cups
SUGAR	1 teaspoon	1 1/2 teaspoons	2 teaspoons
SALT	1/2 teaspoon	1 teaspoon	1 1/2 teaspoons
BREAD FLOUR	1 1/3 cups	2 cups	2 2/3 cups
SEMOLINA FLOUR	2/3 cup	1 cup	1 1/3 cups
POWDERED WHEY OR NONFAT DRY MILK POWDER	2 tablespoons	3 tablespoons	4 tablespoons
CRUMBLED CHÈVRE (GOAT CHEESE)	3/4 cup (3 ounces)	1 cup (4 ounces)	1 1/2 cups (6 ounces)
CHOPPED FRESH CILANTRO	2/3 cup	1 cup	1 1/3 cups
CLOVE GARLIC, MINCED	1 large	2 medium	2 large
RED STAR BRAND ACTIVE DRY YEAST	1 1/2 teaspoons	2 teaspoons	2 1/2 teaspoons

I. Place all ingredients in bread pan, using the least amount of liquid listed in the recipe. Select Medium Crust setting and press Start.

2. Observe the dough as it kneads. After 5 to 10 minutes, if it appears dry and stiff or if your machine sounds as if it's straining to knead it, add more liquid 1 tablespoon at a time until dough forms a smooth, soft, pliable ball that is slightly tacky to the touch.

3. After the baking cycle ends, remove bread from pan, place on cake rack, and allow to cool 1 hour before slicing.

CRUST: Medium
BAKE CYCLE: Standard
OPTIONAL BAKE CYCLES: Delayed Timer/Rapid Bake

NUTRITIONAL INFORMATION PER SLICE
Calories 139/Fat 2.3 grams/Carbohydrates 23.6 grams/Protein 5.2 grams/Fiber 1 gram/Sodium 228 milligrams/Cholesterol 5.7 milligrams

---

Jalapeño Corn Bread

*Y*ou can used canned corn, but drain it well. If you like it hotter, add a tablespoon or two of chopped jalapeños. Then slice into this bread and enjoy a wonderful "south of the border" flavor. Olé!

	SMALL LOAF	MEDIUM LOAF	LARGE LOAF
WATER	½ to ⅝ cup	⅞ to 1 cup	1 to 1⅛ cups
EGG	1	1	2
OIL	1½ tablespoons	2 tablespoons	3 tablespoons
SUGAR	1½ tablespoons	2 tablespoons	3 tablespoons
SALT	½ teaspoon	¾ teaspoon	1 teaspoon
BREAD FLOUR	1⅔ cups	2½ cups	3⅓ cups
CORNMEAL	⅔ cup	1 cup	1⅓ cups
RED STAR BRAND ACTIVE DRY YEAST	1½ teaspoons	2 teaspoons	2½ teaspoons
MONTEREY JACK PEPPER CHEESE, CUT INTO 1/4-INCH CUBES	½ cup (2 ounces)	¾ cup (3 ounces)	1 cup (4 ounces)
CANNED CORN KERNELS, DRAINED	⅓ cup	½ cup	⅔ cup

1. Place all ingredients except the cheese and corn in bread pan, using the least amount of liquid listed in the recipe. Select Light Crust setting and Raisin/Nut cycle. Press Start.

2. Observe the dough as it kneads. After 5 to 10 minutes, if it appears dry and stiff or if your machine sounds as if it's straining to knead it, add more liquid 1 tablespoon at a time until dough forms a smooth, soft, pliable ball that is slightly tacky to the touch.

3. At the beep, add cheese and corn.

4. After the baking cycle ends, remove bread from pan, place on cake rack, and allow to cool 1 hour before slicing.

CRUST: Light
BAKE CYCLE: Raisin/Nut
OPTIONAL BAKE CYCLES: Standard/Whole Wheat/Sweet Bread/Rapid Bake

---

NUTRITIONAL INFORMATION PER SLICE
Calories 171/Fat 4.7 grams/Carbohydrates 26.4 grams/Protein 5.3 grams/Fiber 1.8 grams/Sodium 156 milligrams/Cholesterol 20.6 milligrams

---

Jim's Torta Rustica

I f you're looking for something special for a picnic or tailgate party, look no fur-
ther than this spectacular Italian spinach pie. Lois's husband, Jim, thinks this is
the best recipe in the book! (This is a 2-pound dough recipe. If you don't have one of
the large 2-pound machines, you can cut the dough ingredients in half and make it
twice in your smaller machine. Refrigerate the first dough in an oiled bag while
making the second.)

DOUGH

LARGE LOAF			
WATER	½ cup	SALT	1½ teaspoons
MILK	½ cup	ALL-PURPOSE FLOUR	4 cups
EGGS	2		
OLIVE OIL	¼ cup	RED STAR BRAND ACTIVE DRY YEAST	2 teaspoons
SUGAR	1½ tablespoons		

SPINACH FILLING

LARGE LOAF			
OLIVE OIL	2 tablespoons	PROVOLONE CHEESE, CUBED	1½ cups (6 ounces)
HOT ITALIAN SAUSAGE, CASINGS REMOVED	1 pound	SEASONED BREAD CRUMBS	1 cup
ONION, CHOPPED	1 large	FRESHLY GRATED PARMESEAN CHEESE	½ cup (2 ounces)
EGGS, SLIGHTLY BEATEN	3	PLUM TOMATOES, DICED	1 pound
FROZEN CHOPPED SPINACH, THAWED AND SQUEEZED DRY WITH A KITCHEN TOWEL	2 (10-ounce) packages	SLICED BLACK OLIVES	½ cup
CLOVES GARLIC, MINCED	4	PINE NUTS (OPTIONAL)	¼ cup
		EGG	1
DRIED OREGANO	1 teaspoon	WATER	1 tablespoon
RICOTTA CHEESE	1½ cups	SALT AND PEPPER TO TASTE	

1. Place dough ingredients in bread pan, select Dough setting, and press Start.

1. Place dough ingredients in bread pan, select Dough setting, and press Start.

2. Meanwhile, in a small skillet heat olive oil over medium heat. Add the sausage. As it cooks, break the sausage up into small pieces with a spatula. Cook until no longer pink, about 5 minutes. Remove from pan with slotted spoon and drain on paper towels. Add the onion to the remaining oil in the pan and sauté until softened, about 5 minutes. Set aside.

3. In a large bowl, combine eggs, spinach, garlic, oregano, ricotta cheese, provolone cheese, and salt and pepper to taste. Set aside.

4. When the dough has risen long enough, the machine will beep. Turn off bread machine, remove bread pan, and turn out dough onto a lightly floured countertop or cutting board. Grease a 9-inch springform pan.

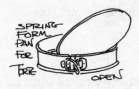

5. Cut the dough into three equal pieces. Set one piece aside and combine the other two into one large ball. With a rolling pin, roll the large ball of dough into a 16-inch-wide circle. Place in prepared pan, gently shaping it to fit the pan. Trim the dough, leaving a 1-inch overhang. (Reserve scraps of dough for decoration.)

6. Sprinkle the bread crumbs and grated Parmesan on the bottom. Then layer in order cooked sausage, onion, spinach mixture, tomatoes, olives, and pine nuts.

7. Roll out the remaining ball of dough into an 11-inch-wide circle. Cut a small hole in the center for ventilation. Place circle of dough on top of pie and crimp edges together to seal.

8. Cover and let rise in a warm oven 30 minutes until puffy. (Hint: To warm slightly, turn oven on Warm setting for 1 minute, then turn it off, and place covered dough in oven to rise. Remove pan from oven before preheating.)

9. Meanwhile, roll out any scraps of dough as thinly as possible and with a small, sharp knife cut dough into desire shapes, such as leaves, flowers, grapevines, hearts, etc. Set aside.

10. Preheat the oven to 375°F. Combine egg and water. Gently brush egg wash over dough. Place decorations on top and brush with egg wash also. Bake pie for 50 to 60 minutes until brown, covering lightly with a sheet of foil after 20 minutes.

11. Remove from oven and cool on a rack for 15 minutes. Remove sides of pan and cool completely on cake rack.

CREATIVE SUGGESTIONS:

1. Substitute your favorite bread recipe for the dough or add your favorite herbs to this recipe to give it more flavor.

2. If you don't care for the hot Italian sausage, you can substitute the mild variety.

3. If you prefer an even hotter taste, use the mild sausage but sprinkle liberally with crushed red pepper flakes to taste.

4. Vary the filling ingredients at will, making sure all are well drained.

5. Too rushed to make and shape the dough? You can achieve similar results by hollowing out a round loaf of French bread, filling as directed above, then wrapping the loaf in foil and baking it in a 350°F oven for 35 to 40 minutes.

6. Serve with a marinara sauce.

7. Add freshly ground nutmeg to the filling to taste.

Serves 10

BAKE CYCLE: Dough

NUTRITIONAL INFORMATION PER SERVING
Calories 629/Fat 35 grams/Carbohydrates 48.4 grams/Protein 31.8 grams/Fiber 4.7 grams/Sodium 1164 milligrams/Cholesterol 169 milligrams

---

Linda's Sun-Dried Tomato Mozzarella Bread

*T*he Linda in the title is Linda Caldwell, a very inventive cook who loves to experiment with all sorts of unique ingredients. This tasty recipe is one of her first and most popular ones. You can use dry, reconstituted, or oil-packed sun-dried tomatoes—just make sure they are well drained. We had the best success using oil-packed tomatoes in our machines. If you have fresh buttermilk on hand that you want to use up, you can substitute it for half of the liquid.

	SMALL LOAF	MEDIUM LOAF	LARGE LOAF
WATER	¾ to ⅞ cup	1¼ to 1⅜ cups	1⅜ to 1½ cups
OLIVE OIL	2 teaspoons	1 tablespoon	4 teaspoons
SALT	¾ teaspoon	1 teaspoon	1½ teaspoons
BREAD FLOUR	2 cups	3 cups	4 cups
VITAL WHEAT GLUTEN (OPTIONAL)	1 tablespoon	1½ tablespoons	2 tablespoons
BUTTERMILK POWDER	1½ tablespoons	2 tablespoons	3 tablespoons
DRIED MINCED ONION	1½ tablespoons	2 tablespoons	3 tablespoons
DRIED BASIL	2 teaspoons	1 tablespoon	4 teaspoons
CHOPPED SUN-DRIED TOMATOES	1½ tablespoons	2 tablespoons	3 tablespoons
MOZZARELLA CHEESE, SHREDDED	¾ cup (3 ounces)	1 cup (4 ounces)	1½ cups (6 ounces)
RED STAR BRAND ACTIVE DRY YEAST	1½ teaspoons	2 teaspoons	2½ teaspoons

1. Place all ingredients in bread pan, using the least amount of liquid listed in the recipe. Select Medium Crust setting and press Start.

2. Observe the dough as it kneads. During the second kneading cycle, if it appears dry and stiff or if your machine sounds as if it's straining to knead it, add more liquid 1 tablespoon at a time until dough forms a smooth, soft, pliable ball that is slightly tacky to the touch.

3. After the baking cycle ends, remove bread from pan, place on cake rack, and allow to cool 1 hour before slicing.

CRUST: Medium
BAKE CYCLE: Standard
OPTIONAL BAKE CYCLES: Sweet Bread/Delayed Timer/Rapid Bake

NUTRITIONAL INFORMATION PER SLICE
Calories 135/Fat 1.9 grams/Carbohydrates 24.6 grams/Protein 4.4 grams/Fiber 1.2 grams/Sodium 207 milligrams/Cholesterol 4.5 milligrams

---

Marlene's Lemon Pepper Bread

*L*ois met her good friend Marlene Casmaer while logged onto America Online in the Cooking Club and they've been sharing recipes every since. This tasty and unusual bread is Marlene's gift to us and all who try it. As she says, "It makes awesome croutons!" It's important to use coarsely ground black pepper. Adjust the amount to suit your own taste.

	SMALL LOAF	MEDIUM LOAF	LARGE LOAF
WATER	⅝ to ¾ cup	1⅛ to 1¼ cups	1½ to 1⅝ cups
OIL	1½ tablespoons	2 tablespoons	3 tablespoons
HONEY	1½ tablespoons	2 tablespoons	3 tablespoons
KOSHER SALT	¾ teaspoon	1 teaspoon	1½ teaspoons
BREAD FLOUR	2 cups	3 cups	4 cups
COARSELY GROUND BLACK PEPPER	1 to 2 teaspoons	2 to 3 teaspoons	3 to 4 teaspoons
GRATED LEMON ZEST	of 1 small	of 1 medium	of 1 large
RED STAR BRAND ACTIVE DRY YEAST	1½ teaspoons	2 teaspoons	2½ teaspoons

1. Place all ingredients in bread pan, using the least amount of liquid listed in the recipe. Select Medium Crust setting and press Start.

2. Observe the dough as it kneads. After 5 to 10 minutes, if it appears dry and stiff or if your machine sounds as if it's straining to knead it, add more liquid 1 tablespoon at a time until dough forms a smooth, soft, pliable ball that is slightly tacky to the touch.

3. After the baking cycle ends, remove bread from pan, place on cake rack, and allow to cool 1 hour before slicing.

CRUST: Medium
BAKE CYCLE: Standard
OPTIONAL BAKE CYCLES: Whole Wheat/Sweet Bread/Delayed Timer/Rapid Bake

---

NUTRITIONAL INFORMATION PER SLICE
Calories 126/Fat 2.2 grams/Carbohydrates 23.3 grams/Protein 3 grams/Fiber 1 gram/Sodium 153 milligrams/Cholesterol 0 milligrams

---

Mexicorn Bread

Mmmm! *Doesn't everyone love creamed corn? When it's coupled with red and green peppers in a bread, how can you go wrong? You might have to adjust the liquid in this, depending on the moisture in the peppers, but don't do it too soon. It starts out as a dry, stiff dough but eventually softens. Give it about 10 minutes before making adjustments. If your peppers disappear, try adding them at the beep on the Raisin/Nut cycle instead.*

	SMALL LOAF	MEDIUM LOAF	LARGE LOAF
MILK		⅛ to ¼ cup	¼ to ⅜ cup
EGG	1	1	2
CREAMED CORN	½ cup	¾ cup	1 cup
BUTTER OR MARGARINE	1 tablespoon	1½ tablespoons	2 tablespoons
SUGAR	1½ tablespoons	2 tablespoons	3 tablespoons
SALT	1 teaspoon	1½ teaspoons	2 teaspoons
BREAD FLOUR	2 cups	3 cups	4 cups
CORNMEAL	⅓ cup	½ cup	⅔ cup
FINELY CHOPPED RED PEPPER	⅓ cup	½ cup	⅔ cup
FINELY CHOPPED GREEN PEPPER	⅓ cup	½ cup	⅔ cup
RED STAR BRAND ACTIVE DRY YEAST	1½ teaspoons	1½ teaspoons	2 teaspoons

I.   Place all ingredients in bread pan, using the least amount of liquid listed in the recipe. Select Medium Crust setting and press Start.

2.   Observe the dough as it kneads. After 5 to 10 minutes, if it appears dry and stiff or if your machine sounds as if it's straining to knead it, add more liquid 1 tablespoon at a time until dough forms a smooth, soft, pliable ball that is slightly tacky to the touch.

3.   After the baking cycle ends, remove bread from pan, place on cake rack, and allow to cool 1 hour before slicing.

CRUST: Medium
BAKE CYCLE: Standard
OPTIONAL BAKE CYCLES: Raisin/Nut/Whole Wheat/Rapid Bake

NUTRITIONAL INFORMATION PER SLICE
Calories 147/Fat 1.8 grams/Carbohydrates 28.6 grams/Protein 4 grams/Fiber 1.5 grams/Sodium 291 milligrams/Cholesterol 15.3 milligrams

---

Pizza Loaf

Pass the pepper flakes, please! This pizza-in-a-bread is the next best thing to the Italian pie. It's also a fun bread to play around with—see our creative suggestions for starters.

	SMALL LOAF	MEDIUM LOAF	LARGE LOAF
MILK	¼ to ⅜ cup	⅝ to ¾ cup	⅝ to ¾ cup
EGG	1	1	2
TOMATO PASTE	6 tablespoons	6-ounce can	¾ cup
OLIVE OIL	2 teaspoons	1 tablespoon	¼ cup
SUGAR	2 teaspoons	1 tablespoon	¼ cup
SALT	½ teaspoon	½ teaspoon	1 teaspoon
BREAD FLOUR	2 cups	3¼ cups	4 cups
DRIED MINCED ONION	1½ teaspoons	2 teaspoons	1 tablespoon
ITALIAN HERB SEASONING	½ teaspoon	1 teaspoon	1 teaspoon
GARLIC POWDER	¼ teaspoon	¼ teaspoon	½ teaspoon
RED PEPPER FLAKES	¼ teaspoon	¼ teaspoon	½ teaspoon
RED STAR BRAND ACTIVE DRY YEAST	1½ teaspoons	1½ teaspoons	2 teaspoons
PEPPERONI	½ cup	¾ cup	1 cup
MOZZARELLA CHEESE	½ cup (2 ounces)	¾ cup (3 ounces)	1 cup (4 ounces)
CHOPPED GREEN PEPPER	¼ cup	⅓ cup	½ cup

1. Place all ingredients in bread pan except pepperoni, cheese, and green pepper, using the least amount of liquid listed in the recipe. Select Light Crust setting and Raisin/Nut cycle. Press Start.

2. Observe the dough as it kneads. After 5 to 10 minutes, if it appears dry and stiff or if your machine sounds as if it's straining to knead it, add more liquid 1 tablespoon at a time until dough forms a smooth, soft, pliable ball that is slightly tacky to the touch.

3. Cut pepperoni and mozzarella cheese into ¼ inch cubes. At the beep add pepperoni, cheese, and green pepper.

4. After the baking cycle ends, remove bread from pan, place on cake rack, and allow to cool 1 hour before slicing.

CREATIVE SUGGESTIONS:

1. Substitute cooked and crumbled Italian sausage for the pepperoni.

2. At the beep, add chopped mushrooms, sliced black olives, Parmesan cheese, chopped pepperoncini, or minced garlic.

3. Instead of adding the extras at the Raisin/Nut beep, you could make this a Spiral Bread (see Pesto Spiral Bread, page 164, for directions).

CRUST: Light
BAKE CYCLE: Raisin/Nut
OPTIONAL BAKE CYCLES: Standard/Whole Wheat/Rapid Bake

NUTRITIONAL INFORMATION PER SLICE
Calories 193/Fat 6.4 grams/Carbohydrates 26.4 grams/Protein 7.2 grams/Fiber 1.5 grams/Sodium 339 milligrams/Cholesterol 23.1 milligrams

---

Reubens

*T*hese pocket sandwiches are terrific for a quick lunch or light dinner. Make them ahead and store them in the freezer. When you feel like having one for lunch or dinner, reheat in the microwave for a couple of minutes. What could be simpler?

DOUGH

	SMALL LOAF	MEDIUM LOAF	LARGE LOAF
MILK	¼ cup	⅜ cup	½ cup
WATER	¼ cup	⅜ cup	⅝ cup
EGG	1	1	2
SHORTENING	2 tablespoons	3 tablespoons	¼ cup
SUGAR	2 tablespoons	3 tablespoons	¼ cup
SALT	1 teaspoon	1½ teaspoons	2 teaspoons
BREAD FLOUR	1½ cups	2¼ cups	3 cups
RYE FLOUR	½ cup	¾ cup	1 cup
CARAWAY SEEDS	1 teaspoon	1½ teaspoons	2 teaspoons
RED STAR BRAND ACTIVE DRY YEAST	1½ teaspoons	2 teaspoons	2½ teaspoons

1.   Place dough ingredients in bread pan, select Dough setting, and press Start.

2.   When the dough has risen long enough, the machine will beep. Turn off bread machine, remove bread pan, and turn out dough onto a lightly floured countertop or cutting board.

FOR THE SMALL RECIPE
Gently roll and stretch dough into a 6-inch log. With a sharp knife, divide dough into 6 pieces.

FOR THE MEDIUM RECIPE
Gently roll and stretch dough into a 9-inch log. With a sharp knife, divide dough into 9 pieces.

FOR THE LARGE RECIPE
Gently roll and stretch dough into a 12-inch long. With a sharp knife, divide dough into 12 pieces.

3.   Grease a baking sheet. Preheat oven to 400°F.

FILLING

	SMALL LOAF	MEDIUM LOAF	LARGE LOAF
THOUSAND ISLAND DRESSING	3 tablespoons	¼ cup	6 tablespoons
THINLY SLICED CORNED BEEF	8 ounces	12 ounces	16 ounces
GRATED SWISS CHEESE	1 cup (4 ounces)	1½ cups (6 ounces)	2 cups (8 ounces)
SAUERKRAUT, WELL DRAINED	¾ cup	1 cup	1½ cups

4. With a rolling pin, roll each piece into a 6-inch circle. Brush each with Thousand Island dressing to within ½-inch of the edges. Cut corned beef into bite-size pieces. Then layer in order corned beef, cheese, and sauerkraut in the center of each circle of dough. Pull the edges of dough up to meet in the center and pinch together well to seal. Place on prepared baking sheet, sealed-side down.

5. Bake for 15 to 20 minutes until light brown. Remove from oven and serve warm. These freeze well for up to 3 months. To reheat, microwave on HIGH power for 1½ to 2 minutes, or wrap in foil and bake in a 325°F oven for 30 minutes.

Small recipe yields 6 rolls
Medium recipe yields 9 rolls
Large recipe yields 12 rolls

BAKE CYCLE: Dough

NUTRITIONAL INFORMATION PER ROLL
Calories 253/Fat 11.2 grams/Carbohydrates 23.1 grams/Protein 14.3 grams/Fiber 1.8 grams/Sodium 1001 milligrams/Cholesterol 49.3 milligrams

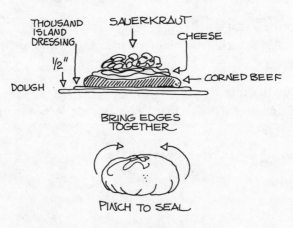

Samosas

This Indian dish works well as an appetizer, a snack, or a full meal. You choose. It's another one we like to keep on hand in the freezer.

DOUGH

	MEDIUM LOAF	
WATER	¾ cup	
EGG	1	
OLIVE OIL	2 tablespoons	
SUGAR	1 tablespoon	
SALT	1 teaspoon	
UNBLEACHED OR ALL-PURPOSE FLOUR	2 cups	
WHOLE WHEAT FLOUR	1 cup	
GROUND CUMIN	1 teaspoon	
GROUND CORIANDER		½ teaspoon
RED STAR BRAND ACTIVE DRY YEAST	2 teaspoons	

I. Place dough ingredients in bread pan, select Dough setting, and press Start.

FILLING

OLIVE OIL	2 tablespoons
CHOPPED ONION	½ cup
RED POTATOES	4 small (4 to 5 ounces each)
CLOVE GARLIC, MINCED	1
FROZEN PEAS, THAWED	½ cup
DICED CARROTS	½ cup
CURRY POWDER	2 teaspoons
CAYENNE PEPPER (OPTIONAL)	Dash
SALT AND PEPPER TO TASTE	

2. Cut potatoes into ¼-inch cubes. In a nonstick skillet over medium heat, sauté the onion and potatoes until tender, about 8 minutes. Add the remaining filling ingredients and cook until heated through, about 5 minutes. Set aside.

3. When the dough has risen long enough, the machine will beep. Turn off bread machine, remove bread pan, and turn out dough onto a lightly floured countertop or cutting board. Grease a large baking sheet.

4. Gently roll and stretch dough into an 8-inch log. With a sharp knife, divide dough into 8 pieces. With a rolling pin, roll each piece into a 6-inch circle. Place ⅓ cup of filling mixture on one half of each circle. Lightly moisten the edge of each circle with a fingertip dipped in water, fold dough in half over filling, and pinch edges to seal well.

GLAZE

EGG	1
WATER	1 tablespoon

5. Preheat the oven to 400°F. Combine egg and water. Gently brush egg wash over dough. Bake for 15 to 20 minutes until brown.

6. Remove from oven and serve warm.

CREATIVE SUGGESTIONS:

1. For appetizer-size samosas, cut dough into 24 pieces and roll into 3-inch circles. Place 2 tablespoons filling on each.

2. For meal-size samosas, cut dough into 4 pieces and roll into 9-inch circles. Place ⅔ cup filling on each.

3. We prefer these with a spicy sauce. Combine 1 cup ketchup or tomato sauce with 1½ teaspoons chili powder, 1½ teaspoons curry powder, and ½ teaspoon dry mustard. Or, if your local supermarket has an ethnic foods section, try them with a spicy chutney.

Serves 8

BAKE CYCLE: Dough

NUTRITIONAL INFORMATION PER SERVING
Calories 193/Fat 5.9 grams/Carbohydrates 30 grams/Protein 5.6 grams/Fiber 3 grams/Sodium 200 milligrams/Cholesterol 35.5 milligrams

Savory Olive Bread

We found that green olives make this a more flavorful bread. Save a slice or two for a sandwich if you can.

	SMALL LOAF	MEDIUM LOAF	LARGE LOAF
WATER	½ to ⅝ cup	⅞ to 1 cup	¾ to ⅞ cup
EGG	1	1	2
OLIVE OIL	2 tablespoons	3 tablespoons	¼ cup
SUGAR	1 teaspoon	1½ teaspoons	2 teaspoons
SALT	½ teaspoon	¾ teaspoon	1 teaspoon
BREAD FLOUR	1⅓ cups	2 cups	2⅔ cups
SEMOLINA FLOUR	⅔ cup	1 cup	1⅓ cups
RED STAR BRAND ACTIVE DRY YEAST	1½ teaspoons	2 teaspoons	2½ teaspoons
CHOPPED AND PITTED GREEN OLIVES, DRAINED	½ cup	¾ cup	1 cup
FINELY DICED COOKED HAM	¼ cup	⅓ cup	½ cup
CHOPPED ONION	¼ cup	⅓ cup	½ cup

1. Place all ingredients except olives, ham, and onion in bread pan, using the least amount of liquid listed in the recipe. Select Medium Crust setting and Raisin/Nut cycle. Press Start.

2. Observe the dough as it kneads. After 5 to 10 minutes, if it appears dry and stiff or if your machine sounds as if it's straining to knead it, add more liquid 1 tablespoon at a time until dough forms a smooth, soft, pliable ball that is slightly tacky to the touch.

3. At the beep, add the olives, ham, and onion.

4. After the baking cycle ends, remove bread from pan, place on cake rack, and allow to cool 1 hour before slicing.

CRUST: Medium
BAKE CYCLE: Raisin/Nut
OPTIONAL BAKE CYCLES: Standard/Whole Wheat

NUTRITIONAL INFORMATION PER SLICE
Calories 154/Fat 4.4 grams/Carbohydrates 23.5 grams/Protein 4.6 grams/Fiber 1.3 grams/Sodium 215 milligrams/Cholesterol 16.7 milligrams

---

8

Dinner Rolls
and
Bread Sticks

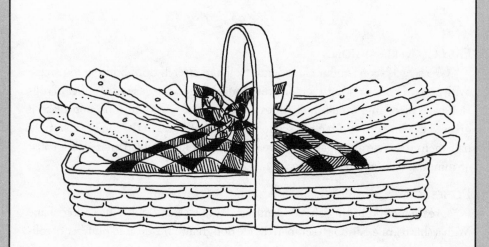

Pan Rolls

Grease a 9×13×2-inch pan or an 8- or 9-inch square pan. Gently roll and stretch dough into a log shape. With a sharp knife or dough scraper, divide dough into the desired number of rolls. Roll each piece into a ball, pull edges under to make smooth tops, and place in prepared pan ½ to 1 inch apart. Cover and let rise until doubled in size, about 30 to 45 minutes. Bake as directed in recipe.

Cloverleaf Rolls

Grease a 12-cup muffin pan. Gently roll and stretch into a log shape. With a sharp knife or dough scraper, divide dough into the desired number of rolls. Cut each roll into thirds. Roll each piece into small balls; pull edges under to make smooth tops. Place 3 balls in each greased muffin cup. Cover and let rise until doubled in size, about 30 to 45 minutes. Bake as directed in recipe.

Easy Cloverleaf Rolls

Grease a 12-cup muffin pan. Gently roll and stretch dough into a log shape. With a sharp knife or dough scraper, divide dough into the desired number of rolls. Roll each piece into a ball, pull edges under to make smooth tops, and place in greased muffin cups. With clean scissors dipped in flour, cut the top of each roll in half, then crosswise into quarters. Cover and let rise until doubled in size, about 30 to 45 minutes. Bake as directed in recipe.

Posies

Grease a large baking sheet. Gently roll and stretch dough into a log shape. With a sharp knife or dough scraper, divide dough into the desired number of rolls.

Roll each piece into a ball, pull edges under to make smooth tops, and flatten slightly. With scissors, snip six or eight ¼-inch-deep cuts around the edge of each ball. Place on prepared baking sheet. Brush tops with an egg glaze. Sprinkle with sesame or poppy seeds. Let rise until doubled in size, about 30 to 45 minutes. Bake as directed in recipe.

TWISTS

Grease a large baking sheet. Gently roll and stretch dough into a log shape. With a sharp knife or dough scraper, divide dough into the desired number of rolls. Roll each piece into a 12-inch rope. Fold rope in half and twist, pinching the end to seal. Place on prepared baking sheet. Brush with melted butter or margarine. Let rise until doubled in size, about 30 to 45 minutes. Bake as directed in recipe.

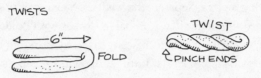

KNOTS

Grease a large baking sheet. Gently roll and stretch dough into a log shape. With a sharp knife or dough scraper, divide dough into the desired number of rolls. Roll each piece into a 10-inch rope. Tie each rope into a loose knot. Place on prepared baking sheet. Brush with melted butter or margarine. Let rise until doubled in size, about 30 to 45 minutes. Bake as directed in recipe.

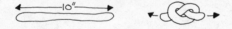

SNAILS

Grease a large baking sheet. Gently roll and stretch dough into a log shape. With a sharp knife or dough scraper, divide dough into the desired number of rolls. Roll each piece into a 12-inch rope. Hold one end of the rope (the center of the snail) in place on the baking sheet. Loosely coil the rest of the rope around the center; tuck the end underneath. Cover and let rise until doubled in size, about 30 to 45 minutes. Bake as directed in recipe. (Optional: Before baking, brush rolls with beaten egg; sprinkle with sesame or poppy seeds.)

PARKER HOUSE ROLLS

Grease a large baking sheet. With a rolling pin, roll out dough to a ¼-inch thickness. With a 2- to 2½-inch biscuit cutter, cut out rolls. Brush each with melted butter. Holding both ends of a clean pen or pencil (or a chopstick), press it into each roll slightly off center to make a crease. Fold the larger side over the smaller side; press the edges together lightly. Place on prepared baking sheet. Cover and let rise until doubled in size, about 30 to 45 minutes. Bake as directed in recipe.

BUTTERHORNS AND CRESCENT ROLLS

Grease a large baking sheet. With a sharp knife or dough scraper, divide large dough in quarters, medium dough into thirds, or small dough in half. Roll each piece into an 8- or 9-inch circle. With a knife or pizza cutter, divide each circle into 8 wedges, as if cutting a pizza. Separate the wedges. Starting at the wide end, roll up each wedge toward the point. Place on baking sheet with points underneath. For crescent rolls, curve each roll into a crescent shape by bringing the points slightly toward each other. Cover and let rise until doubled in size, about 30 to 45 minutes. Bake as directed in recipe.

FAN TANS

Butter a 12-cup muffin tin. With a rolling pin, roll dough into a 9×12-inch rectangle. Brush with melted butter. With a pizza cutter or sharp knife, cut 6 lengthwise strips about 1½ inches wide. Stack strips on top of each other, then cut crosswise into twelve 1-inch pieces. Place cut-side down in prepared muffin cups. Cover and let rise almost doubled in size, about 20 to 30 minutes. Bake as directed in recipe.

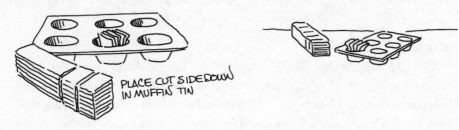

PLACE CUT SIDE DOWN IN MUFFIN TIN

Annie's Dinner Rolls

*T*here are some wonderful people and recipes in cyberspace. These buttery dinner rolls are from our online friend Annie Miner.

	SMALL LOAF	MEDIUM LOAF	LARGE LOAF
WATER	½ cup	¾ cup	⅞ cup
EGG	1	1	2
BUTTER OR MARGARINE	3 tablespoons	4 tablespoons	6 tablespoons
SUGAR	3 tablespoons	¼ cup	6 tablespoons
SALT	¾ teaspoon	1 teaspoon	1½ teaspoons
ALL-PURPOSE FLOUR	2 cups	3 cups	4 cups
RED STAR BRAND ACTIVE DRY YEAST	1½ teaspoons	2 teaspoons	2½ teaspoons
MELTED BUTTER or MARGARINE	2 tablespoons	3 tablespoons	¼ cup

1.   Place all ingredients except melted butter in bread pan, select Dough setting, and press Start.

2.   When the dough has risen long enough, the machine will beep. Turn off bread machine, remove bread pan, and turn out dough onto a lightly floured countertop or cutting board.

3.   With a rolling pin, roll out the dough ½ inch thick. Cut rolls with 3-inch biscuit cutter, rerolling the scraps of dough and cutting more rolls until all the dough has been used.

4.   Place rolls on a large baking sheet and brush each with melted butter.

5.   Let rise in a warm oven 30 to 45 minutes until doubled in size. (Hint: To warm oven slightly, turn oven on Warm setting for 1 minute, then turn it off, and place covered dough in oven to rise. Remove pan from oven before preheating.)

6.   Preheat oven to 375°F. Bake for 12 to 15 minutes until golden-brown.

7.   Remove from oven and serve warm.

Small recipe yields 9 to 10 rolls
Medium recipe yields 13 to 15 rolls
Large recipe yields 18 to 20 rolls

BAKE CYCLE: Dough

NUTRITIONAL INFORMATION PER ROLL
Calories 145/Fat 4.6 grams/Carbohydrates 22.4 grams/Protein 3.2 grams/Fiber .8
grams/Sodium 212 milligrams/Cholesterol 14.2 milligrams

Aunt Catherine's Buttermilk Rolls

L inda married into a family of marvelous Midwestern cooks—even her new father-in-law impressed her with his barbecuing skills. but it was Aunt Catherine's dinner rolls that she heard her husband rave about most of all. Here's that wonderful family recipe adapted for the bread machine. May they become legendary in your family, too.

	SMALL LOAF	MEDIUM LOAF	LARGE LOAF
BUTTERMILK	⅜ cup	½ cup	¾ cup
WATER	⅜ cup	½ cup	⅞ cup
SHORTENING	2 tablespoons	3 tablespoons	¼ cup
SUGAR	1 tablespoon	1½ tablespoons	2 tablespoons
SALT	1 teaspoon	1¼ teaspoons	2 teaspoons
ALL-PURPOSE FLOUR	2 cups	3 cups	4 cups
RED STAR BRAND ACTIVE DRY YEAST	1 teaspoon	1½ teaspoons	2 teaspoons

I. Place ingredients in bread pan, select Dough setting, and press Start.

2. When the dough has risen long enough, the machine will beep. Turn off bread machine, remove bread pan, and turn out dough onto a lightly floured countertop or cutting board.

FOR THE SMALL RECIPE

Grease an 8- or 9-inch square baking pan. Gently roll and stretch dough into a 9-inch rope. With a sharp knife, divide dough into 9 pieces; roll each into a ball and place in pan.

FOR THE MEDIUM RECIPE

Grease a 9×13×2-inch baking pan. Gently roll and stretch dough into a 12-inch rope. With a sharp knife, divide dough into 12 pieces; roll each into a ball and place in pan.

FOR THE LARGE RECIPE

Grease two 8- or 9-inch square baking pans. Gently roll and stretch dough into an 18-inch rope. With a sharp knife, divide dough into 18 pieces; roll each into a ball and place in pans.

3. Cover and let rise in a warm oven 30 to 45 minutes until doubled in size. (Hint: To warm oven slightly, turn oven on Warm setting for 1 minute, then turn it off, and place covered dough in oven to rise. Remove pan from oven before preheating.)

4. Preheat oven to 400°F. Bake for 12 to 15 minutes until golden.

5. Remove from oven and serve warm.

Small recipe yields 9 rolls
Medium recipe yields 12 rolls
Large recipe yields 18 rolls

BAKE CYCLE: Dough

NUTRITIONAL INFORMATION PER ROLL
Calories 123/Fat 3.1 grams/Carbohydrates 20.6 grams/Protein 2.9 grams/Fiber .7 grams/Sodium 200 milligrams/Cholesterol .3 milligrams

---

Bread Sticks Extraordinaire

*T*hanks to our good friend Bev Janson, we submit these pudgy bread sticks for your enjoyment. Bev came up with the unique idea of using our popular French Bread Extraordinaire recipe for the bread sticks, brushing the dough with buttermilk and then coating the bread sticks with a mixture of seeds and nuts.

	SMALL LOAF	MEDIUM LOAF	LARGE LOAF
BUTTERMILK	¼ cup	⅓ cup	½ cup
UNSALTED SUNFLOWER SEEDS	2 tablespoons	3 tablespoons	4 tablespoons
SESAME SEEDS	2 tablespoons	3 tablespoons	4 tablespoons
OLD-FASHIONED OATS	2 tablespoons	3 tablespoons	4 tablespoons
POPPY SEEDS	2 tablespoons	3 tablespoons	4 tablespoons
FINELY CHOPPED PINE NUTS	2 tablespoons	3 tablespoons	4 tablespoons
French Bread Extraordinaire dough, small, medium, and large recipes (see page 19) (see Note below)			
COARSE KOSHER SALT, TO TASTE (OPTIONAL)			

I. Grease a large baking sheet.

FOR THE SMALL RECIPE

Gently roll and stretch dough into an 8-inch log. With a sharp knife, divide dough into 8 pieces and roll each into an 8- to 10-inch-long bread stick.

FOR THE MEDIUM RECIPE

Gently roll and stretch dough into a 12-inch log. With a sharp knife, divide dough into 12 pieces and roll each into an 8- to 10-inch-long bread stick.

FOR THE LARGE RECIPE

Gently roll and stretch dough into a 16-inch log. With a sharp knife, divide dough into 16 pieces and roll each into an 8- to 10-inch-long bread stick.

2. In a jelly-roll pan, combine the seeds, oats, and nuts.

3. Brush each bread stick liberally with buttermilk on all sides. Roll each in the seed mixture to coat thoroughly. Place on prepared baking sheet.

4. Let bread sticks rise in a warm oven 30 minutes. (Hint: To warm oven slightly, turn oven on Warm setting for 1 minute, then turn it off, and place dough in oven to rise. Remove pan from oven before preheating.)

5. Preheat oven to 450°F. Just before baking, place three handfuls of ice cubes in a jelly-roll pan and place it on the bottom shelf of the oven. This will create steam and produce a crisper crust. Place the bread stick pan on the shelf above it. Bake for 15 to 20 minutes.

6. Remove from oven and cool on wire racks.

NOTE: You can shorten the French Bread Extraordinaire recipe by omitting the two risings in Step 2 of the French Bread Extraordinaire recipe (see page 19).

Small recipe yields 8 bread sticks
Medium recipe yields 12 bread sticks
Large recipe yields 16 bread sticks

BAKE CYCLE: Dough

NUTRITIONAL INFORMATION PER BREAD STICK
Calories 179/Fat 3.9 grams/Carbohydrates 30.3 grams/Protein 5.8 grams/Fiber 1.7 grams/Sodium 274 milligrams/Cholesterol .2 milligrams

---

ROLLING BREAD STICKS

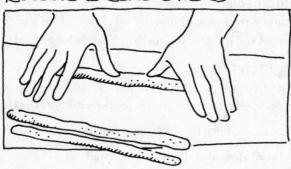

Butter Rolls

*R*ich, *meltingly flavorful, and tender, these rolls will fill the bill at any meal. The dough is so easy to work with, you'll find yourself making these dinner rolls time and again for family, friends, and dinner guests.*

	SMALL LOAF	MEDIUM LOAF	LARGE LOAF
MILK	½ cup	¾ cup	⅞ cup
EGG	1	1	2
SOFTENED BUTTER	¼ cup	6 tablespoons	½ cup
SUGAR	2 tablespoons	3 tablespoons	¼ cup
SALT	1 teaspoon	1½ teaspoons	2 teaspoons
ALL-PURPOSE FLOUR	2 cups	3 cups	4 cups
RED STAR BRAND ACTIVE DRY YEAST	1½ teaspoons	2 teaspoons	2½ teaspoons

1. Place dough ingredients in bread pan, select Dough setting, and press Start.

2. When the dough has risen long enough, the machine will beep. Turn off bread machine, remove bread pan, and turn out dough onto a lightly floured countertop or cutting board.

3. Lightly grease a large baking sheet or muffin pan.

For the Small Recipe
Gently roll and stretch dough into an 8-inch rope. With a sharp knife, divide dough into 8 pieces; shape as desired (see pages 112–114) and place on prepared baking sheet or muffin pan.

For the Medium Recipe
Gently roll and stretch dough into a 12-inch rope. With a sharp knife, divide dough into 12 pieces; shape as desired (see pages 112–114) and place on prepared baking sheet or muffin pan.

For the Large Recipe
Gently roll and stretch dough into a 16-inch rope. With a sharp knife, divide dough into 16 pieces; shape as desired (see pages 112–114) and place on prepared baking sheet or muffin pan.

4. Cover and let rise in a warm oven 15 minutes. (Hint: To warm oven slightly, turn oven on Warm setting for 1 minute, then turn it off, and place covered dough in oven to rise. Remove pan from oven before preheating.)

5. Preheat oven to 400°F. Bake for 12 to 15 minutes until golden.

6. Remove from oven and serve warm.

Small recipe yields 8 rolls
Medium recipe yields 12 rolls
Large recipe yields 16 rolls

BAKE CYCLE: Dough

NUTRITIONAL INFORMATION PER ROLL
Calories 190/Fat 6.6 grams/Carbohydrates 27.8 grams/Protein 4.5 grams/Fiber 1 gram/Sodium 329 milligrams/Cholesterol 34 milligrams

---

Corrine's Lemon Sour Cream Rolls

These luscious rolls are so versatile, you can serve them in the morning with breakfast, in the afternoon with tea, or in the evening with dinner. It's a recipe that was created to share with special friends. Count yourself very lucky if you have a Corrine Davis in your life, too—a feisty friend with a loving heart and an open door.

	SMALL LOAF	MEDIUM LOAF	LARGE LOAF
SOUR CREAM	⅔ cup	1 cup	1⅓ cups cups
EGG	1	2	2
SUGAR	¼ cup	⅜ cup	½ cup
SALT	½ teaspoon	¾ teaspoon	1 teaspoon
ALL-PURPOSE FLOUR	2 cups	3¼ cups	4 cups
GRATED LEMON PEEL	1½ tablespoons	2 tablespoons	3 tablespoons
RED STAR BRAND ACTIVE DRY YEAST	1½ teaspoons	2 teaspoons	2½ teaspoons

1. Place dough ingredients in bread pan, select Dough setting, and press Start.

2. When the dough has risen long enough, the machine will beep. Turn off bread machine, remove bread pan, and turn out dough onto a lightly floured countertop or cutting board.

FOR THE SMALL RECIPE

Grease an 8- or 9-inch square dark baking pan. Gently roll and stretch dough into a 9-inch log. With a sharp knife, divide dough into 9 pieces; roll each into a ball and place in pan.

FOR THE MEDIUM RECIPE

Grease a 9×13×2-inch dark baking pan. Gently roll and stretch dough into a 12-inch log. With a sharp knife, divide dough into 12 pieces; roll each into a ball and place in pan.

FOR THE LARGE RECIPE

Grease two 8- or 9-inch square dark baking pans. Gently roll and stretch dough into an 18-inch rope. With a sharp knife, divide dough into 18 pieces; roll each into a ball and place in pans.

3. Cover and let rise in a warm oven 30 to 45 minutes until doubled in size. (Hint: To warm oven slightly, turn oven on Warm setting for 1 minute, then turn it off, and place covered dough in oven to rise. Remove pan from oven before preheating.)

4. Preheat oven to 375°F. Bake for 15 to 20 minutes until golden.

5. Remove from oven and serve warm.

Small recipe yields 9 rolls
Medium recipe yields 12 rolls
Large recipe yields 18 rolls

BAKE CYCLE: Dough

NUTRITIONAL INFORMATION PER ROLL
Calories 159/Fat 3.7 grams/Carbohydrates 26.9 grams/Protein 4.1 grams/Fiber .9 grams/Sodium 147 milligrams/Cholesterol 24.1 milligrams

---

Garlic Cheese Bread Sticks

I f you plan to make these for family or friends, you'd better make the large batch. In fact, these disappear so fast that no matter how many you make, it won't be enough.

DOUGH

	SMALL LOAF	MEDIUM LOAF	LARGE LOAF
WATER	¾ cup	1 cup	1⅜ cups
BUTTER OR MARGARINE	2 teaspoons	1 tablespoon	4 teaspoons
SUGAR	1 teaspoon	1½ teaspoons	2 teaspoons
SALT	1 teaspoon	1½ teaspoons	2 teaspoons
BREAD FLOUR	2 cups	3 cups	4 cups
RED STAR BRAND ACTIVE DRY YEAST	1½ teaspoons	2 teaspoons	2½ teaspoons

1.   Place ingredients in bread pan, except for the melted butter, olive oil, garlic, and Parmesan cheese. Select Dough setting and press Start.

2.   When the dough has risen long enough, the machine will beep. Turn off bread machine, remove bread pan, and turn out dough onto a lightly floured countertop or cutting board.

3.   Grease a large baking sheet. You'll need two for the Large recipe.

FOR THE SMALL RECIPE
   With a rolling pin, roll the dough into a 9×10-inch rectangle.

FOR THE MEDIUM RECIPE
   With a rolling pin, roll the dough into a 9×14-inch rectangle.

FOR THE LARGE RECIPE
   With a rolling pin, roll the dough into two 9×10-inch rectangles.

4.   Place dough on prepared baking sheet(s). With a pizza wheel, cut the dough rectangle(s) lengthwise into six 1½-inch-wide strips, then cut in half crosswise to create 12 bread sticks. Separate slightly.

5.   Cover and let rise in a warm oven 30 to 45 minutes until doubled in size. (Hint: To warm oven slightly, turn oven on Warm setting for 1 minute, then turn it off, and place covered dough in oven to rise. Remove pan from oven before preheating.)

	SMALL LOAF	MEDIUM LOAF	LARGE LOAF
MELTED BUTTER OR MARGARINE	2 tablespoons	3 tablespoons	¼ cup
OLIVE OIL	2 tablespoons	3 tablespoons	¼ cup
CLOVE GARLIC, MINCED	1	2	2
FRESHLY GRATED PARMESEAN CHEESE	1 tablespoon	4 teaspoons	2 tablespoons

6. Combine topping ingredients and brush half the mixture over the bread sticks.

7. Preheat oven to 375°F. Bake for 15 to 20 minutes. Remove from oven and brush each again with remaining garlic butter. Serve warm.

CREATIVE SUGGESTIONS:

1. For thinner bread sticks, cut the dough rectangle(s) lengthwise into nine 1-inch-wide strips.

2. For an herb flavor, add a dash of Italian herb seasoning to the garlic butter.

3. Lightly sprinkle some kosher salt on top of the bread sticks before baking.

4. For a chewier, softer bread stick, add ¼ cup (small recipe), ⅓ cup (medium recipe), or ½ cup (large recipe) instant potato flakes and 2 tablespoons more water.

Small recipe yields 12 bread sticks
Medium recipe yields 12 bread sticks
Large recipe yields 24 bread sticks

BAKE CYCLE: Dough

NUTRITIONAL INFORMATION PER BREAD STICK
Calories 158/Fat 4.8 grams/Carbohydrates 24.5 grams/Protein 3.6 grams/Fiber 1 gram/Sodium 310 milligrams/Cholesterol .3 milligrams

Heavenly Herb Rolls

When you pop these in the oven, your guests will wander into the kitchen and want to know what that heavenly aroma is. These dinner rolls go well with any meal—from backyard barbecue to formal banquet.

	SMALL LOAF	MEDIUM LOAF	LARGE LOAF
MILK	⅝ cup	1 cup	1¼ cups
OIL	2 tablespoons	3 tablespoons	¼ cup
SUGAR	1 teaspoon	1½ teaspoons	2 teaspoons
SALT	½ teaspoon	¾ teaspoon	1 teaspoon
ALL-PURPOSE FLOUR	2 cups	3 cups	4 cups
CHOPPED ONION	¼ cup	⅓ cup	½ cup
DRIED DILL	½ teaspoon	¾ teaspoon	1 teaspoon
DRIED BASIL	½ teaspoon	¾ teaspoon	1 teaspoon
DRIED OREGANO	½ teaspoon	¾ teaspoon	1 teaspoon
RED STAR BRAND ACTIVE DRY YEAST	1½ teaspoons	2 teaspoons	2½ teaspoons

1. Place dough ingredients in bread pan, select Dough setting, and press Start.

2. When the dough has risen long enough, the machine will beep. Turn off bread machine, remove bread pan, and turn out dough onto a lightly floured countertop or cutting board.

3. Grease a large baking sheet. You'll need two for the large recipe.

FOR THE SMALL RECIPE
Gently roll and stretch dough into a 9-inch log. With a sharp knife, divide dough into 9 pieces; roll each into a ball and place on prepared baking sheet.

FOR THE MEDIUM RECIPE
Gently roll and stretch dough into an 14-inch log. With a sharp knife, divide dough into 14 pieces; roll each into a ball and place on prepared baking sheet.

FOR THE LARGE RECIPE
Gently roll and stretch dough into a 18-inch log. With a sharp knife, divide dough into 18 pieces; roll each into a ball and place on prepared baking sheet.

4. Cover and let rise in a warm oven 30 to 45 minutes until doubled. (Hint: To warm oven slightly, turn oven on Warm setting for 1 minute, then turn it off, and place covered dough in oven to rise. Remove pan from oven before preheating.)

5. Preheat oven to 425°F. Bake for 12 to 15 minutes until golden-brown.

6. Remove from oven and serve warm.

Small recipe yields 9 rolls
Medium recipe yields 14 rolls
Large recipe yields 18 rolls

BAKE CYCLE: Dough

NUTRITIONAL INFORMATION PER ROLL
Calories 106/Fat 2.6 grams/Carbohydrates 17.4 grams/Protein 2.8 grams/Fiber .7 grams/Sodium 96.5 milligrams/Cholesterol .6 milligrams

---

Honey Whole Wheat Rolls

*S*ometimes nothing goes better with a meal than these rich-tasting whole wheat rolls. We also like to split them in half and use them for small sandwiches— tuna salad, ham and cheese, turkey and avocado . . . a feast in a fist.

	SMALL LOAF	MEDIUM LOAF	LARGE LOAF
BUTTERMILK	¾ cup	1 cup	1⅝ cups
OIL	2 tablespoons	3 tablespoons	¼ cup
HONEY	2 tablespoons	3 tablespoons	¼ cup
SALT	¾ teaspoon	1 teaspoon	1½ teaspoons
WHOLE WHEAT FLOUR	1⅓ cups	2 cups	2⅔ cups
ALL-PURPOSE FLOUR	⅔ cup	1 cup	1⅓ cups
RED STAR BRAND ACTIVE DRY YEAST	1½ teaspoons	1½ teaspoons	2 teaspoons

I. Place ingredients in bread pan, select Dough setting, and press Start.

2. When the dough has risen long enough, the machine will beep. Turn off bread machine, remove bread pan, and turn out dough onto a lightly floured countertop or cutting board.

FOR THE SMALL RECIPE

Grease an 8- or 9-inch square baking pan. Gently roll and stretch dough into a 9-inch rope. With a sharp knife, divide dough into 9 pieces; roll each into a ball and place in pan.

FOR THE MEDIUM RECIPE

Grease a 9×13×2-inch baking pan. Gently roll and stretch dough into a 12-inch rope. With a sharp knife, divide dough into 12 pieces; roll each into a ball and place in pan.

FOR THE LARGE RECIPE

Grease two 8- or 9-inch square baking pans. Gently roll and stretch dough into an 18-inch rope. With a sharp knife, divide dough into 18 pieces; roll each into a ball and place in pans.

3. Cover and let rise in a warm oven 30 to 45 minutes until doubled in size. (Hint: To warm oven slightly, turn oven on Warm setting for 1 minute, then turn it off, and place covered dough in oven to rise. Remove pan from oven before preheating.)

4. Preheat oven to 400°F. Bake for 12 to 15 minutes.

5. Remove from oven and serve warm.

Small recipe yields 9 rolls
Medium recipe yields 12 rolls
Large recipe yields 18 rolls

BAKE CYCLE: Dough

NUTRITIONAL INFORMATION PER ROLL
Calories 160/Fat 4 grams/Carbohydrates 27.7 grams/Protein 4.5 grams/Fiber 2.9 grams/Sodium 198 milligrams/Cholesterol .7 milligrams

---

Jalapeño Cheese Rolls

*H*ere's a dinner roll that bites back! If you like them hot, double the amount of peppers. If you prefer a milder version, omit the peppers or switch to the canned diced green chilies.

	SMALL	MEDIUM	LARGE
MILK	³⁄₈ cup	½ cup	¾ cup
WATER	¼ cup	½ cup	¾ cup
SUGAR	1½ tablespoons	2 tablespoons	3 tablespoons
SALT	1 teaspoon	1½ teaspoons	2 teaspoons
ALL-PURPOSE FLOUR	2 cups	3 cups	4 cups
GRATED MONTEREY JACK CHEESE WITH JALAPEÑO PEPPERS	¾ cup (3 ounces)	1 cup (4 ounces)	1½ cups (6 ounces)
SEEDED AND CHOPPED, FRESH, OR CANNED JALAPEÑO PEPPERS	1½ teaspoons	2 teaspoons	1 tablespoon
RED STAR BRAND ACTIVE DRY YEAST	1½ teaspoons	1½ teaspoons	2 teaspoons

1. Place dough ingredients in bread pan, select Dough setting, and press Start.

2. When the dough has risen long enough, the machine will beep. Turn off bread machine, remove bread pan, and turn out dough onto a lightly floured countertop or cutting board.

3. Grease a muffin pan. You'll need two for the large recipe.

FOR THE SMALL RECIPE

Gently roll and stretch dough into a 12-inch rope. With a sharp knife, divide dough into 12 pieces; roll each into a ball and place in pan.

FOR THE MEDIUM RECIPE

Gently roll and stretch dough into an 18-inch rope. With a sharp knife, divide dough into 18 pieces; roll each into a ball and place in pan.

For the Large Recipe

Gently roll and stretch dough into a 24-inch rope. With a sharp knife, divide dough into 24 pieces; roll each into a ball and place in pans.

4. Cover and let rise in a warm oven 30 to 45 minutes until doubled. (Hint: To warm oven slightly, turn oven on Warm setting for 1 minute, then turn it off, and place covered dough in oven to rise. Remove pan from oven before preheating.)

5. Preheat oven to 375°F. Bake for 12 to 15 minutes until golden.

6. Remove from oven and serve warm.

Small recipe yields 12 rolls
Medium recipe yields 18 rolls
Large recipe yields 24 rolls

BAKE CYCLE: Dough

NUTRITIONAL INFORMATION PER ROLL
Calories 108/Fat 2.2 grams/Carbohydrates 17.7 grams/Protein 4 grams/Fiber .6 grams/Sodium 220 milligrams/Cholesterol 5.8 milligrams

---

Orange Rye Rolls

Try something a little different in a dinner roll tonight. Bake up a batch of these and see your family smile.

	SMALL	MEDIUM	LARGE
BUTTERMILK	⅞ cup	1⅛ cup	1⅜ cups
OIL	1 tablespoon	1½ tablespoons	2 tablespoons
HONEY	1½ tablespoons	2 tablespoons	3 tablespoons
SALT	1 teaspoon	1½ teaspoons	2 teaspoons
ALL-PURPOSE FLOUR	1⅓ cups	2 cups	2⅔ cups
RYE FLOUR	⅔ cup	1 cup	1⅓ cups
GRATED ORANGE RIND	2 teaspoons	1 tablespoon	4 teaspoons
CARAWAY SEEDS	1 teaspoon	1½ teaspoons	2 teaspoons
RED STAR BRAND ACTIVE DRY YEAST	1½ teaspoons	1½ teaspoons	2 teaspoons

1. Place dough ingredients in bread pan, select Dough setting, and press Start.

2. When the dough has risen long enough, the machine will beep. Turn off bread machine, remove bread pan, and turn out dough onto a lightly floured countertop or cutting board.

3. Grease a large baking sheet.

FOR THE SMALL RECIPE
Gently roll and stretch dough into an 8-inch log. With a sharp knife, divide dough into 8 pieces; roll each into a 10-inch-long rope and coil into snail shape on the prepared baking sheet.

FOR THE MEDIUM RECIPE
Gently roll and stretch dough into a 12-inch log. With a sharp knife, divide dough into 12 pieces; roll each into a 10-inch-long rope and coil into snail shape on the prepared baking sheet.

FOR THE LARGE RECIPE
Gently roll and stretch dough into a 16-inch log. With a sharp knife, divide dough into 16 pieces; roll each into a 10-inch-long rope and coil into snail shape on the prepared baking sheet.

4. Cover and let rise in a warm oven 30 to 45 minutes until doubled. (Hint: To warm oven slightly, turn oven on Warm setting for 1 minute, then turn it off, and place covered dough in oven to rise. Remove pan from oven before preheating.)

5. Preheat oven to 375°F. Bake for 12 to 15 minutes until golden-brown.

6. Remove from oven and serve warm.

Small recipe yields 8 rolls
Medium recipe yields 12 rolls
Large recipe yields 16 rolls

BAKE CYCLE: Dough

NUTRITIONAL INFORMATION PER ROLL
Calories 143/Fat 2.3 grams/Carbohydrates 26.6 grams/Protein 3.8 grams/Fiber 2 grams/Sodium 289 milligrams/Cholesterol .8 milligrams

Petite Brioche

French brioche are those cute little rolls with the topknot. They're the perfect accompaniment to a cup of steaming coffee at breakfast or just as good scooped out and filled with a seafood salad. To make these rich egg rolls, you should use fluted brioche tins or a muffin pan. Also note that the dough is easiest to handle if it's refrigerated for 4 to 12 hours before shaping. As rich as they are, they dry out quickly, so these brioche should be eaten the same day they're baked. Wait . . . don't toss out the day-old remainders! Turn them into mini French toasts or a lush bread pudding.

	SMALL	MEDIUM	LARGE
EGGS	3	4	6
BUTTER	½ cup	¾ cup	1 cup
SUGAR	1½ tablespoons	2 tablespoons	3 tablespoons
SALT	¾ teaspoon	1 teaspoon	1½ teaspoons
ALL-PURPOSE FLOUR	2¼ cups	3⅓ cups	4½ cups
RED STAR BRAND ACTIVE DRY YEAST	1½ teaspoons	2 teaspoons	2½ teaspoons
EGG YOLK BEATEN WITH I TABLESPOON MILK	1	1	1

I. Place all ingredients in bread pan except egg yolk and milk mixture, select Dough setting, and press Start.

2. When the dough has risen long enough, the machine will beep. Turn off bread machine, remove bread pan, and turn out dough onto a lightly floured countertop or cutting board. Place the dough in an oiled plastic bag and refrigerate it from 4 hours to overnight. Chilling the dough makes it easier to shape and improves the flavor.

3. After the dough has been chilled, butter small brioche tins or a muffin pan.

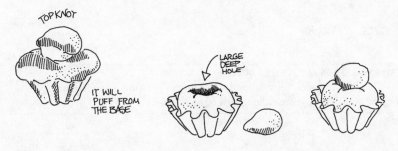

FOR THE SMALL RECIPE

With a sharp knife, divide the cold dough into 4 equal pieces. Set aside one piece. Cut the remaining 3 pieces into 4 segments. Roll these 12 pieces into balls and place 1 in each prepared brioche tin, making a large hole in the center of each with your finger. With a sharp knife, cut the remaining piece of dough into 12 pieces about the size of a large marble. Roll each into a ball and place in the hole in each roll.

FOR THE MEDIUM RECIPE

With a sharp knife, divide the cold dough into 4 equal pieces. Set aside 1 piece. Cut the remaining 3 pieces into 6 segments. Roll these 18 pieces into balls and place 1 in each prepared brioche tin, making a large hole in the center of each with your finger. With a sharp knife, cut the remaining piece of dough into 18 small pieces about the size of a large marble. Roll each into a ball and place in the hole in each roll.

FOR THE LARGE RECIPE

With a sharp knife, divide the cold dough into 4 equal pieces. Set aside 1 piece. Cut the remaining 3 pieces into 8 segments. Roll these 24 pieces into balls and place 1 in each prepared brioche tin, making a hole in the center of each with your finger. With a sharp knife, cut the remaining piece of dough into 24 small pieces about the size of a large marble. Roll each into a ball and place in the hole in each roll.

4. Place the brioche tins on a large baking sheet. Let the rolls rise in a warm oven 60 to 90 minutes until almost doubled in size. (Hint: To warm oven slightly, turn oven on Warm setting for 1 minute, then turn it off, and place dough in oven to rise. Remove pan from oven before preheating.)

5. After rolls have risen, gently brush the egg yolk mixture over the top of each roll.

6. Preheat oven to 375°F. Bake for 10 to 15 minutes until golden-brown.

7. Remove from oven, turn rolls out of pans, and cool on wire rack.

Small recipe yields 12 rolls
Medium recipe yields 18 rolls
Large recipe yields 24 rolls

BAKE CYCLE: Dough

NUTRITIONAL INFORMATION PER ROLL
Calories 178/Fat 9.3 grams/Carbohydrates 19.1 grams/Protein 4.3 grams/Fiber .7 grams/Sodium 137 milligrams/Cholesterol 80 milligrams

---

Sweet Hawaiian Rolls

*S*ave your pennies! These luscious rolls are every bit as good as any you'll find in the market. They tend to burn so be sure and cover them with foil after ten minutes in the oven.

	SMALL	MEDIUM	LARGE
MILK	¼ cup	¼ cup	½ cup
EGG	1	2	2
EGG YOLK	1	1	2
BUTTER OR MARGARINE	2 tablespoons	3 tablespoons	¼ cup
POTATO, BOILED AND MASHED	1 small (4 ounces)	1 medium (6 ounces)	1 large (8 ounces)
SUGAR	6 tablespoons	½ cup + 1 tablespoon	¾ cup
SALT	½ teaspoon	¾ teaspoon	1 teaspoon
ALL-PURPOSE FLOUR	2¼ cups	3⅜ cups	4½ cups
RED STAR BRAND ACTIVE DRY YEAST	1½ teaspoons	2 teaspoons	2½ teaspoons

1.   Place dough ingredients in bread pan, select Dough setting, and press Start.

2.   When the dough has risen long enough, the machine will beep. Turn off bread machine, remove bread pan, and turn out dough onto a lightly floured countertop or cutting board.

FOR THE SMALL RECIPE

Grease an 8- or 9-inch square baking pan. Gently roll and stretch dough into a 9-inch log. With a sharp knife, divide dough into 9 pieces; roll each into a ball and place in pan.

FOR THE MEDIUM RECIPE

Grease a 9×13×2-inch baking pan. Gently roll and stretch dough into a 12-inch log. With a sharp knife, divide dough into 12 pieces; roll each into a ball and place in pan.

FOR THE LARGE RECIPE

Grease two 8- or 9-inch square baking pans. Gently roll and stretch dough into an 18-inch rope. With a sharp knife, divide dough into 18 pieces; roll each into a ball and place in pans.

3. Cover and let rise in a warm oven 30 to 45 minutes until doubled in size. (Hint: To warm oven slightly, turn oven on Warm setting for 1 minute, then turn it off, and place covered dough in oven to rise. Remove pan from oven before preheating.)

4. Preheat oven to 350°F. Bake for 15 to 20 minutes, covering rolls with foil after the first 10 minutes to prevent burning.

5. Remove from oven and serve warm.

Small recipe yields 9 rolls
Medium recipe yields 12 rolls
Large recipe yields 18 rolls

BAKE CYCLE: Dough

NUTRITIONAL INFORMATION PER ROLL
Calories 217/Fat 3.9 grams/Carbohydrates 39.5 grams/Protein 5.6 grams/Fiber 1.3 grams/Sodium 185 milligrams/Cholesterol 53.6 milligrams

Tomato Basil Bread Sticks

*T*he perfect accompaniment to pasta or soup, these tomato-y bread sticks look smashing in a tall glass on the table. They are a little taste of Italy in every bite.

DOUGH

	SMALL	MEDIUM	LARGE
WATER	³⁄₈ cup	½ cup	½ cup
EGG	1	1	2
TOMATO PASTE	³⁄₈ cup	½ cup	¾ cup
OLIVE OIL	1½ tablespoons	2 tablespoons	3 tablespoons
SUGAR	2 teaspoons	1 tablespoon	4 teaspoons
SALT	½ teaspoon	¾ teaspoon	1 teaspoon
ALL-PURPOSE FLOUR	2 cups	3 cups	4 cups
DRIED MINCED ONION	1 teaspoon	1½ teaspoons	2 teaspoons
DRIED BASIL	1½ teaspoons	2 teaspoons	1 tablespoon
GARLIC POWDER	¼ teaspoon	heaping ¼ teaspoon	½ teaspoon
GROUND NUTMEG	¼ teaspoon	heaping ¼ teaspoon	½ teaspoon
RED STAR BRAND ACTIVE DRY YEAST	1½ teaspoons	2 teaspoons	2½ teaspoons

1. Place dough ingredients in bread pan, select Dough setting, and press Start.

2. When the dough has risen long enough, the machine will beep. Turn off bread machine, remove bread pan, and turn out dough onto a lightly floured countertop or cutting board. Gently roll and stretch dough into a 20-inch rope.

3. Grease 2 baking sheets. Preheat oven to 350°F.

FOR THE SMALL RECIPE
With a sharp knife, divide dough into 24 pieces. (Hint: First cut the dough into 12 equal pieces, then cut each of those in half.)

FOR THE MEDIUM RECIPE
With a sharp knife, divide dough into 32 pieces. (Hint: First cut the dough into 8 equal pieces, then cut each of those into 4 small pieces.)

With a sharp knife, divide dough into 48 pieces. (Hint: First cut the dough into 12 equal pieces, then cut each of those into 4 small pieces.)

TOPPING

EGG	1
WATER	1 teaspoon
COARSE SALT TO TASTE	

4. Roll each piece of dough into an 8-inch stick; place on prepared baking sheets. Combine 1 egg and 1 teaspoon water for the topping and brush mixture over each bread stick. Sprinkle with coarse salt, if desired.

5. Bake for 20 to 25 minutes. Remove from oven. Remove bread sticks from pans and cool on wire racks. Once cool, store at room temperature in paper bags. They will stay fresh for 2 to 3 days.

CREATIVE SUGGESTIONS:

1. For crisper, thinner bread sticks, roll each piece of dough into 16-inch sticks.

2. Put your pasta machine to use! Break off 2-inch balls of dough, flatten to $1/4$-inch thickness, and dust well with flour. Feed dough through the fettucine cutting blades. Place cut strips on greased baking sheets. Bake at 350°for 15 to 20 minutes. Cool on wire racks.

Small recipe yields 24 bread sticks
Medium recipe yields 32 bread sticks
Large recipe yields 48 bread sticks

BAKE CYCLE: Dough

NUTRITIONAL INFORMATION PER BREAD STICK
Calories 46/Fat 1.3 grams/Carbohydrates 7.3 grams/Protein 1.4 grams/Fiber .5 grams/Sodium 120 milligrams/Cholesterol 13.3 milligrams

---

9
Bagels, Buns, and Breads with a Twist

Allyson and Andrew's Pretzel Bread

*H*ere's a fun bread that children can help shape. You could even break off a small piece of dough and let them practice on it first. Bake up their creation as a snack, along with the bread.

DOUGH

	SMALL LOAF	MEDIUM LOAF	LARGE LOAF
WATER	¾ cup	1 cup	1⅜ cups
OIL	1½ tablespoons	2 tablespoons	3 tablespoons
SUGAR .	2 teaspoons	1 tablespoon	4 teaspoons
SALT	½ teaspoon	¾ teaspoon	1 teaspoon
BREAD FLOUR	2 cups	3 cups	4 cups
RED STAR BRAND ACTIVE DRY YEAST	1½ teaspoons	2 teaspoons	2½ teaspoons

1. Place dough ingredients in bread pan, select Dough setting, and press Start.

2. When the dough has risen long enough, the machine will beep. Turn off bread machine, remove bread pan, and turn out dough onto a lightly floured countertop or cutting board.

3. Grease a large baking sheet.

FOR THE SMALL RECIPE
Gently roll and stretch dough into a 24-inch rope.

FOR THE MEDIUM RECIPE
Gently roll and stretch dough into a 30-inch rope.

FOR THE LARGE RECIPE
With a sharp knife, cut dough in half. Gently roll and stretch each piece into a 24-inch rope.

4. Shape the dough into a giant pretzel(s) by bringing both ends of the rope up toward the top and crossing them (forming something that looks like a bunny's head with ears). Bring the "ears" towards you to rest on the base of the pretzel (the bunny's chin), pressing them down slightly. Place on prepared baking sheet.

5. Let rise in a warm oven 30 to 45 minutes until doubled in size. (Hint: To warm oven slightly, turn oven on Warm setting for 1 minute, then turn it off, and place covered dough in oven to rise. Remove pan from oven before preheating.)

TOPPING

EGG	1	1	1
WATER	1 tablespoon	1 tablespoon	1 tablespoon
COARSE KOSHER SALT			

6. Combine the egg and water. Gently brush egg wash over top of pretzel, then sprinkle generously with coarse salt before it dries.

7. Preheat oven to 375°F. Bake for 30 to 35 minutes until golden-brown.

8. Remove from oven and cool on wire rack.

BAKE CYCLE: Dough

NUTRITIONAL INFORMATION PER SERVING
Calories 124/Fat 2.6 grams/Carbohydrates 21.4 grams/Protein 3.3 grams/Fiber .8 grams/Sodium 157 milligrams/Cholesterol 15.2 milligrams

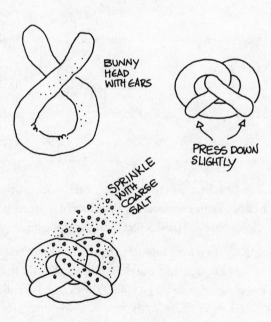

Bagels

If you're going to go to the effort of making bagels at home when there are so many great bagel bakeries in town these days, then they'd better be well worth the effort! We did a great deal of reading, asked bakers for their secrets, watched videos, and tested various methods in order to create a satisfactory version for the bread machine. Cakey or doughy bagels that tasted like a hamburger bun with a hole in it were unacceptable. They had to be dense and chewy like the real thing. We feel this recipe merits your time. Once you master these, do try the many variations that follow. A word of support: A good-looking bagel takes some practice to master, so please don't try this recipe once, then quit in despair because yours didn't look like the bakery variety. Our first efforts didn't either—our families thought they were shriveled up doughnuts that we'd dropped in the dishwater. We stayed with it long enough to bake up bagels to be proud of, and you can, too!

DOUGH

	SMALL	MEDIUM	LARGE
WATER	¾ cup	1 cup	1⅜ cups
DIASTATIC MALT POWDER	1 teaspoon	1½ teaspoons	2 teaspoons
OR	or	or	or
BARLEY MALT SYRUP	1 tablespoon	1½ tablespoons	2 tablespoons
KOSHER SALT	1 teaspoon	1½ teaspoons	2 teaspoons
VITAL WHEAT GLUTEN	2 tablespoons	3 tablespoons	4 tablespoons
BREAD FLOUR	2 cups	3 cups	4 cups
RED STAR BRAND ACTIVE DRY YEAST	2 teaspoons	3 teaspoons	4 teaspoons

1. Before measuring the first cup of flour, place gluten in measuring cup, then add flour to measure 1 cup. Continue measuring additional flour as you normally do. Place dough ingredients in bread pan. Select Dough setting and press Start.

2. When the dough has risen long enough, the machine will beep. Turn off bread machine, remove bread pan, and turn out dough onto a lightly floured countertop or cutting board. Bagel dough should be stiff. If the dough is at all sticky, knead in extra flour until it is no longer sticky to the touch. Cover dough and let rest for 10 minutes.

3. Grease a large baking sheet.

For the Small Recipe

Gently roll and stretch dough into a 4- to 6-inch log. With a sharp knife, divide dough into 4 to 6 pieces; roll each into a *smooth* ball and flatten slightly.

For the Medium Recipe

Gently roll and stretch dough into a 6- to 8-inch log. With a sharp knife, divide dough into 6 to 8 pieces; roll each into a *smooth* ball and flatten slightly.

For the Large Recipe

Gently roll and stretch dough into an 8- to 10-inch log. With a sharp knife, divide dough into 8 to 10 pieces; shape each into a *smooth* ball and flatten slightly.

4. With thumbs, make a hole in the center of each piece of dough. Using your two index fingers to start, rotate your hands around each other to stretch the bagel until the hole is large enough to put your hand through. Shape and smooth the bagel. Place on prepared baking sheet, cover, and let rise 10 more minutes. The bagel should be about 3½ to 4 inches in diameter at this point and the hole in the center will have shrunk down to about 1 to 1½ inches wide.

BOILING WATER

WATER	2 quarts
BARLEY MALT SYRUP	2 tablespoons

5. In a large kettle, combine 2 quarts of water and the barley malt syrup; bring almost to a boil over high heat. Watch it carefully. The syrup will cause it to boil over if left unattended. As soon as it begins to boil, remove the pan from the burner, reduce the heat to medium, then return the pan and keep the water at a gentle simmer.

6. Preheat oven to 425°F.

7. With a slotted spoon, spatula, or skimmer, place 2 bagels in the simmering water for 30 seconds, turning once. Remove and drain on a slotted broiler pan or clean dish towel.

GLAZE

EGG WHITE COMBINED WITH 1 TABLESPOON WATER (OPTIONAL)	1

TOPPING

SESAME SEEDS, POPPY SEEDS, CARAWAY SEEDS, FLAX SEEDS, ONION FLAKES, KOSHER SALT, OR MINCED SUNFLOWER SEEDS (OPTIONAL)

8. After draining, place bagels on prepared baking sheet. If desired, gently brush glaze on each bagel and sprinkle with topping of choice. Bake 15 to 20 minutes until deep golden-brown.

MAKE A HOLE

STRETCH THE HOLE WIDER THAN YOUR HAND

HOLE WILL SHRINK TO 1—1½"

9. Remove from oven and cool on wire racks. These should be eaten the same day. Slice and freeze any leftovers for up to 1 month.

CREATIVE SUGGESTIONS:

1. There are so many unique bagels you can create. Be daring! Try your favorite savory bread recipe and turn it into a bagel. Use this recipe as your guideline for the liquid and flour amounts. Omit all or part of the fat listed in the recipe as well. Ever had a chicken sandwich on a tomato, basil, mozzarella bagel? It's mahhhhvelous!

2. It's easy to create mini bagels for snacks and lunchboxes by cutting the dough into twice as many pieces as the recipe lists and shaping them into mini versions of the original.

3. If you roll the dough out and cut with a doughnut cutter, you'll end up with "bagel holes," too!

4. To brown both sides of the bagels, turn them over halfway through the baking time. You could also wait and add your glaze and topping at this time.

HELPFUL HINTS:

The secret to smooth, nice looking bagels is to start with a very smooth ball before shaping.
The longer the bagels boil, the thicker the skin.
Have a watch or clock with a second hand nearby for timing the boiling.
High-gluten bread flour is what gives the bagel its wonderful chewiness.
If you don't want to make all the bagels in one day, refrigerate any leftover dough for up to 2 days.
Adding barley malt syrup to the water rather than just sugar gives them their shine, their golden color, and that special flavor. If your grocer doesn't carry it, your local health food store will, or check the Sources section (page 259).

Small recipe yields 4 to 6 bagels
Medium recipe yields 6 to 8 bagels
Large recipe yields 8 to 10 bagels

BAKE CYCLE: Dough

NUTRITIONAL INFORMATION PER BAGEL
Calories 197/Fat .5 grams/Carbohydrates 39.7 grams/Protein 7 grams/Fiber 1.6 grams/Sodium 208 milligrams/Cholesterol 0 milligrams

---

146

Bialys

No need to travel to Poland or even your local bagel shop to sample these wonderful rolls. Now you can bake them with ease right in your own home! They're great as is or split in half and toasted for a sandwich.

DOUGH

	SMALL	MEDIUM	LARGE
WATER	¾ cup	1 cup	1⅜ cups
OIL	1 tablespoon	1½ tablespoons	2 tablespoons
SUGAR	2 teaspoons	1 tablespoon	4 teaspoons
SALT	1 teaspoon	1½ teaspoons	2 teaspoons
BREAD FLOUR	2 cups	3 cups	4 cups
RED STAR BRAND ACTIVE DRY YEAST	1½ teaspoons	2 teaspoons	2½ teaspoons

1. Place dough ingredients in bread pan, select Dough setting, and press Start.

2. When the dough has risen long enough, the machine will beep. Turn off bread machine, remove bread pan, and turn out dough onto a lightly floured countertop or cutting board.

FOR THE SMALL RECIPE

Gently roll and stretch dough into a 10-inch rope. With a sharp knife, divide dough into 10 pieces; roll each into a ball.

FOR THE MEDIUM RECIPE

Gently roll and stretch dough into a 15-inch rope. With a sharp knife, divide dough into 15 pieces; roll each into a ball.

FOR THE LARGE RECIPE

Gently roll and stretch dough into a 20-inch rope. With a sharp knife, divide dough into 20 pieces; roll each into a ball.

FILLING

	SMALL	MEDIUM	LARGE
MINCED ONION	3 tablespoons	4½ tablespoons	6 tablespoons
POPPY SEEDS	2 teaspoons	1 tablespoon	4 teaspoons
OIL	1 teaspoon	1½ teaspoons	2 teaspoons
SALT	One pinch	⅛ teaspoon	¼ teaspoon

3. Cover balls with a towel and let rest 10 minutes. Meanwhile, combine the topping ingredients and set aside.

4. With a rolling pin, roll each ball into 3½-inch circles. Place on ungreased baking sheets. Cover with a towel and let rise in a warm oven until almost doubled in size, about 30 to 45 minutes. (Hint: To warm oven slightly, turn oven on Warm setting for 1 minute, then turn it off, and place covered dough in oven to rise. Remove pan from oven before preheating.)

5. With thumbs or the bottom of a shot glass, gently depress the center of each roll. Fill with about 1 teaspoon of the onion mixture. Cover and let rise for 15 minutes more while preheating the oven to 450°F.

6. Bake for 20 to 25 minutes until golden-brown. Remove from oven and cool on a rack.

Small recipe yields 10 rolls
Medium recipe yields 15 rolls
Large recipe yields 20 rolls

BAKE CYCLE: Dough

NUTRITIONAL INFORMATION PER ROLL
Calories 112/Fat 2.1 grams/Carbohydrates 20.2 grams/Protein 2.7 grams/Fiber .8 grams/Sodium 228 milligrams/Cholesterol 0 milligrams

---

Cinnamon Raisin Bagels

O*nce you've mastered the basic bagel recipe, try these. Is there anyone who doesn't love cinnamon raisin bagels?*

DOUGH

	SMALL	MEDIUM	LARGE
WATER	¾ cup	1 cup	1⅜ cups
DIASTATIC MALT POWDER	2 teaspoons	3 teaspoons	4 teaspoons
OR	or	or	or
BARLEY MALT SYRUP	2 tablespoons	3 tablespoons	4 tablespoons
KOSHER SALT	1 teaspoon	1½ teaspoons	2 teaspoons
VITAL WHEAT GLUTEN	2 tablespoons	3 tablespoons	4 tablespoons
BREAD FLOUR	2 cups	3 cups	4 cups
CINNAMON	1 teaspoon	1½ teaspoons	2 teaspoons
RAISINS OR CURRANTS	½ cup	¾ cup	1 cup
RED STAR BRAND ACTIVE DRY YEAST	2 teaspoons	3 teaspoons	4 teaspoons

1. Before measuring the first cup of flour, place gluten in measuring cup, then add flour to measure 1 cup. Continue measuring additional flour as you normally do. Place dough ingredients in bread pan. Select Dough setting and press Start.

2. When the dough has risen long enough, the machine will beep. Turn off bread machine, remove bread pan, and turn out dough onto a lightly floured countertop or cutting board. Bagel dough should be stiff. If the dough is at all sticky, knead in extra flour until it is no longer sticky to the touch. Cover dough and let rest 10 minutes.

3. Grease a large baking sheet.

FOR THE SMALL RECIPE

Gently roll and stretch dough into a 4- to 6-inch log. With a sharp knife, divide dough into 4 to 6 pieces; roll each into a *smooth* ball and flatten slightly.

FOR THE MEDIUM RECIPE

Gently roll and stretch dough into a 6- to 8-inch log. With a sharp knife, divide dough into 6 to 8 pieces; roll each into a *smooth* ball and flatten slightly.

FOR THE LARGE RECIPE

Gently roll and stretch dough into an 8- to 10-inch log. With a sharp knife, divide dough into 8 to 10 pieces; shape each into a *smooth* ball and flatten slightly.

4. With thumbs, make a hole in the center of each piece of dough. Using your two index fingers to start, rotate your hands around each other to stretch the bagel until the hole is large enough to put your hand through. Shape and smooth the bagel. Place on prepared baking sheet, cover, and let rise 10 more minutes. The bagel should be about 3½ to 4 inches in diameter at this point and the hole in the center will have shrunk down to about 1 to 1½ inches wide. Place on prepared baking sheet, cover, and let rise 10 more minutes.

BOILING WATER

WATER	2 quarts
BARLEY MALT SYRUP	2 tablespoons

5. In a large kettle, combine 2 quarts of water and the barley malt syrup; bring almost to a boil over high heat. Watch it carefully. The syrup will cause it to boil over if left unattended. As soon as it begins to boil, remove the pan from the burner, reduce the heat to medium, then return the pan and keep the water at a gentle simmer.

6. Preheat oven to 425°F.

7. With a slotted spoon, spatula, or skimmer, place 2 bagels in the simmering water for 30 seconds, turning once. Remove and drain on a slotted broiler pan or clean dish towel.

8. After draining, place bagels on prepared baking sheet. Bake 15 to 20 minutes until deep golden-brown.

9. Remove from oven and cool on wire racks. These should be eaten the same day. Slice and freeze any leftovers for up to 1 month.

CREATIVE SUGGESTION: For Whole Wheat Cinnamon Raisin Bagels, substitute honey for the barley malt syrup and whole wheat flour for half of the bread flour.

Small recipe yields 4 to 6 bagels
Medium recipe yields 6 to 8 bagels
Large recipe yields 8 to 10 bagels

BAKE CYCLE: Dough

NUTRITIONAL INFORMATION PER BAGEL
Calories 158/Fat .4 grams/Carbohydrates 33.7 grams/Protein 4.9 grams/Fiber 1.6 grams/Sodium 183 milligrams/Cholesterol 0 milligrams

Egg Bagels

These plain bagels are wonderful when split and filled with tuna salad.

DOUGH

	SMALL	MEDIUM	LARGE
WATER	½ cup	⅝ cup	⅞ cup
EGG YOLKS	2	3	4
OIL	1½ tablespoons	2 tablespoons	3 tablespoons
DIASTATIC MALT POWDER	1 teaspoon	1½ teaspoons	2 teaspoons
OR	or	or	or
BARLEY MALT SYRUP	1 tablespoon	1½ tablespoons	2 tablespoons
KOSHER SALT	1 teaspoon	1½ teaspoons	2 teaspoons
VITAL WHEAT GLUTEN	2 tablespoons	3 tablespoons	4 tablespoons
BREAD FLOUR	2 cups	3 cups	4 cups
RED STAR BRAND ACTIVE DRY YEAST	2 teaspoons	3 teaspoons	4 teaspoons

I.   Before measuring the first cup of flour, place gluten in measuring cup, then add flour to measure 1 cup. Continue measuring additional flour as you normally do. Place dough ingredients in bread pan. Select Dough setting and press Start.

2.   When the dough has risen long enough, the machine will beep. Turn off bread machine, remove bread pan, and turn out dough onto a lightly floured countertop or cutting board. Bagel dough should be stiff. If the dough is at all sticky, knead in extra flour until it is no longer sticky to the touch. Cover dough and let rest 10 minutes.

3.   Grease a large baking sheet.

FOR THE SMALL RECIPE

Gently roll and stretch dough into a 4- to 6-inch log. With a sharp knife, divide dough into 4 to 6 pieces; roll each into a *smooth* ball and flatten slightly.

FOR THE MEDIUM RECIPE

Gently roll and stretch dough into a 6- to 8-inch log. With a sharp knife, divide dough into 6 to 8 pieces; roll each into a *smooth* ball and flatten slightly.

Gently roll and stretch dough into an 8- to 10-inch log. With a sharp knife, divide dough into 8 to 10 pieces; shape each into a *smooth* ball and flatten slightly.

4. With thumbs, make a hole in the center of each piece of dough. Using your two index fingers to start, rotate your hands around each other to stretch the bagel until the hole is large enough to put your hand through. Shape and smooth the bagel. Place on prepared baking sheet, cover, and let rise 10 more minutes. The bagel should be about 3½ to 4 inches in diameter at this point and the hole in the center will have shrunk down to about 1 to 1½ inches wide.

BOILING WATER

WATER	2 quarts
BARLEY MALT SYRUP	2 tablespoons

5. In a large kettle, combine 2 quarts of water and the barley malt syrup; bring almost to a boil over high heat. Watch it carefully. The syrup will cause it to boil over if left unattended. As soon as it begins to boil, remove the pan from the burner, reduce the heat to medium, then return the pan and keep the water at a gentle simmer.

6. Preheat oven to 425°F.

7. With a slotted spoon, spatula, or skimmer, place 2 bagels in the simmering water for 30 seconds, turning once. Remove and drain on a slotted broiler pan or clean dish towel.

GLAZE

EGG WHITE COMBINED WITH 1 TABLESPOON WATER (OPTIONAL)	1

TOPPING

SESAME SEEDS, POPPY SEEDS, CARAWAY SEEDS, FLAX SEEDS, ONION FLAKES, KOSHER SALT, OR MINCED SUNFLOWER SEEDS (OPTIONAL)

8. After draining, place bagels on prepared baking sheet. If desired, gently brush glaze on each bagel and sprinkle with topping of choice. Bake 15 to 20 minutes until deep golden-brown.

9. Remove from oven and cool on wire racks. These should be eaten the same day. Slice and freeze any leftovers for up to 1 month.

Small recipe yields 4 to 6 bagels
Medium recipe yields 6 to 8 bagels
Large recipe yields 8 to 10 bagels

BAKE CYCLE: Dough

NUTRITIONAL INFORMATION PER BAGEL
Calories 166/Fat 4 grams/Carbohydrates 26.6 grams/Protein 5.4 grams/Fiber 1.1 grams/Sodium 185 milligrams/Cholesterol 53.2 milligrams

---

Lynn's Sandwich Buns

Lynn Dominguez, a longtime family friend of Linda's, offered the instructions for making these rolls years ago. We caught her by surprise when we asked if we could add them to the book. Thank goodness she said "Yes"—wait until you try them! These rolls are wonderful hot out of the oven. They're also terrific sliced in half for sandwiches. Fill with some thinly sliced ham and a dollop of mustard . . . you'll see what we mean. (It's best to use a cheese slicer to get the thin slices of cheese called for in the recipe, and don't worry if your strips aren't exactly ½ inch wide.)

	SMALL	MEDIUM	LARGE
WATER	³⁄₈ cup	½ cup	⁵⁄₈ cup
MILK	³⁄₈ cup	½ cup	¾ cup
OIL	1 tablespoon	1½ tablespoons	2 tablespoons
SUGAR	2 tablespoons	3 tablespoons	¼ cup
SALT	1 teaspoon	1½ teaspoons	2 teaspoons
BREAD FLOUR	2 cups	3 cups	4 cups
RED STAR BRAND ACTIVE DRY YEAST	1½ teaspoons	1½ teaspoons	2 teaspoons
CHEDDAR CHEESE	¾ cup (3 ounces)	1 cup (4 ounces)	1½ cups (6 ounces)
(EXTRA CHEESE FOR TOPPING)			

1. Place all ingredients except cheese in bread pan, select Dough setting, and press Start.

2. When the dough has risen long enough, the machine will beep. Turn off bread machine, remove bread pan, and turn out dough onto a lightly floured countertop or cutting board. Grease a large baking sheet.

FOR THE SMALL RECIPE

Gently roll and stretch dough into a 4-inch log. With a sharp knife, divide dough into 4 pieces; roll each into a 12-inch-long rope.

FOR THE MEDIUM RECIPE

Gently roll and stretch dough into a 6-inch log. With a sharp knife, divide dough into 6 pieces; roll each into a 12-inch-long rope.

FOR THE LARGE RECIPE

Gently roll and stretch dough into an 8-inch log. With a sharp knife, divide dough into 8 pieces; roll each into a 12-inch-long rope.

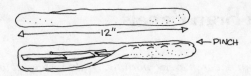

3. Flatten each rope. Thinly slice cheese and cut into ½-inch wide strips. Then, if you're right-handed, with your right thumb press strips of cheese into the dough while you pinch the edges of the dough together well with the left hand to seal the cheese inside. (Lefties, reverse the procedure: left thumb presses and right hand pinches.) Tie each sealed rope into a loose knot and place on prepared cookie sheet.

4. Cover and let rise in a warm oven 30 to 45 minutes until doubled in size. (Hint: To warm oven slightly, turn oven on Warm setting for 1 minute, then turn it off, and place covered dough in oven to rise. Remove pan from oven before preheating.)

5. Preheat oven to 375°F. Bake for 15 to 20 minutes, until golden-brown.

6. Meanwhile, cut several wide paper-thin slices of cheese, enough to cover each roll. Set aside.

7. Remove rolls from oven and top each with 1 or 2 thin slices of cheese. Return the rolls to the oven and bake 5 to 10 minutes more, until the cheese is bubbly and brown.

8. Remove rolls from oven and either serve warm or cool on wire rack and use later for sandwiches.

CREATIVE SUGGESTIONS:

1. Substitute your favorite bread recipe for the dough.

2. Substitute pepper cheese for the Cheddar or add some diced jalapeños to give some "heat" to these rolls.

3. Substitute low-fat cheese for the Cheddar to trim the fat grams.

Small recipe yields 4 rolls
Medium recipe yields 6 rolls
Large recipe yields 8 rolls

BAKE CYCLE: Dough

NUTRITIONAL INFORMATION PER ROLL
Calories 385/Fat 12 grams/Carbohydrates 55 grams/Protein 13 grams/Fiber 1.9 grams/Sodium 689 milligrams/Cholesterol 25.6 milligrams

---

Oat Bran Bagels

*H*ere's *an easy way to eat your oat bran every morning. Make up several large batches of these at once, slice them when they cool, and place them in the freezer.*

DOUGH

	SMALL	MEDIUM	LARGE
OLD-FASHIONED OATS	¼ cup	⅓ cup	½ cup
WATER	¾ cup	1 cup	1⅜ cups
DIASTATIC MALT POWDER	1 teaspoon	1½ teaspoons	2 teaspoons
OR	or	or	or
HONEY	1 tablespoon	1½ tablespoons	2 tablespoons
KOSHER SALT	1 teaspoon	1½ teaspoons	2 teaspoons
VITAL WHEAT GLUTEN	2 tablespoons	3 tablespoons	4 tablespoons
BREAD FLOUR	1½ cups	2⅓ cups	3 cups
OAT BRAN	¼ cup	⅓ cup	½ cup
RED STAR BRAND ACTIVE DRY YEAST	2 teaspoons	3 teaspoons	4 teaspoons

1. Before measuring the first cup of flour, place gluten in measuring cup then add flour to measure 1 cup. Continue measuring additional flour as you normally do. Place dough ingredients in bread pan. Select Dough setting and press Start.

2. When the dough has risen long enough, the machine will beep. Turn off bread machine, remove bread pan, and turn out dough onto a lightly floured countertop or cutting board. Bagel dough should be stiff. If the dough is at all sticky, knead in extra flour until it is no longer sticky to the touch. Cover dough and let rest 10 minutes.

3. Grease a large baking sheet.

FOR THE SMALL RECIPE
Gently roll and stretch dough into a 4- to 6-inch log. With a sharp knife, divide dough into 4 to 6 pieces; roll each into a *smooth* ball and flatten slightly.

FOR THE MEDIUM RECIPE
Gently roll and stretch dough into a 6- to 8-inch log. With a sharp knife, divide dough into 6 to 8 pieces; roll each into a *smooth* ball and flatten slightly.

Gently roll and stretch dough into an 8- to 10-inch log. With a sharp knife, divide dough into 8 to 10 pieces; shape each into a *smooth* ball and flatten slightly.

4. With thumbs, make a hole in the center of each piece of dough. Using your two index fingers to start, rotate your hands around each other to stretch the bagel until the hole is large enough to put your hand through. Shape and smooth the bagel. Place on prepared baking sheet, cover, and let rise 10 more minutes. The bagel should be about 3½ to 4 inches in diameter at this point and the hole in the center will have shrunk down to about 1 to 1½ inches wide.

BOILING WATER

WATER	2 quarts
BARLEY MALT SYRUP	2 tablespoons

5. In a large kettle, combine 2 quarts of water and the barley malt syrup; bring almost to a boil over high heat. Watch it carefully. The syrup will cause it to boil over if left unattended. As soon as it begins to boil, remove the pan from the burner, reduce the heat to medium, then return the pan and keep the water at a gentle simmer.

6. Preheat oven to 425°F.

7. With a slotted spoon, spatula, or skimmer, place 2 bagels in the simmering water for 30 seconds, turning once. Remove and drain on a slotted broiler pan or clean dish towel.

GLAZE

EGG WHITE COMBINED WITH 1 TABLESPOON WATER (OPTIONAL)	1

TOPPING

OLD-FASHIONED OATS, SESAME SEEDS, POPPY SEEDS, CARAWAY SEEDS, FLAX SEEDS, ONION FLAKES, KOSHER SALT, OR MINCED SUNFLOWER SEEDS (OPTIONAL)

8. After draining, place bagels on prepared baking sheet. If desired, gently brush glaze on each bagel and sprinkle with topping of choice. Bake 15 to 20 minutes until deep golden-brown.

9. Remove from oven and cool on wire racks. These should be eaten the same day. Slice and freeze any leftovers for up to 1 month.

Small recipe yields 4 to 6 bagels
Medium recipe yields 6 to 8 bagels
Large recipe yields 8 to 10 bagels

BAKE CYCLE: Dough

NUTRITIONAL INFORMATION PER BAGEL
Calories 116/Fat .6 grams/Carbohydrates 24.4 grams/Protein 4.3 grams/Fiber 1.5 grams/Sodium 179 milligrams/Cholesterol 0 milligrams

---

Onion Bagels

These savory bagels are hard to pass up. Try them with our Vegetable Herb Spread (see page 246).

DOUGH

	SMALL	MEDIUM	LARGE
MINCED ONION	¾ cup	1 cup	1½ cups
BUTTER OR MARGARINE	1 tablespoon	1½ tablespoons	2 tablespoons
VITAL WHEAT GLUTEN	2 tablespoons	3 tablespoons	4 tablespoons
BREAD FLOUR	2 cups	3 cups	4 cups
WATER	¾ cup	1 cup	1⅜ cups
DIASTATIC MALT POWDER	1 teaspoon	1½ teaspoons	2 teaspoons
OR	or	or	or
SUGAR	1 tablespoon	1½ tablespoons	2 tablespoons
KOSHER SALT	1 teaspoon	1½ teaspoons	2 teaspoons
RED STAR BRAND ACTIVE DRY YEAST	2 teaspoons	3 teaspoons	4 teaspoons

1.   In a small skillet, sauté onion in butter until softened, about 5 minutes. Add half to the bread pan. Set aside the remaining half for the topping.

2.   Place gluten in measuring cup, then add flour to measure 1 cup. Continue measuring additional flour as you normally do. Place all the dough ingredients (including half the onion mixture) in bread pan. Select Dough setting and press Start.

3.   When the dough has risen long enough, the machine will beep. Turn off bread machine, remove bread pan, and turn out dough onto a lightly floured counter top or cutting board. Bagel dough should be stiff. If the dough is at all sticky, knead in extra flour until it is no longer sticky to the touch. Cover dough and let rest 10 minutes.

4.   Grease a large baking sheet.

FOR THE SMALL RECIPE
Gently roll and stretch dough into a 4- to 6-inch log. With a sharp knife, divide dough into 4 to 6 pieces; roll each into a *smooth* ball and flatten slightly.

Gently roll and stretch dough into a 6- to 8-inch log. With a sharp knife, divide dough into 6 to 8 pieces; roll each into a *smooth* ball and flatten slightly.

Gently roll and stretch dough into an 8- to 10-inch log. With a sharp knife, divide dough into 8 to 10 pieces; shape each into a *smooth* ball and flatten slightly.

5. With thumbs, make a hole in the center of each piece of dough. Using your two index fingers to start, rotate your hands around each other to stretch the bagel until the hole is large enough to put your hand through. Shape and smooth the bagel. Place on prepared baking sheet, cover and let rise 10 more minutes. The bagel should be about 3½ to 4 inches in diameter at this point and the hole in the center will have shrunk down to about 1 to 1½ inches wide.

BOILING WATER

WATER	2 quarts
BARLEY MALT SYRUP	2 tablespoons

6. In a large kettle, combine 2 quarts of water and the barley malt syrup; bring almost to a boil over high heat. Watch it carefully. The syrup will cause it to boil over if left unattended. As soon as it begins to boil, remove the pan from the burner, reduce the heat to medium, then return the pan and keep the water at a gentle simmer.

7. Preheat oven to 425°F.

8. With a slotted spoon, spatula, or skimmer, place 2 bagels in the simmering water for 30 seconds, turning once. Remove and drain on a broiler pan or clean dish towel.

GLAZE

EGG WHITE COMBINED WITH 1 TABLESPOON WATER (OPTIONAL)	1

9. After draining, place bagels on prepared baking sheet. Bake 15 to 20 minutes, turning once halfway through the baking period. After turning the bagels over, gently brush glaze on each bagel and sprinkle with remaining onion mixture.

10. Remove from oven and cool on wire racks. These should be eaten the same day. Slice and freeze any leftovers for up to 1 month.

CREATIVE SUGGESTION: For onion–poppy seed bagels, add poppy seeds to the onion mixture after cooking.

Small recipe yields 4 to 6 bagels
Medium recipe yields 6 to 8 bagels
Large recipe yields 8 to 10 bagels

BAKE CYCLE: Dough

NUTRITIONAL INFORMATION PER BAGEL
Calories 144/Fat 1.5 grams/Carbohydrates 27.4 grams/Protein 4.8 grams/Fiber 1.3 grams/Sodium 191 milligrams/Cholesterol 0 milligrams

---

Onion Lover's Twist

This onion bread recipe was adapted from the Grand Prize Winner in the 1970 Pillsbury Bake-Off® Contest. The original version is a classic. Once you try this modern update, you'll see why. It's every bit as good, but with the convenience of the bread machine, oh so much easier to make.

	SMALL LOAF	MEDIUM LOAF	LARGE LOAF
WATER	¼ cup	½ cup	½ cup
MILK	¼ cup	¼ cup	½ cup
EGG	1	1	2
BUTTER OR MARGARINE	2 tablespoons	3 tablespoons	4 tablespoons
SUGAR	2 tablespoons	3 tablespoons	¼ cup
SALT	¾ teaspoon	1 teaspoon	1½ teaspoons
BREAD FLOUR	2 cups	3 cups	4 cups
RED STAR BRAND ACTIVE DRY YEAST	1½ teaspoons	2 teaspoons	2½ teaspoons

1. Place dough ingredients in bread pan, select Dough setting, and press Start.

FILLING

	SMALL LOAF	MEDIUM LOAF	LARGE LOAF
BUTTER OR MARGARINE	1 tablespoon	1½ tablespoons	2 tablespoons
FINELY CHOPPED ONION	½ cup	¾ cup	1 cup
GRATED PARMESEAN CHEESE	1½ teaspoons	2 teaspoons	1 tablespoon
SESAME OR POPPY SEEDS	1½ teaspoons	2 teaspoons	1 tablespoon
GARLIC SALT	½ teaspoon	¾ teaspoon	½ to 1 teaspoon
PAPRIKA	½ teaspoon	¾ teaspoon	1 teaspoon

2. In a small saucepan, melt the butter for the filling. Stir in the rest of the filling ingredients. Set aside.

3. When the dough has risen long enough, the machine will beep. Turn off bread machine, remove bread pan, and turn out dough onto a lightly floured countertop or cutting board.

4. Grease a large baking sheet. You'll need 2 for the large recipe.

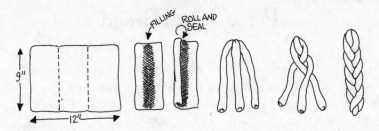

FOR THE SMALL RECIPE

With a rolling pin, roll dough to a 9×12-inch rectangle. With a sharp knife, cut rectangle crosswise into three 9×4-inch strips. Place filling lengthwise down the center of each strip. Starting at the long edge, roll up each strip, and pinch edges firmly to seal.

FOR THE MEDIUM RECIPE

With a rolling pin, roll dough to a 12×15-inch rectangle. With a sharp knife, cut rectangle crosswise into three 12×5-inch strips. Place filling lengthwise down the center of each strip. Starting at the long edge, roll up each strip and pinch edges firmly to seal.

FOR THE LARGE RECIPE

With a rolling pin, roll dough into two 9×12-inch rectangles. With a sharp knife, cut each rectangle crosswise into three 9×4-inch strips. Place filling lengthwise down the center of each strip. Starting at the long edge, roll up each strip and pinch edges firmly to seal.

5. Place the three strips on prepared baking sheet(s). Braid them together and pinch the ends to seal. (See Challah recipe, page 222, for illustration.)

6. Cover and let rise in a warm oven 30 to 45 minutes until doubled in size. (Hint: To warm oven slightly, turn oven on Warm setting for 1 minute, then turn it off, and place covered dough in oven to rise. Remove pan from oven before preheating.)

7. Preheat oven to 350°F. Bake for 20 to 25 minutes until golden-brown.

8. Remove from oven and cool on wire rack.

Small recipe yields 1 loaf; Medium recipe yields 1 loaf; Large recipe yields 2 loaves

Recipe adapted and printed with the permission of "The Pillsbury Company"

BAKE CYCLE: Dough

NUTRITIONAL INFORMATION PER SLICE
Calories 137/Fat 4.1 grams/Carbohydrates 21.3 grams/Protein 3.4 grams/Fiber .9 grams/Sodium 197 milligrams/Cholesterol 13.6 milligrams

---

Pesto Spiral Bread

*T*his bread takes a little more time and effort, but it's worth it. Your friends will find it hard to believe you baked it in your machine. Credit goes to the bread bakers on Prodigy, who first came up with the idea of "Swirl Breads." To make a swirl bread, you remove dough from the machine after the "punch down," very quickly roll it out, spread it with a filling, roll it into a rope, and coil it back into the bread pan to rise and bake. This is a whole new category of breads! Here's one we came up with that we thought was a natural.

	SMALL LOAF	MEDIUM LOAF	LARGE LOAF
SMALL, MEDIUM, AND LARGE LOAVES SEMOLINA BREAD (SEE RECIPES, PAGE 25)			
PESTO SAUCE	¼ cup	⅓ cup	½ cup
CHOPPED SUN-DRIED TOMATOES	3 tablespoons	¼ cup	6 tablespoons
ROASTED AND COARSELY CHOPPED PINE NUTS (OPTIONAL)	2 tablespoons	3 tablespoons	¼ cup

1. Place all ingredients for Semolina Bread in bread pan, using the least amount of liquid listed in the recipe. Select Medium Crust setting and press Start.

2. Observe the dough as it kneads. After 5 to 10 minutes, if it appears dry and stiff or if your machine sounds as if it's straining to knead it, add more liquid 1 tablespoon at a time until dough forms a smooth, soft, pliable ball that is slightly tacky to the touch.

3. Just before the last rising cycle, the machine will "punch down" the dough. Once that happens, immediately remove the dough from the bread pan, being careful not to lift out the pan as well, which will shut off some machines. You can also remove the mixing blade at this time, if possible.

For Small Loaf
Quickly roll dough into an 11×15-inch rectangle. Don't be too concerned with the exact measurement. Rolling it out quickly is more important. Spread dough with pesto and sprinkle on chopped tomatoes and pine nuts.

For Medium Loaf
Quickly roll dough into a 13×18-inch rectangle. Don't be too concerned with the exact measurement. Rolling it out quickly is more important. Spread with pesto and sprinkle on chopped tomatoes and pine nuts.

FOR LARGE LOAF

Quickly roll dough into 16×20-inch rectangle. Don't be too concerned with the exact measurement. Rolling it out quickly is more important. Spread with pesto and sprinkle on chopped tomatoes and pine nuts.

4. Starting with long edge, roll up into a rope and quickly pinch edges to seal.

5. Coil dough back into bread pan; close lid.

6. After the baking cycle ends, remove bread from pan, place on cake rack, and allow to cool 1 hour before slicing.

HINTS:

· It helps to look up in your machine's manual just exactly when that last "punch down" before the final rising occurs. Set a timer so you don't miss it.

· When removing and replacing dough, close the lid of the machine as rapidly as possible. The longer it is open, the more heat escapes.

· Be careful not to dislodge or remove the bread pan when pulling the dough out. In some machines, that will shut them off.

· Time is of the essence when working with the dough. The longer you take to roll it out and fill it, the less time it will have to rise to its full height. So be prepared to move quickly! Have all the ingredients measured and at hand. Quickly roll the dough out and don't worry about forming the perfect rectangle—you should be more concerned with speed than perfection here.

· If your pesto sauce is extremely oily, drain in a colander before measuring.

· If your bread didn't rise high enough, next time try it on the Whole Wheat cycle, which has a little bit longer rising cycle.

· If you miscalculate or forget to remove the dough on time, all is not lost. You can remove the dough anytime during that last rising cycle, shape it as directed, and place it into a greased loaf pan. (For the small loaf, use a greased 8×4-inch pan; for the medium, use a greased 9×5-inch pan; for the large loaf, use two greased 8×4-inch pans.) Cover and let the bread rise until doubled in size, then bake in a 350° oven for 45 to 50 minutes, until golden-brown.

CRUST: Medium
BAKE CYCLE: Standard
OPTIONAL BAKE CYCLES: Whole Wheat

NUTRITIONAL INFORMATION PER SLICE
Calories 164/Fat 4.3 grams/Carbohydrates 24.9 grams/Protein 4.4 grams/Fiber 1.3 grams/Sodium 230 milligrams/Cholesterol 0 milligrams

Pumpernickel Bagels

I f you're a pumpernickel bread lover, you'll enjoy these change-of-pace bagels.

DOUGH

	SMALL	MEDIUM	LARGE
WATER	¾ cup	1 to 1⅛ cups	1½ cups
MOLASSES	2 tablespoons	3 tablespoons	¼ cup
KOSHER SALT	1 teaspoon	1½ teaspoons	2 teaspoons
VITAL WHEAT GLUTEN	2 tablespoons	3 tablespoons	4 tablespoons
BREAD FLOUR	⅔ cup	1 cup	1⅓ cups
WHOLE WHEAT FLOUR	⅔ cup	1 cup	1⅓ cups
RYE FLOUR	⅔ cup	1 cup	1⅓ cups
COCOA POWDER	2 tablespoons	3 tablespoons	¼ cup
CARAWAY SEEDS	1 teaspoon	1½ teaspoons	2 teaspoons
RED STAR BRAND ACTIVE DRY YEAST	2 teaspoons	3 teaspoons	4 teaspoons

1. Before measuring the first cup of flour, place gluten in measuring cup, then add flour to measure 1 cup. Continue measuring additional flour as you normally do. Place dough ingredients in bread pan. Select Dough setting and press Start.

2. When the dough has risen long enough, the machine will beep. Turn off bread machine, remove bread pan, and turn out dough onto a lightly floured countertop or cutting board. Bagel dough should be stiff. If the dough is at all sticky, knead in extra flour until it is no longer sticky to the touch. Cover dough and let rest 10 minutes.

3. Grease a large baking sheet.

FOR THE SMALL RECIPE

Gently roll and stretch dough into a 4- to 6-inch log. With a sharp knife, divide dough into 4 to 6 pieces; roll each into a *smooth* ball and flatten slightly.

FOR THE MEDIUM RECIPE

Gently roll and stretch dough into a 6- to 8-inch log. With a sharp knife, divide dough into 6 to 8 pieces; roll each into a *smooth* ball and flatten slightly.

FOR THE LARGE RECIPE

Gently roll and stretch dough into an 8 to 10-inch log. With a sharp knife, divide dough into 8 to 10 pieces; shape each into a *smooth* ball and flatten slightly.

4. With thumbs, make a hole in the center of each piece of dough. Using your two index fingers to start, rotate your hands around each other to stretch the bagel until the hole is large enough to put your hand through. Shape and smooth the bagel. Place on prepared baking sheet, cover and let rise 10 more minutes. The bagel should be about 3½ to 4 inches in diameter at this point and the hole in the center will have shrunk down to about 1 to 1½ inches wide.

BOILING WATER

WATER	2 quarts
BARLEY MALT SYRUP	2 tablespoons

5. In a large kettle, combine 2 quarts of water and the barley malt syrup; bring almost to a boil over high heat. Watch it carefully. The syrup will cause it to boil over if left unattended. As soon as it begins to boil, remove the pan from the burner, reduce the heat to medium, then return the pan and keep the water at a gentle simmer.

6. Preheat oven to 425°F.

7. With a slotted spoon, spatula, or skimmer, place 2 bagels in the simmering water for 30 seconds, turning once. Remove and drain on a slotted broiler pan or clean dish towel.

GLAZE

EGG WHITE COMBINED WITH I TABLESPOON WATER (OPTIONAL)	1

TOPPING

SESAME SEEDS, POPPY SEEDS, CARAWAY SEEDS, FLAX SEEDS, ONION FLAKES, KOSHER SALT, OR MINCED SUNFLOWER SEEDS (OPTIONAL)

8. After draining, place bagels on prepared baking sheet. If desired, gently brush glaze on each bagel and sprinkle with topping of choice. Bake 15 to 20 minutes until deep golden-brown.

9. Remove from oven and cool on wire racks. These should be eaten the same day. Slice and freeze any leftovers for up to 1 month.

Small recipe yields 4 to 6 bagels
Medium recipe yields 6 to 8 bagels
Large recipe yields 8 to 10 bagels

BAKE CYCLE: Dough

NUTRITIONAL INFORMATION PER BAGEL
Calories 128/Fat .8 grams/Carbohydrates 26.4 grams/Protein 4.7 grams/Fiber 3.5 grams/Sodium 180 milligrams/Cholesterol 0 milligrams

Spinach Parmesan Spiral Bread

Here's another spiral loaf that's guaranteed to please. If you're hesitant to try this, we suggest you try a very simple version first. Using a favorite white bread recipe, remove dough as directed, roll it out, brush it quickly with a little melted butter, and sprinkle with some cinnamon sugar and optional ingredients such as raisins or nuts, then roll it up and coil back into the bread pan.

DOUGH

	SMALL LOAF	MEDIUM LOAF	LARGE LOAF
MILK	⅝ cup	⅝ cup	1 cup
LOW-FAT COTTAGE CHEESE	½ cup	¾ cup	1 cup
BUTTER OR MARGARINE	1 tablespoon	1½ tablespoons	2 tablespoons
SUGAR	1½ tablespoons	2 tablespoons	3 tablespoons
SALT	1 teaspoon	1½ teaspoons	2 teaspoons
DRIED OREGANO	¾ teaspoon	1 teaspoon	1½ teaspoons
BREAD FLOUR	2 cups	3 cups	4 cups
RED STAR BRAND ACTIVE DRY YEAST	1½ teaspoons	1½ teaspoons	2 teaspoons

1. Place all dough ingredients in bread pan, using the least amount of liquid listed in the recipe. Select Medium Crust setting and press Start.

2. Observe the dough as it kneads. After 5 to 10 minutes, if it appears dry and stiff or if your machine sounds as if it's straining to knead it, add more liquid 1 tablespoon at a time until dough forms a smooth, soft, pliable ball that is slightly tacky to the touch.

FILLING

	SMALL LOAF	MEDIUM LOAF	LARGE LOAF
FINELY CHOPPED ONION	¼ cup	⅓ cup	½ cup
CLOVES GARLIC, MINCED	2	3	4
OLIVE OIL	1½ tablespoons	2 tablespoons	3 tablespoons
FROZEN CHOPPED SPINACH, THAWED, WELL DRAINED	1 cup	1½ cups	2 cups
FRESHLY GRATED PARMESEAN CHEESE	½ cup (2 ounces)	¾ cup (3 ounces)	1 cup (4 ounces)
FRESHLY GRATED BLACK PEPPER TO TASTE			

3. Meanwhile, in a skillet over medium heat sauté the onion and garlic in the olive oil briefly until just golden. Add spinach and stir just to warm it. Remove pan from heat and stir in Parmesan cheese and black pepper. Set aside to cool to room temperature.

4. Just before the last rising cycle, the machine will "punch down" the dough. Once that happens, immediately remove the dough from the bread pan, being careful not to lift out the pan as well, which will shut off some machines. You can also remove the mixing blade at this time, if possible.

FOR THE SMALL RECIPE

Quickly roll dough into an 11×15-inch rectangle. Don't be too concerned with the exact measurement. Rolling it out quickly is more important. Spread with the spinach filling.

FOR THE MEDIUM RECIPE

Roll dough quickly into a 13×18-inch rectangle. Don't be too concerned with the exact measurement. Rolling it out quickly is more important. Spread with the spinach filling.

FOR THE LARGE RECIPE

Roll dough quickly into a 16×20-inch rectangle. Don't be too concerned with the exact measurement. Rolling it out quickly is more important. Spread with the spinach filling.

5. Starting with long edge, roll up into a rope and quickly pinch edges to seal.

6. Coil dough back into bread pan; close lid.

7. After the baking cycle ends, remove bread from pan, place on cake rack, and allow to cool 1 hour before slicing.

HINTS:

· It helps to look up in your machine's manual just exactly when that last "punch down" before the final rising occurs. Set a timer so you don't miss it.

· When removing and replacing dough, close the lid of the machine as rapidly as possible. The longer it is open, the more heat escapes.

· Be careful not to dislodge or remove the bread pan when pulling the dough out. In some machines, that will shut them off.

· Time is of the essence when working with the dough. The longer you take to roll it out and fill it, the less time it will have to rise to its full height. So be prepared to move quickly! Have all the ingredients measured and at hand. Quickly roll the dough out and don't worry about forming the perfect rectangle—you should be more concerned with speed than perfection here.

· If your bread didn't rise high enough, next time try it on the Whole Wheat cycle, which has a little bit longer rising cycle.

· If you miscalculate or forget to remove the dough on time, all is not lost. You can remove the dough anytime during that last rising cycle, shape it as directed, and place it into a greased loaf pan. (For the small loaf, use a greased 8×4-inch pan; for the medium, use a greased 9×5-inch pan; for the large loaf, use two greased 8×4-inch pans.) Cover and let the bread rise until doubled in size, then bake in a 350°F oven for 50 minutes until golden-brown.

CRUST: Medium
BAKE CYCLE: Standard
OPTIONAL BAKE CYCLES: Whole Wheat

NUTRITIONAL INFORMATION PER SLICE
Calories 173/Fat 4.7 grams/Carbohydrates 25.6 grams/Protein 7.1 grams/Fiber 1.4 grams/Sodium 395 milligrams/Cholesterol 4.2 milligrams

---

Whole Wheat Bagels

H*ere's another wholesome bagel recipe to start your day just right.*

DOUGH

	SMALL	MEDIUM	LARGE
WATER	¾ cup	1 cup	1½ cups
DIASTATIC MALT POWDER	1 teaspoon	1½ teaspoons	2 teaspoons
OR	or	or	or
HONEY	1 tablespoon	1½ tablespoons	2 tablespoons
KOSHER SALT	1 teaspoon	1½ teaspoons	2 teaspoons
VITAL WHEAT GLUTEN	2 tablespoons	3 tablespoons	4 tablespoons
BREAD FLOUR	1 cup	1½ cups	2 cups
WHOLE WHEAT FLOUR	1 cup	1¼ cups	1⅔ cups
WHEAT GERM OR BRAN	3 tablespoons	¼ cup	⅓ cup
RED STAR BRAND ACTIVE DRY YEAST	2 teaspoons	3 teaspoons	4 teaspoons

I.   Before measuring the first cup of flour, place gluten in measuring cup, then add flour to measure 1 cup. Continue measuring additional flour as you normally do. Place dough ingredients in bread pan. Select Dough setting and press Start.

2.   When the dough has risen long enough, the machine will beep. Turn off bread machine, remove bread pan, and turn out dough onto a lightly floured countertop or cutting board. Bagel dough should be stiff. If the dough is at all sticky, knead in extra flour until it is no longer sticky to the touch. Cover dough and let rest 10 minutes.

3.   Grease a large baking sheet.

FOR THE SMALL RECIPE
Gently roll and stretch dough into a 4- to 6-inch log. With a sharp knife, divide dough into 4 to 6 pieces; roll each into a *smooth* ball and flatten slightly.

FOR THE MEDIUM RECIPE
Gently roll and stretch dough into a 6- to 8-inch log. With a sharp knife, divide dough into 6 to 8 pieces; roll each into a *smooth* ball and flatten slightly.

FOR THE LARGE RECIPE
Gently roll and stretch dough into an 8- to 10-inch log. With a sharp knife, divide dough into 8 to 10 pieces; shape each into a *smooth* ball and flatten slightly.

4. With thumbs, make a hole in the center of each piece of dough. Using your two index fingers to start, rotate your hands around each other to stretch the bagel until the hole is large enough to put your hand through. Shape and smooth the bagel. Place on prepared baking sheet, cover and let rise 10 more minutes. The bagel should be about 3½ to 4 inches in diameter at this point and the hole in the center will have shrunk down to about 1 to 1½ inches wide.

BOILING WATER

WATER	2 quarts
BARLEY MALT SYRUP	2 tablespoons

5. In a large kettle, combine 2 quarts of water and the barley malt syrup; bring almost to a boil over high heat. Watch it carefully. The syrup will cause it to boil over if left unattended. As soon as it begins to boil, remove the pan from the burner, reduce the heat to medium, then return the pan and keep the water at a gentle simmer.

6. Preheat oven to 425°F.

7. With a slotted spoon, spatula, or skimmer, place 2 bagels in the simmering water for 30 seconds, turning once. Remove and drain on a slotted broiler pan or clean dish towel.

GLAZE

EGG WHITE COMBINED WITH 1 TABLESPOON WATER (OPTIONAL)	1

TOPPING

SESAME SEEDS, POPPY SEEDS, CARAWAY SEEDS, FLAX SEEDS, ONION FLAKES, KOSHER SALT, OR MINCED SUNFLOWER SEEDS (OPTIONAL)

8. After draining, place bagels on prepared baking sheet. If desired, gently brush glaze on each bagel and sprinkle with topping of choice. Bake 15 to 20 minutes until deep golden-brown.

9. Remove from oven and cool on wire racks. These should be eaten the same day. Slice and freeze any leftovers for up to 1 month.

Small recipe yields 4 to 6 bagels
Medium recipe yields 6 to 8 bagels
Large recipe yields 8 to 10 bagels

BAKE CYCLE: Dough

NUTRITIONAL INFORMATION PER ROLL
Calories 120/Fat .5 grams/Carbohydrates 25 grams/Protein 4.7 grams/Fiber 2.5 grams/Sodium 179 milligrams/Cholesterol 0 milligrams

10

Pizzas and Flat Breads

Basic Pizza Dough

Both of us make this simple pizza dough at least once a week . . . so often that it's now easier than picking up a phone and ordering one!

	SMALL	MEDIUM	LARGE
WATER	¾ cup	1 cup	1⅜ cups
OLIVE OIL	1½ tablespoons	2 tablespoons	3 tablespoons
SUGAR	2 teaspoons	1 tablespoon	4 teaspoons
SALT	¾ teaspoon	1 teaspoon	1½ teaspoons
UNBLEACHED OR ALL-PURPOSE FLOUR	2 cups	3 cups	4 cups
RED STAR BRAND ACTIVE DRY YEAST	1½ teaspoons	2 teaspoons	2½ teaspoons

1. Place all ingredients in bread pan, select Dough setting, and press Start.

2. When the dough has risen long enough, the machine will beep. Turn off bread machine, remove bread pan, and turn out dough onto a lightly floured countertop or cutting board. For the Large recipe, cut dough in half. Wrap dough in plastic wrap that has been lightly coated with olive oil. Set aside to rest for 15 minutes. (With the Large recipe, it is not necessary to use both crusts at one time. At this point the extra dough can be placed in an oiled plastic bag and kept in the freezer or it can be refrigerated up to 3 days for later use.)

FOR THE SMALL RECIPE
    Lightly oil one 12- to 14-inch pizza pan to within 1 inch of the edge.

FOR THE MEDIUM RECIPE
    Lightly oil one 14- to 16-inch pizza pan to within 1 inch of the edge.

FOR THE LARGE RECIPE
    Lightly oil one or two 12- to 14-inch pizza pans to within 1 inch of the edge.

3. Using a rolling pin, roll the dough into a circle slightly smaller than the pizza pan you plan to use. (We prefer the pizza pans that have small holes all over. They produce a very crisp crust.) Place the dough on the pizza pan and gently stretch it to fit. Shape dough around the edge to form a small rim.

4. Cover dough and let rise on the countertop for 20 to 30 minutes. Meanwhile, preheat oven to 450°F.

5. Spread your toppings of choice on pizza and bake on the middle shelf of the oven for 15 to 20 minutes.

6. Remove from oven and serve warm.

CREATIVE SUGGESTIONS:

1. To add more flavor to the dough, consider adding Parmesan cheese, minced onion and garlic, herbs of choice, crushed red or black pepper, poppy seeds, Cajun spices, sesame seeds, sun-dried tomatoes, or pesto sauce to the dough.

2. In a hurry? Speed up the process by turning off the bread machine after 10 minutes of kneading. Allow the dough to rise for 30 minutes in the machine, then proceed as directed from Step 2 on.

HELPFUL HINTS:

1. Use only bleached or unbleached all-purpose flour for an easy-to-handle pizza dough. Using bread flour with its higher gluten content makes the dough more elastic and harder to stretch and shape, especially when rolling out a thin crust. If you must use bread flour, it helps to refrigerate the dough for several hours or overnight to relax it.

2. Avoid using fast-acting yeasts if you intend to refrigerate your pizza dough for several hours or more.

3. When oiling the pizza pan, do not oil the outer rim. A dry edge helps the dough adhere when you're stretching it to fit the pan.

4. You can customize these crusts to your own preference; it's all in how you handle the dough. If you prefer a thin crust, roll the small dough to fit a 14- to 16-inch pizza pan or use the Medium recipe and cut the dough in half to form two crusts instead of one. Reduce the rising time after shaping as well. If it's a thick-crust pizza you desire, do the reverse—use smaller pizza pans and let the dough rise longer.

Small recipe yields 1 pizza crust
Medium recipe yields 1 pizza crust
Large recipe yields 2 pizza crusts

BAKE CYCLE: Dough

NUTRITIONAL INFORMATION PER SLICE (⅛ PIE)
Calories 119/Fat 2.2 grams/Carbohydrates 21.3 grams/Protein 2.9 grams/Fiber .8 grams/Sodium 153 milligrams/Cholesterol 0 milligrams

Bubbly Pizza Shell

We've had many requests to create a recipe for a prebaked pizza crust. It really wasn't that difficult. Here's our version, which we think rivals the store-bought product because it's fresh. If you keep one or two in the freezer, they'll come in handy for a last-minute veggie pizza or spur-of-the-moment appetizers. If you divide the dough into smaller pieces, you can also make individual shells for single-serving pizzas.

DOUGH

	SMALL	MEDIUM	LARGE
WATER	¾ cup	1 cup	1⅜ cups
OLIVE OIL	1½ tablespoons	2 tablespoons	3 tablespoons
SALT	1 teaspoon	1½ teaspoons	2 teaspoons
SUGAR	1 teaspoon	1½ teaspoons	2 teaspoons
BREAD FLOUR	2 cups	3 cups	4 cups
RED STAR BRAND ACTIVE DRY YEAST	1½ teaspoons	2 teaspoons	2½ teaspoons

1. Place dough ingredients in bread pan, select Dough setting, and press Start.

2. When the dough has risen long enough, the machine will beep. Turn off bread machine, remove bread pan, and turn out dough onto a lightly floured countertop or cutting board.

FOR THE SMALL RECIPE
   With a sharp knife, divide dough in half. Grease two 12-inch pizza pans.

FOR THE MEDIUM RECIPE
   Grease one 14-inch pizza pan.

FOR THE LARGE RECIPE
   With a sharp knife, cut dough into 4 pieces. Grease four 12-inch pizza pans.

3. Wrap dough in plastic wrap that has been lightly coated with olive oil. Set aside and let rest 15 minutes.

4. Preheat oven to 500°F.

5. Using a rolling pin, roll each piece of dough into circles large enough to fit the prepared pizza pans. Place dough on pizza pans. (We prefer the pizza pans that have small holes all over. They produce a very crisp crust.) Prick entire surface of the dough with a fork to prevent large bubbles during baking.

176

TOPPING

	SMALL	MEDIUM	LARGE
TOMATO PASTE	2 tablespoons	3 tablespoons	¼ cup
GARLIC CLOVES, CRUSHED	1	2 medium	2 large
GRATED MOZZARELLA CHEESE	¼ cup (1 ounce)	6 tablespoons (1½ ounces)	½ cup (2 ounces)
FRESHLY GRATED PARMESAN CHEESE	1 tablespoon	1½ tablespoons	2 tablespoons

6. In a small bowl, combine tomato paste and garlic. Brush this mixture over each pizza shell. Sprinkle evenly with the cheeses. Let dough rise on the countertop for 15 minutes.

7. Place pizza shell on the middle rack of the oven. Bake 7 to 8 minutes. Remove from oven and place on wire rack to cool. Repeat for each pizza.

8. Pizza shells can be used immediately or sealed well in plastic wrap or large plastic bags and frozen up to 1 month for later use. There's no need to thaw the crust first. Just add toppings and bake as directed in the recipe.

Small recipe yields two 12-inch pizza shells
Medium recipe yields one 14-inch pizza shell
Large recipe yields four 12-inch pizza shells

BAKE CYCLE: Dough

NUTRITIONAL INFORMATION PER SLICE (⅛ PIE)
Calories 230/Fat 4.7 grams/Carbohydrates 39.8 grams/Protein 6.5 grams/Fiber 1.8 grams/Sodium 451 milligrams/Cholesterol 3.5 milligrams

---

Flat Bread

Here's a chewy flat bread that is good plain or even better layered with thinly sliced meat, onion, tomato, a mild yogurt sauce, and then rolled up into a sandwich.

	SMALL	MEDIUM	LARGE
OLD-FASHIONED OATS	½ cup	¾ cup	1 cup
WATER	⅞ cup	1¼ cups	1⅝ cups
OLIVE OIL	3 tablespoons	4½ tablespoons	6 tablespoons
SUGAR	3 tablespoons	4½ tablespoons	6 tablespoons
SALT	1 teaspoon	1½ teaspoons	2 teaspoons
BREAD FLOUR	2 cups	3 cups	4 cups
RED STAR BRAND ACTIVE DRY YEAST	1½ teaspoons	2 teaspoons	2½ teaspoons

1. Place dough ingredients in bread pan, select Dough setting, and press Start.

2. When the dough has risen long enough, the machine will beep. Turn off bread machine, remove bread pan, and turn out dough onto a lightly floured countertop or cutting board.

3. Lightly grease 2 large baking sheets.

FOR THE SMALL RECIPE

Gently roll and stretch dough into a 6-inch log. With a sharp knife, divide dough into 6 pieces.

FOR THE MEDIUM RECIPE

Gently roll and stretch dough into a 9-inch log. With a sharp knife, divide dough into 9 pieces.

FOR THE LARGE RECIPE

Gently roll and stretch dough into a 12-inch log. With a sharp knife, divide dough into 12 pieces.

4. Roll each piece into a smooth ball. With a rolling pin, roll each ball into 7- to 8-inch circle. Set aside on lightly floured countertop; cover with a towel. Let breads rise about 30 minutes until slightly puffy.

5. Preheat oven to 350°F. Place 2 breads at a time on prepared baking sheet. Bake for 6 to 8 minutes until slightly golden. Do not overbake. They need to be soft and pliable to roll up well. Repeat with rest of breads.

6. Remove from oven and stack baked breads on clean kitchen towel. Cover with a second kitchen towel. Cool to room temperature before removing towels. Repeat baking and cooling process with remaining breads.

7. Store breads in sealed plastic bags to keep soft. They keep from 3 to 4 days.

Small recipe yields 6 flat breads
Medium recipe yields 9 flat breads
Large recipe yields 12 flat breads

BAKE CYCLE: Dough

NUTRITIONAL INFORMATION PER FLATBREAD
Calories 263/Fat 7.6 grams/Carbohydrates 42.6 grams/Protein 5.6 grams/Fiber 2 grams/Sodium 357 milligrams/Cholesterol 0 milligrams

---

Focaccia

Here's a very basic focaccia recipe with a multitude of suggestions on ways to jazz it up. We're sure once you experiment with a few of the creative suggestions, you'll come up with many of your own.

DOUGH

	MEDIUM
WATER	1 cup
OLIVE OIL	¼ cup
SUGAR	1 teaspoon
SALT	1 teaspoon
ALL-PURPOSE cups FLOUR	3 to 3¼
RED STAR BRAND ACTIVE	2 teaspoons

1. Place dough ingredients in bread pan, select Dough setting, and press Start.

2. When the dough has risen long enough, the machine will beep. Turn off bread machine, remove bread pan, and turn out dough onto a lightly floured countertop or cutting board. Cover and let rest 15 minutes.

TOPPING

OLIVE OIL	2 to 3 tablespoons
CLOVES GARLIC, MINCED	1 to 2
KOSHER SALT TO TASTE	

3. Combine the olive oil and garlic for the topping; set aside.

4. Brush a 10×15×1-inch jelly-roll pan with a little olive oil. Gently stretch and press dough to fit evenly into pan. If you do not have a jelly-roll pan, you can shape the dough into a 10×15-inch rectangle and place it on an oiled baking sheet.

5. Cover and let rise in a warm oven 30 to 45 minutes until doubled in size. (Hint: To warm oven slightly, turn oven on Warm setting for 1 minute, then turn it off, and place covered dough in oven to rise. Remove pan from oven before preheating.)

6. Preheat oven to 375°F. With fingers, poke holes all over dough. Drizzle the garlic oil on top. Sprinkle with kosher salt to taste. Bake for 25 to 30 minutes until brown.

7. Remove from oven, cool on wire rack briefly, cut into squares, and serve warm.

CREATIVE SUGGESTIONS:

1. Replace the kosher salt in the topping with ½ cup freshly grated imported Parmesan cheese.

2. Add to the topping fresh herbs of choice, such as rosemary, oregano, basil, thyme, or parsley.

3. Omit the topping. In a large covered skillet on low heat, sauté 2 large sliced onions in 2 tablespoons olive oil until very soft, about 20 minutes. Add some minced garlic and freshly ground black pepper during the last 5 minutes of cooking time. Top the focaccia dough with the onion mixture and fresh rosemary (optional); bake as directed.

4. To the topping add a layer of thinly sliced onion rings and a layer of thinly sliced fresh tomatoes, freshly ground black pepper to taste, chopped fresh basil, and freshly grated imported Parmesan cheese. Bake as directed.

5. Omit the topping. Brush the dough with 3 tablespoons of a good Italian salad dressing, sprinkle with some Italian herb seasoning and chopped sun-dried tomatoes to taste. Bake as directed.

6. Omit the topping. Bake the focaccia dough plain. Meanwhile, combine 1 cup very soft butter or margarine with ¼ cup olive oil; ¼ cup dried bread crumbs; 2 tablespoons chopped fresh parsley; 1 large clove garlic, minced; 1 teaspoon kosher salt; and freshly ground black pepper to taste. Remove baked focaccia from the oven and allow to cool on a rack for at least 30 minutes. Spread with butter mixture. Place under the broiler just briefly to brown. Watch closely to prevent burning.

7. Add a pinch of crushed red pepper flakes to the olive oil–garlic topping mixture.

8. Omit the kosher salt in the topping. Add ⅓ cup coarsely chopped black olives, ⅓ cup chopped roasted red peppers, and 3 ounces of crumbled feta, goat, or smoked mozzarella cheese. Bake as directed.

9. To the topping add ¼ cup finely julienned sun-dried tomatoes, 2 tablespoons thinly sliced green onions, 3 tablespoons chopped fresh basil, 3 tablespoons freshly grated Parmesan cheese, and freshly ground black pepper to taste. Bake as directed.

10. To the dough add ¼ cup chopped fresh onion and 2 teaspoons of Italian herb seasoning.

Serves 12

BAKE CYCLE: Dough

NUTRITIONAL INFORMATION PER SERVING
Calories 176/Fat 7.1 grams/Carbohydrates 24.3 grams/Protein 3.4 grams/Fiber 1 gram/Sodium 179 milligrams/Cholesterol 0 milligrams

---

Jerry's Poway Pizza

*T*he idea for combining barbecue chicken and asparagus on a pizza came from Jerry Lovelady, a longtime friend of Linda's and an inventive cook. This is sure to become a Friday night favorite! (If asparagus is out of season, canned or frozen will suffice.)

DOUGH

	MEDIUM
WATER	1 cup
OLIVE OIL	2 tablespoons
SALT	1 teaspoon
SUGAR	1½ teaspoons
ALL-PURPOSE FLOUR	1½ cups
WHOLE WHEAT FLOUR	1½ cups
RED STAR BRAND ACTIVE DRY YEAST	2 teaspoons

1. Place dough ingredients in bread pan, select Dough setting, and press Start.

2. When the dough has risen long enough, the machine will beep. Turn off bread machine, remove bread pan, and turn out dough onto a lightly floured countertop or cutting board. Wrap dough in plastic wrap that has been lightly coated with olive oil. Set aside to rest for 15 minutes.

TOPPING

HALF BREASTS OF CHICKEN, SKINNED AND BONED	3 half breasts
OIL	1 tablespoon
YOUR FAVORITE BARBECUE SAUCE	1¼ to 1½ cups
THINLY SLICED MUENSTER CHEESE	4 ounces
MEDIUM ONION, THINLY SLICED	½
COOKED FRESH ASPARAGUS, CUT INTO BITE-SIZE PIECES	½ pound
SHREDDED MOZZARELLA CHEESE, TO TASTE	1 to 1½ cups (4 to 6 ounces)

3. Cut chicken into bite-sized pieces. In a skillet, cook the chicken in the oil over medium heat until no longer pink, about 3 minutes. Add the barbecue sauce and simmer over low heat until the chicken is cooked through, about 15 minutes. Set aside.

4. Lightly oil one 14- to 16-inch pizza pan to within 1 inch of the edge.

5. Using a rolling pin, roll the dough into a circle slightly smaller than the pizza pan you plan to use. (We prefer the pizza pans that have small holes all over. They produce a very crisp crust.) Place the dough on the pizza pan and gently stretch it to fit. Shape dough around the edge to form a small rim.

6. If you prefer a thicker pizza crust, cover the dough and let it rise in a warm oven 30 to 45 minutes until doubled in size. (Hint: To warm oven slightly, turn oven on Warm setting for 1 minute, then turn it off, and place covered dough in oven to rise. Remove pan from oven before preheating.)

7. If you prefer a thin crust, skip Step 6 and use the 16-inch pan.

8. Cover the pizza dough with thin slices of Muenster cheese. Spread the chicken and barbecue sauce on top of the cheese. Scatter the onion and asparagus evenly over the chicken, then sprinkle the mozzarella cheese over all.

9. Preheat the oven to 450°F.

10. Bake the pizza in the middle of the oven for 15 minutes until the crust is golden-brown. Serve hot.

Recipe yields one 14- to 16-inch pizza

BAKE CYCLE: Dough

NUTRITIONAL INFORMATION PER SLICE (⅛ PIE)
Calories 411/Fat 16.7 grams/Carbohydrates 41.8 grams/Protein 24.2 grams/Fiber 4.7 grams/Sodium 775 milligrams/Cholesterol 52.7 milligrams

---

Light Whole Wheat Pizza Dough

*T*his crisp, flavorful, and almost fat-free pizza crust will help ease the guilt pangs one normally feels when eating pizza, especially if you top it with good things like grilled vegetables and fresh herbs.

	SMALL	MEDIUM	LARGE
WATER	¾ cup	1 cup	1⅜ cup
UNSWEETENED APPLESAUCE	1 tablespoon	1½ tablespoons	2 tablespoons
SUGAR	1½ teaspoons	2 teaspoons	1 tablespoon
SALT	¾ teaspoon	1 teaspoon	1½ teaspoons
WHOLE WHEAT FLOUR	1⅓ cups	2 cups	2⅔ cups
UNBLEACHED OR ALL-PURPOSE FLOUR	⅔ cup	1 cup	1⅓ cups
RED STAR BRAND ACTIVE DRY YEAST	1½ teaspoons	2 teaspoons	2½ teaspoons

1. Place all ingredients in bread pan, select Dough setting, and press Start.

2. When the dough has risen long enough, the machine will beep. Turn off bread machine, remove bread pan, and turn out dough onto a lightly floured countertop or cutting board. For the Large recipe, cut dough in half. Wrap dough in plastic wrap that has been lightly coated with olive oil. Set aside to rest for 15 minutes. (With the Large recipe, it is not necessary to use both crusts at one time. At this point the extra dough can be placed in an oiled plastic bag and kept in the freezer or it can be refrigerated up to 3 days for later use.)

FOR THE SMALL RECIPE
Lightly oil one 12- to 14-inch pizza pan to within 1 inch of the edge.

FOR THE MEDIUM RECIPE
Lightly oil one 14- to 16-inch pizza pan to within 1 inch of the edge.

FOR THE LARGE RECIPE
Lightly oil one or two 12- to 14-inch pizza pans to within 1 inch of the edge.

3. Using a rolling pin, roll the dough into a circle slightly smaller than the pizza pan you plan to use. (We prefer the pizza pans that have small holes all over. They produce a very crisp crust.) Place the dough on the pizza pan and gently stretch it to fit. Shape dough around the edge to form a small rim.

4. Cover dough and let rise on the countertop for 20 to 30 minutes. Meanwhile, preheat oven to 450°F.

5. Spread your toppings of choice on pizza and bake on the middle shelf of the oven for 15 to 20 minutes.

6. Remove from oven and serve warm.

Small recipe yields 1 pizza crust
Medium recipe yields 1 pizza crust
Large recipe yields 2 pizza crusts

BAKE CYCLE: Dough

NUTRITIONAL INFORMATION PER SLICE (⅛ PIE)
Calories 167/Fat .4 grams/Carbohydrates 34.4 grams/Protein 4.7 grams/Fiber 1.4 grams/Sodium 268 milligrams/Cholesterol 0 milligrams

---

Morris's Onion Pletzel

*W*hat's a pletzel? you ask. The best way to find out is to make this tasty bread. Serve it up as an appetizer or with a salad for lunch and enjoy.

DOUGH

	SMALL	MEDIUM	LARGE
WATER	¾ cup	1 cup	1⅜ cups
OIL	1 tablespoon	1½ tablespoons	2 tablespoons
SUGAR	1 teaspoon	1½ teaspoons	2 teaspoons
SALT	¼ teaspoon	¼ teaspoon	½ teaspoon
ALL-PURPOSE FLOUR	2 cups	3 cups	4 cups
RED STAR BRAND ACTIVE DRY YEAST	1½ teaspoons	2 teaspoons	2½ teaspoons

1. Place dough ingredients in bread pan, select Dough setting, and press Start.

2. When the dough has risen long enough, the machine will beep. Turn off bread machine, remove bread pan, and turn out dough onto a lightly floured counter top or cutting board.

3. Grease a large baking sheet. You'll need two for the Large.

FOR THE SMALL RECIPE
With a rolling pin, roll dough into a ¼-inch-thick rectangle about 7×11 inches. Place on prepared baking sheet.

FOR THE MEDIUM RECIPE
With a rolling pin, roll dough into a ¼-inch-thick rectangle about 9×15 inches. Place on prepared baking sheet.

FOR THE LARGE RECIPE
Cut dough in half. With a rolling pin, roll dough into two ¼-inch-thick rectangles about 7×11 inches. Place on prepared baking sheets.

4. Cover and let rise in a warm oven 30 to 45 minutes until doubled in size. (Hint: To warm oven slightly, turn oven on Warm setting for 1 minute, then turn it off, and place covered dough in oven to rise. Remove pan from oven before preheating.)

TOPPING

	SMALL LOAF	MEDIUM LOAF	LARGE LOAF
OLIVE OIL	1 tablespoon	1½ tablespoons	2 tablespoons
CHOPPED ONION	1 cup	1½ cups	2 cups
EGG, BEATEN	1	1	1
COARSE KOSHER SALT			

5. Meanwhile, in a skillet over low heat sauté the onion in oil until almost brown, about 20 minutes. Set aside.

6. Brush the dough with beaten egg. Sprinkle cooked onion and kosher salt over dough.

7. Preheat oven to 375°F. Bake for 20 to 25 minutes until the crust is light brown.

8. Remove from oven and serve warm or cool on wire racks.

CREATIVE SUGGESTION: Morris says you can turn these savory pletzels into sweet ones by replacing the onion topping with cinnamon sugar.

Small recipe yields 1 flat bread
Medium recipe yields 1 flat bread
Large recipe yields 2 flat breads

BAKE CYCLE: Dough

NUTRITIONAL INFORMATION PER SERVING
Calories 198/Fat 3.6 grams/Carbohydrates 34.7 grams/Protein 5.6 grams/Fiber 1.5 grams/Sodium 142 milligrams/Cholesterol 26.6 milligrams

Pacific Northwest Pizza

Here's a pizza that will knock your socks off! A slice or two with a fresh fruit salad makes a perfect summer meal or it can be gussied up with greens and a tomato rose in the center for a luncheon party. To cut the calories and fat grams in half, omit the cream cheese layer.

DOUGH

	SMALL
WATER	¾ cup
OLIVE OIL	1½ tablespoons
SALT	½ teaspoon
SUGAR	2 teaspoons
ALL-PURPOSE FLOUR	2 cups
RED STAR BRAND ACTIVE DRY YEAST	2 teaspoons

1. Place dough ingredients in bread pan, select Dough setting, and press Start.

TOPPING

BUTTER	1 tablespoon
VIDALIA ONIONS OR ANY TYPE OF SWEET ONION, THINLY SLICED	2
OLIVE OIL	2 to 3 teaspoons
COOKED, CANNED, OR SMOKED SALMON, FLAKED	12 to 16 ounces
FRESH LEMON JUICE, TO TASTE	1 to 2 teaspoons
PACKAGE CREAM CHEESE, SOFTENED	1 (8-ounce)
MAYONNAISE	¼ cup
MILK	1 tablespoon
DRIED DILL WEED	⅛ teaspoon
RIPE TOMATOES, CHOPPED,	1½ medium
GREEN PEPPER, CHOPPED	1 medium
CHOPPED BLACK OLIVES	½ cup
HARD-BOILED EGG, CHOPPED	1
FRESHLY GROUND BLACK PEPPER, TO TASTE	

2. Meanwhile, in a small skillet over medium heat, melt the butter. Add the sweet onions and sauté until soft and golden, about 30 minutes. Remove from heat and cool.

3.   When the dough has risen long enough, the machine will beep. Turn off bread machine, remove bread pan, and turn out dough onto a lightly floured countertop or cutting board.

4.   Wrap dough in plastic wrap that has been lightly coated with olive oil. Set aside to rest for 15 minutes.

5.   Preheat the oven to 500°F.

6.   Using a rolling pin, roll out the pizza dough on a floured surface to approximately 14 inches in diameter. Use the oiled plastic wrap that covered the dough to lightly grease a 14-inch pizza pan. (We prefer the pizza pans that have small holes all over. They produce a very crisp crust.) Place the dough on the prepared pan and stretch to fit.

7.   Brush the dough with olive oil, then prick the entire surface of the dough with a fork.

8.   Bake the pizza dough in the middle of the oven for 7 to 8 minutes until golden-brown. Place on a rack to cool to room temperature. (For a softer crust, cover the cooling pizza with a clean dish towel.)

9.   In a small bowl, combine the salmon and lemon juice; set aside.

10. With an electric mixer, cream together the cream cheese, mayonnaise, milk, and dill.

11. Spread cream cheese mixture over the pizza crust, leaving a 1-inch outer rim.

12. Spread cooled onions evenly over the cream cheese mixture and sprinkle flaked salmon on top.

13. Starting at the outer edge of the salmon, create concentric rings of chopped tomato, green pepper, and olives on top of the salmon layer. Sprinkle the chopped hard-boiled egg in the center.

14. Sprinkle freshly ground black pepper on top.

15. Serve immediately or cover with plastic wrap, refrigerate and serve cold later the same day.

Recipe yields one 14-inch pizza

BAKE CYCLE: Dough

> NUTRITIONAL INFORMATION PER SLICE (⅛ PIE)
> Calories 434/Fat 26.3 grams/Carbohydrates 30.5/Protein 18.9 grams/Fiber 2.48 grams/Sodium 420 milligrams/Cholesterol 86.3 milligrams

Pesto Pizza

If you have the pizza shell in the freezer, then nothing could be quicker than throwing this together as an appetizer when unexpected guests arrive at your door.

I. Preheat oven to 350°F.

BASIL OR TOMATO PESTO SAUCE	¾ cup
SLICED PEPPERONI (OPTIONAL)	¼ pound
PLUM TOMATOES, SLICED	2 to 3
FRESHLY GROUND BLACK PEPPER	to taste
RED ONION, THINLY SLICED	¼ medium
SLICED BLACK OLIVES, DRAINED	1 small can (4 ounces)
PINE NUTS (OPTIONAL)	¼ cup
FRESHLY GRATED IMPORTED PARMESAN CHEESE	½ cup (2 ounces)
PREBAKED PIZZA SHELL (SEE RECIPE, PAGES 176—77)	One medium

2. Layer ingredients on prebaked pizza shell in order given. Place on lightly oiled baking sheet.

3. Bake for 15 minutes. Remove from the oven, cut into squares or thin wedges, and serve.

CREATIVE SUGGESTION: This pizza can also be served cold. In a small bowl, whisk together 2 tablespoons olive oil and 1 tablespoon balsamic vinegar together with a pinch of oregano. Toss the tomatoes and onions in this mixture before adding them to the pizza.

Recipe yields 16 thin appetizer slices

BAKE CYCLE: Dough

NUTRITIONAL INFORMATION PER SLICE (⅟₁₆ PIE)
Calories 232/Fat 13.3 grams/Carbohydrates 21.7 grams/Protein 6.9 grams/Fiber 1.4 grams/Sodium 500 milligrams/Cholesterol 7 milligrams

Pizza Olé

Italy meets Mexico in this flavorful south-of-the-border pizza.

REFRIED BEANS	1 can (16 ounces)
PREBAKED PIZZA SHELL (SEE RECIPE, PAGES 176–77)	One medium
GROUND BEEF	1 pound
YELLOW ONION, CHOPPED	½
CHILI POWDER	2 teaspoons
SALSA	1 cup
SLICED BLACK OLIVES	1 small can (2.5 ounces)
SHREDDED MONTEREY JACK CHEESE	½ cup (2 ounces)
SHREDDED CHEDDAR CHEESE	½ cup (2 ounces)
GARNISH: GUACAMOLE, CHOPPED TOMATOES, SOUR CREAM, SHREDDED LETTUCE, CHOPPED JALAPEÑO PEPPERS, HOT SAUCE (OPTIONAL)	

1. Preheat oven to 400°F.

2. Spread refried beans over pizza shell to within 1 inch of the edge.

3. In a skillet over medium heat, cook the meat and onion until the meat is brown, about 10 minutes. Remove from heat, drain, and stir in chili powder.

4. Spread meat mixture over refried beans. Layer the rest of the ingredients on top in the order given. Place on lightly oiled baking sheet.

5. Bake for 15 minutes. Remove from the oven and serve with garnish, if desired.

CREATIVE SUGGESTION: You can turn up the heat on this southwestern pizza by using spicy refried beans, a dash of cayenne pepper in the hamburger, hot salsa, and by substituting pepper cheese for the Monterey Jack cheese.

Recipe yields 8 slices

BAKE CYCLE: Dough

NUTRITIONAL INFORMATION PER SLICE (⅛ PIE)
Calories 535/Fat 22.8 grams/Carbohydrates 54.3 grams/Protein 28.2 grams/Fiber 8.2 grams/Sodium 975 milligrams/Cholesterol 66.5 milligrams

---

Roasted Peppers and Garlic Pizza

S *tuck in a pizza rut? Here's a trendy version that's a pleasing switch from pep-peroni pizza.*

CHOPPED FRESH BASIL	3 tablespoons
LARGE CLOVES GARLIC, MINCED	4 to 6
VIDALIA ONION OR OTHER SWEET ONION, THINLY SLICED	1
CRUMBLED GOAT CHEESE	1½ cups (6 ounces)
CHOPPED SUNDRIED TOMATOES, DRAINED	⅓ cup
FRESH ROASTED PEPPERS, SLICED IN THIN STRIPS (IF USING BOTTLED PEPPERS, DRAIN WELL)	1 cup
PREBAKED PIZZA SHELL (SEE RECIPE, PAGES 176–77)	One medium

1. Preheat oven to 350°F.

2. Layer ingredients on prebaked pizza shell in order given. Place on lightly oiled baking sheet.

3. Bake for 20 minutes. Serve warm.

Recipe yields 8 slices

BAKE CYCLE: Dough

NUTRITIONAL INFORMATION PER SLICE (⅛ PIE)
Calories 319/Fat 10.5 grams/Carbohydrates 43.7 grams/Protein 11.8 grams/Fiber 2.7 grams/Sodium 648 milligrams/Cholesterol 24.3 milligrams

---

Salt-Free Pizza Dough

*T*his pizza dough sans *salt* bakes up beautifully. *The Italian seasoning adds enough flavor that you'll never miss the salt.*

	SMALL	MEDIUM	LARGE
WATER	⅝ cup	1 cup	1⅜ cups
OLIVE OIL	1½ tablespoons	2 tablespoons	3 tablespoons
SUGAR	¾ teaspoon	1 teaspoon	1½ teaspoons
ITALIAN SEASONING	¾ teaspoon	1 teaspoon	1½ teaspoons
UNBLEACHED OR ALL-PURPOSE FLOUR	2 cups	3 cups	4 cups
RED STAR BRAND ACTIVE DRY YEAST	1½ teaspoons	2 teaspoons	2½ teaspoons

1. Place all ingredients in bread pan, select Dough setting, and press Start.

2. When the dough has risen long enough, the machine will beep. Turn off bread machine, remove bread pan, and turn out dough onto a lightly floured countertop or cutting board. For large recipe, cut dough in half. Wrap dough in plastic wrap that has been lightly coated with olive oil. Set aside to rest for 15 minutes. (With the Large recipe, it is not necessary to use both crusts at one time. At this point the extra dough can be placed in an oiled plastic bag and kept in the freezer or it can be refrigerated up to 3 days for later use.)

FOR THE SMALL RECIPE

Lightly oil one 12- to 14-inch pizza pan to within 1 inch of the edge.

FOR THE MEDIUM RECIPE

Lightly oil one 14- to 16-inch pizza pan to within 1 inch of the edge.

FOR THE LARGE RECIPE

Lightly oil one or two 12- to 14-inch pizza pans to within 1 inch of the edge.

3. Using a rolling pin, roll the dough into a circle slightly smaller than the pizza pan you plan to use. (We prefer the pizza pans that have small holes all over. They produce a very crisp crust.) Place the dough on the pizza pan and gently stretch it to fit. Shape dough around the edge to form a small rim.

4. Cover dough and let rise on the countertop for 20 to 30 minutes. Meanwhile, preheat oven to 450°F.

5. Spread your toppings of choice on pizza and bake on the middle shelf of the oven for 15 to 20 minutes.

6. Remove from oven and serve warm.

Small recipe yields 1 pizza crust
Medium recipe yields 1 pizza crust
Large recipe yields 2 pizza crusts

BAKE CYCLE: Dough

NUTRITIONAL INFORMATION PER SLICE (⅛ PIE)
Calories 191/Fat 3.8 grams/Carbohydrates 33.5 grams/Protein 4.7 grams/Fiber 1.4 grams/Sodium 1.2 milligrams/Cholesterol 0 milligrams

Thin-Crust Pizza Dough

*T*his recipe was inspired by a recipe in the King Arthur Flour Baker's Catalog. The original called for using their Italian-style flour and baking it on the bottom of two 14-inch pizza pans. If you haven't discovered their catalog yet, do yourself a favor and drop them a card requesting one. For the address, see Sources, page 260.

	SMALL	MEDIUM	LARGE
RED STAR BRAND ACTIVE DRY YEAST	1½ teaspoons	2 teaspoons	2½ teaspoons
SUGAR	1 teaspoon	2 teaspoons	1 tablespoon
WARM WATER	½ cup	1 cup	1⅜ cups
OLIVE OIL	1 tablespoon	2 tablespoons	3 tablespoons
UNBLEACHED FLOUR	1½ cups	3 cups	4½ cups
SALT	¾ teaspoon	1½ teaspoons	2¼ teaspoons
NONFAT DRY MILK	1½ teaspoons	1 tablespoon	1½ tablespoons

1. Place first three ingredients in bread pan and allow to sit for 10 minutes, until bubbly.

2. Add rest of ingredients, select Dough setting, and press Start. *Allow dough to knead for 5 minutes only.* Remove dough from machine. For the Medium recipe, cut dough in half. For the Large recipe, cut dough into three pieces.

3. Wrap dough in plastic wrap that has been lightly coated with olive oil. Set aside to rest for 15 minutes. (It is not necessary to use all the crusts at one time. At this point the extra[s] can be placed in an oiled plastic bag and kept in the freezer or they can be refrigerated up to 3 days for later use.)

4. Using a rolling pin, roll each piece of dough into a 14-inch circle. Lightly grease one, two, or three 14-inch pizza pans with the oil-coated plastic wrap. (We prefer the pizza pans that have small holes all over. They produce a very crisp crust.) Place dough on pizza pan(s) and gently stretch to fit.

5. Cover dough and let rise on the countertop for half an hour. Meanwhile, preheat oven to 450°F for ½ hour.

6. Uncover dough and place on the middle rack of the oven. Bake 5 minutes.

7. Remove crust from oven and cover with toppings of choice. (Note: You'll probably want to use half the amount of ingredients you usually use to avoid overwhelming the thin crust.)

8. Place pan(s) back in oven for 5 more minutes. Rotate pan(s) from top to bottom, back to front, and bake for 5 minutes more until crust(s) are golden-brown and toppings are bubbly.

9. Remove from oven and serve warm.

CREATIVE SUGGESTION: For a different taste and texture, substitute semolina flour for ⅓ of the unbleached flour.

Small recipe yields 1 pizza crust
Medium recipe yields 2 pizza crusts
Large recipe yields 3 pizza crusts

BAKE CYCLE: Dough

NUTRITIONAL INFORMATION PER SLICE (⅛ PIE)
Calories 104/Fat 1.9 grams/Carbohydrates 18.6 grams/Protein 2.6 grams/Fiber .7 grams/Sodium 202 milligrams/Cholesterol .1 milligrams

Veggie Pizza

*T*here are as many ways to vary this pizza as there are veggies in the vegetable bin. We enjoyed it best using a garlic-flavored hummus.

HUMMUS	1 cup
PREBAKED PIZZA SHELL (SEE RECIPE, PAGES 176—77)	One medium
CHOPPED PLUM TOMATOES	2 cups (about 5 medium tomatoes)
CHOPPED ONION	½ cup
SLICED ZUCCHINI	1 cup
CHOPPED GARLIC	1 tablespoon
GREEN BELL PEPPER, CUT IN STRIPS	½ medium
SALT AND PEPPER TO TASTE	
OLIVE OIL	1 tablespoon
FRESHLY GRATED PARMESAN CHEESE	¼ cup (1 ounce)
SHREDDED MOZZARELLA CHEESE	1 cup (4 ounces)

1. Spread hummus evenly over pizza shell to within 1 inch of the edge.

2. In a large bowl, combine the tomatoes, onion, zucchini, garlic, green pepper, and salt and pepper to taste. Drizzle with olive oil and toss lightly. Spoon mixture onto pizza shell. Top with grated cheeses.

3. Bake in 400°F oven for 10 to 12 minutes to heat through.

Serves 4

NUTRITIONAL INFORMATION PER SLICE (⅛ PIE)
Calories 380/Fat 14.2 grams/Carbohydrates 50.1 grams/Protein 16 grams/Fiber 3.3 grams/Sodium 774 milligrams/Cholesterol 18 milligrams

PARMIGIANO·REGGIANO

II
Sweet Rolls
and
Desserts

Apricot Sweet Rolls

*T*he generous amount of filling in these sweet rolls rank them as out of the ordinary. If you prefer a more traditional version, simply cut the filling amounts in half.

DOUGH

	MEDIUM
BUTTERMILK	¾ cup
EGG	1
BUTTER OR MARGARINE	4 tablespoons
SUGAR	¼ cup
SALT	1 teaspoon
ALL-PURPOSE FLOUR	3 cups
RED STAR BRAND ACTIVE DRY YEAST	2 teaspoons

1. In a small bowl with an electric mixer, beat the cream cheese until smooth. Add the egg, sugar, and lemon peel and beat until well blended. Stir in apricots, walnuts, and coconut.

2. Place dough ingredients in bread pan, select Dough setting, and press Start.

3. When the dough has risen long enough, the machine will beep. Turn off bread machine, remove bread pan, and turn out dough onto a lightly floured countertop or cutting board.

4. Grease a 9×13×2-inch baking pan. With a rolling pin, roll the dough into a 12×18-inch rectangle.

FILLING

PACKAGE CREAM CHEESE, SOFTENED	1 (8-ounce)
PACKAGE CREAM CHEESE, SOFTENED	1 (3-ounce)
EGG	1
SUGAR	⅓ cup
GRATED LEMON PEEL	1½ teaspoons
SNIPPED DRIED APRICOTS	¾ cup
CHOPPED WALNUTS	⅓ cup
FLAKED COCONUT (OPTIONAL)	⅓ cup

5. Spread cream cheese filling over dough, leaving a 1-inch border on one of the long edges. Starting with the other long edge, roll up the dough; pinch edges to seal. Slide a 12-inch piece of dental floss or heavy thread underneath the dough. By bringing the ends of the floss up and crisscrossing them on top, pull in opposite directions and cut the dough into twelve 1½-inch segments. Place cut-side up in prepared pan.

6. Cover and let rise in a warm oven 30 to 45 minutes until doubled in size. (Hint: To warm oven slightly, turn oven on Warm setting for 1 minute, then turn it off, and place covered dough in oven to rise. Remove pan from oven before preheating.)

GLAZE

CONFECTIONERS' SUGAR	1 cup
LEMON JUICE	1 tablespoon

7. Preheat oven to 350°F. Bake for 25 to 30 minutes until golden-brown. Meanwhile, stir together glaze ingredients until smooth; set aside.

8. Remove rolls from oven and immediately transfer rolls to a large platter or serving plate. Allow to cool at least 5 minutes then drizzle with glaze. Serve warm.

CREATIVE SUGGESTION: If you don't care for dried apricots or have none on hand, this recipe adapts well to any dried fruit of choice, such as peaches, apples, pineapple, and so on.

Yields 12 rolls

BAKE CYCLE: Dough

NUTRITIONAL INFORMATION PER ROLL
Calories 372/Fat 15.7 grams/Carbohydrates 51.6 grams/Protein 7.4 grams/Fiber 2 grams/Sodium 335 milligrams/Cholesterol 64.4 milligrams

Berry Bread Cake

*D*id you overestimate how much bread you needed yesterday and you're now left with one too many loaves? Here's a delicious solution to your problem, guaranteed to make that straggler disappear faster than you can say "Alikazam."

BUTTER OR MARGARINE, SOFTENED	½ cup
GROUND CINNAMON	½ teaspoon
LOAF OF LEFTOVER BREAD, THINLY SLICED, CRUSTS REMOVED	1 pound
PACKAGES OF FROZEN BERRIES, THAWED	2 (10-ounce)
SUGAR (OPTIONAL)	4 to 6 tablespoons
SWEETENED WHIPPED CREAM	

1. Combine butter and cinnamon in a small bowl.

2. Trim crusts from bread and lightly spread both sides of each slice with the cinnamon-butter mixture.

3. In a blender or food processor, purée the frozen berries, adding sugar if necessary to sweeten to taste.

4. Line a 9×5-inch loaf pan with plastic wrap. Cut bread to fit pan and layer with puréed fruit, beginning and ending with the purée. Press down well with a large spoon to compress the bread.

5. Cover with plastic wrap and refrigerate for at least 8 hours, or overnight.

6. Uncover and invert cake onto a serving dish. Cut into slices and serve with a dollop of whipped cream.

Serves 8

NUTRITIONAL INFORMATION PER SERVING
Calories 419/Fat 22 grams/Carbohydrates 51 grams/Protein 5.9 grams/Fiber 4.4 grams/Sodium 444 milligrams/Cholesterol 40.7 milligrams

Bread Ice Cream

I f you thumb through the pages of this book, you'll find recipes for bread soup, bread salad, and bread cake. Here's one for bread ice cream you'll have to try to believe.

SWEET, BROWN BREAD (SEE NOTE)	8 ounces (2½ cups cubed)
DARK BROWN SUGAR	1 cup
EGG	1
HEAVY CREAM	1½ cups
MILK	¾ cup
VANILLA EXTRACT	1 teaspoon

1.   Place bread and brown sugar in food processor. Process briefly until reduced to coarse crumbs. Pour onto a large rimmed baking pan.

2.   Place bread crumbs in oven 4 inches from broiler. Watch carefully to avoid burning; stir often. Toast until sugar melts and bubbles, about 5 minutes. Remove from oven and cool.

3.   In a large bowl, whisk the egg until light and fluffy, 2 minutes. Whisk in the cream and milk, stirring 1 to 2 minutes more. Stir in the vanilla.

4.   Pour into ice cream maker and freeze following manufacturer's directions.

5.   As the ice cream begins to stiffen, add the baked bread crumbs then continue churning until the ice cream is done.

Yields 1 quart

NOTE: Try using Irish Soda Bread, Boston Brown Bread, Chock-o-Nut Bread, Delores's Raisin Walnut Bread, New England Maple Syrup Bread, Scandinavian Rye Bread, or Rum Raisin Bread.

NUTRITIONAL INFORMATION PER CUP SERVING
Calories 394/Fat 23.5 grams/Carbohydrates 43.5 grams/Protein 4.1 grams/Fiber .2 grams/Sodium 115 milligrams/Cholesterol 118 milligrams

Butterscotch Apple Bread Pudding

This combination of apples, raisins, butterscotch, and bread seems like a natural. The bread should be a few days old or briefly dried in a warm oven.

DAY OLD BREAD OF CHOICE	6 cups
BUTTERSCOTCH CHIPS	½ cup
PEELED AND CUBED APPLES	3 cups
GOLDEN RAISINS (OPTIONAL)	½ cup
EGGS	6
MILK	3 cups
SUGAR	½ cup
SALT	½ teaspoon
BUTTERSCOTCH ICE CREAM TOPPING	1 cup
VANILLA ICE CREAM, FROZEN FAT-FREE VANILLA YOGURT, OR WHIPPED CREAM (OPTIONAL)	

1. Preheat oven to 350°F. Butter a 3-quart mold or casserole.

2. Cut bread into ½-inch cubes. In the prepared casserole, layer half the bread, half the butterscotch chips, half the apples, and half the raisins. Repeat the layers.

3. In a mixing bowl, whisk together eggs, milk, sugar, and salt. Pour over the bread and fruit mixture then top with butterscotch topping.

4. Bake for 60 to 70 minutes until set.

5. Serve warm with vanilla ice cream, yogurt, or whipped cream, as desired.

CREATIVE SUGGESTION: You can cut the fat grams considerably by using one of the delicious fat-free butterscotch toppings or fruit dips now on the market. You'll never notice the difference!

Serves 6 to 8

NUTRITIONAL INFORMATION PER SERVING (⅛)
Calories 471/Fat 13.5 grams/Carbohydrates 50 grams/Protein 11.2 grams/Fiber 2.7 grams/ Sodium 397 milligrams/Cholesterol 175 milligrams

Cinnamon Crisps

Try these flat, crispy cinnamon rolls. They're unique!

DOUGH

	SMALL	MEDIUM	LARGE
MILK	⅜ cup	¾ cup	⅞ cup
EGG	1	1	2
BUTTER OR MARGARINE	2 tablespoons	3 tablespoons	¼ cup
SUGAR	3 tablespoons	¼ cup	6 tablespoons
DARK BROWN SUGAR	3 tablespoons	¼ cup	6 tablespoons
SALT	¾ teaspoon	1 teaspoon	1½ teaspoons
ALL-PURPOSE FLOUR	2 cups	3 cups	4 cups
CINNAMON	1 teaspoon	1½ teaspoons	2 teaspoons
RED STAR BRAND ACTIVE DRY YEAST	½ teaspoon	¾ teaspoon	1 teaspoon

1. Place dough ingredients in bread pan, select Dough setting, and press Start.

2. When the dough has risen long enough, the machine will beep. Turn off bread machine, remove bread pan, and turn out dough onto a lightly floured countertop or cutting board.

FOR THE SMALL RECIPE

Gently roll and stretch dough into a 24-inch log. With a sharp knife, divide dough into 24 pieces.

FOR THE MEDIUM RECIPE

Gently roll and stretch dough into two 18-inch logs. With a sharp knife, divide dough into 36 pieces.

FOR THE LARGE RECIPE

Gently roll and stretch dough into two 24-inch logs. With a sharp knife, divide dough into 48 pieces.

3. Roll each piece into a 12-inch rope. Hold one end of the rope in place and loosely coil the rest of the rope around the center; tuck the end underneath. Flatten each roll slightly with hand or rolling pin. Set aside on lightly floured countertop.

4. Preheat a large griddle to 400°F.

TOPPING

	SMALL	MEDIUM	LARGE
DARK BROWN SUGAR	¼ cup	⅓ cup	½ cup
GRANULATED SUGAR	¼ cup	⅓ cup	½ cup
CINNAMON	2 teaspoons	1 tablespoon	4 teaspoons
BUTTER OR MARGARINE, MELTED	¼ cup	⅓ cup	½ cup

5. In a shallow bowl, combine the sugars and cinnamon.

6. Dunk each roll into the melted butter then dredge in cinnamon sugar mixture. Place on hot griddle and cook 4 minutes per side. When you turn the rolls over, press down firmly on each roll with a spatula to flatten it.

7. Cool briefly on wire racks. These are best served while still warm and crispy.

Small recipe yields 24 rolls
Medium recipe yields 36 rolls
Large recipe yields 48 rolls

BAKE CYCLE: Dough

NUTRITIONAL INFORMATION PER ROLL
Calories 84/Fat 2.2 grams/Carbohydrates 14.7 grams/Protein 1.5 grams/Fiber .4 grams/Sodium 95.8 milligrams/Cholesterol 6.1 milligrams

Dennis's Bear Claws

*L*inda's husband, Dennis, has a weakness for these breakfast treats. Each time he passes through the kitchen, another slice disappears. These almond-filled pastries are more work than most sweet rolls, but husbands like Dennis are worth it!

DOUGH

	SMALL	MEDIUM	LARGE
MILK	⅜ cup	⅝ cup	1 cup
EGG	1	1	2
BUTTER, SOFTENED	½ cup	¾ cup	1 cup
SUGAR	3 tablespoons	¼ cup	6 tablespoons
SALT	½ teaspoon	1 teaspoon	1 teaspoon
ALL-PURPOSE FLOUR	2 cups	3 cups	4 cups
RED STAR BRAND ACTIVE DRY YEAST	1½ teaspoons	2 teaspoons	2½ teaspoons

I. Place dough ingredients in bread pan, select Dough setting, and press Start.

FILLING

	SMALL	MEDIUM	LARGE
SLIVERED ALMONDS	1½ cups (6 ounces)	2 cups (8 ounces)	3 cups (12 ounces)
LIGHT BROWN SUGAR	⅓ cup	½ cup	⅔ cup
BUTTER	¼ cup	6 tablespoons	½ cup
EGG	1	1	2
MILK	2 tablespoons	3 tablespoons	¼ cup
VANILLA EXTRACT	½ teaspoon	1 teaspoon	1 teaspoon
ALMOND EXTRACT	¼ teaspoon	½ teaspoon	½ teaspoon

2. For the filling, place the almonds in a food processor and process until finely ground. Add the rest of the ingredients and process until mixture becomes a paste.

3. When the dough has risen long enough, the machine will beep. Turn off bread machine, remove bread pan, and turn out dough onto a lightly floured countertop or cutting board. Grease a large baking sheet.

207

FOR THE SMALL RECIPE

With a rolling pin, roll the dough into a 6×20-inch rectangle. Gently spread the filling *lengthwise* over half of the dough. Fold the other half of the dough over the filling and pinch the edges to seal. With a sharp knife, cut the 3×20-inch rectangle into four 3×5-inch pieces. Pinch the cut edges to seal.

FOR THE MEDIUM RECIPE

With a rolling pin, roll the dough into a 6×30-inch rectangle. Gently spread the filling *lengthwise* over half of the dough. Fold the other half of the dough over the filling and pinch the edges to seal. With a sharp knife, cut the 3×30-inch rectangle into six 3×5-inch pieces. Pinch the cut edges to seal.

FOR THE LARGE RECIPE

With a rolling pin, roll the dough into two 6×20-inch rectangles. Gently spread the filling *lengthwise* over half of each dough. Fold the other half of the dough over the filling and pinch the edges to seal. With a sharp knife, cut the 3×20-inch rectangles into eight 3×5-inch pieces. Pinch the cut edges to seal.

4. Place the rectangles on the prepared baking sheet. With a sharp knife, make four cuts on the sealed long edge about 2 inches long. Curve each bear claw to fan out the "claws." Cover and let rise in a warm oven 30 to 45 minutes until puffy. (Hint: To warm oven slightly, turn oven on Warm setting for 1 minute, then turn it off, and place covered dough in oven to rise. Remove pan from oven before preheating.)

TOPPING

	SMALL	MEDIUM	LARGE
EGGS, BEATEN	1	1	2
SLICED ALMONDS	½ cup	¾ cup	1 cup
MILK	1½ tablespoons	2 tablespoons	3 tablespoons

5. Preheat oven to 375°F. Gently brush each bear claw with the beaten egg. Sprinkle the sliced almonds and sugar over each. Bake for 15 to 20 minutes until golden-brown.

6. Remove from oven and cool on wire rack.

GLAZE

	SMALL	MEDIUM	LARGE
CONFECTIONERS' SUGAR	½ cup	¾ cup	1 cup
MILK	1½ teaspoons	2¼ teaspoons	3 teaspoons

7. Once cooled, combine the glaze ingredients and drizzle over each bear claw.

Small recipe yields 4 rolls
Medium recipe yields 6 rolls
Large recipe yields 8 rolls

BAKE CYCLE: Dough

NUTRITIONAL INFORMATION PER ROLL
Calories 1039/Fat 67.7 grams/Carbohydrates 91.6 grams/Protein 22.8 grams/Fiber 8.5 grams/Sodium 426 milligrams/Cholesterol 201 milligrams

---

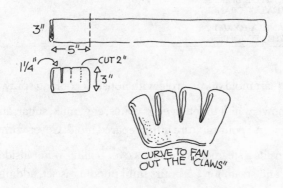

CURVE TO FAN OUT THE "CLAWS"

Guilt-Free Bread Pudding

*N*ow here's a lighter, healthier version of the traditional bread pudding.

EGG WHITES	4
EGG	1
NONFAT OR LOW-FAT MILK	2 cups
BROWN SUGAR	3 tablespoons
FLAVORED EXTRACT, SUCH AS LEMON, ORANGE, PINEAPPLE, BANANA, ALMOND, RUM, COCONUT, PEPPERMINT, OR VANILLA	1 teaspoon
CUBED, DAY-OLD BREAD OF CHOICE	4 cups
CHOPPED FRESH FRUIT OF CHOICE, SUCH AS CHERRIES, APPLES, BERRIES, PINEAPPLES, BANANAS, OR ORANGES	1 cup
FROZEN FAT-FREE VANILLA YOGURT OR FAT-FREE FROZEN WHIPPED TOPPING	

I. Spray a 1½-quart mold or casserole with nonstick cooking spray.

2. In a mixing bowl, whisk together egg whites, egg, milk, sugar, and extract. Add the bread and fruit and pour mixture into prepared mold. Cover with foil.

3. Place mold inside a steamer or on a rack over boiling water inside a large kettle. Cover the kettle and steam for 1½ hours until pudding is set, adding more boiling water to kettle as needed.

4. Serve warm with frozen yogurt or frozen whipped topping as desired.

Serves 4 to 6

NUTRITIONAL INFORMATION PER SERVING Calories 157/Fat 1.8 grams/Carbohydrates 25.6 grams/Protein 9.6 grams/Fiber .8 grams/Sodium 233 milligrams/Cholesterol 2.2 milligrams

Peaches and Cream Kuchen

W hen peaches are in season, buy several for this fabulous dessert. If you can't wait until then, you can use frozen peach slices instead. We love to serve this slightly warm from the oven.

DOUGH

	SMALL	MEDIUM	LARGE
WATER	¼ cup	⅝ cup	¾ cup
EGGS	1	1	2
BUTTER OR MARGARINE	¼ cup	⅓ cup	½ cup
SUGAR	¼ cup	⅓ cup	½ cup
SALT	¼ teaspoon	¼ teaspoon	½ teaspoon
ALL-PURPOSE FLOUR	2 cups	3 cups	4 cups
RED STAR BRAND ACTIVE DRY YEAST	1½ teaspoons	2 teaspoons	2½ teaspoons

1. Place dough ingredients in bread pan, select Dough setting, and press Start.

2. When the dough has risen long enough, the machine will beep. Turn off bread machine, remove bread pan, and turn out dough onto a lightly floured countertop or cutting board.

FOR THE SMALL RECIPE

Grease a 9×13×2-inch baking pan. With a rolling pin, roll dough into an 11×15-inch rectangle. Place in bottom of pan and press 1 inch up the sides.

FOR THE MEDIUM RECIPE

Grease an 11×17-inch jelly-roll pan. With a rolling pin, roll dough into a 13×19-inch rectangle. Place in bottom of pan and press 1 inch up the sides.

FOR THE LARGE RECIPE

Grease two 9×13×2-inch baking pans. Cut dough in half. With a rolling pin, roll dough into two 11×15-inch rectangles. Place in bottom of pans and press 1 inch up the sides.

	SMALL	MEDIUM	LARGE
COTTAGE CHEESE	¾ cup	1 cup	1½ cup
SOUR CREAM	½ cup	¾ cup	1 cup
EGGS	2	3	4
BROWN SUGAR	¼ cup	⅓ cup	½ cup
VANILLA	1 teaspoon	1½ teaspoons	2 teaspoons
ALL-PURPOSE FLOUR	3 tablespoons	4 tablespoons	5 tablespoons

TOPPING

	SMALL	MEDIUM	LARGE
RIPE PEACHES	4 to 5	6 to 7	8 to 9
OR	or	or	or
FROZEN SLICED PEACHES	1½ pounds	2¼ pounds	3 pounds
SUGAR	½ cup	¾ cup	1 cup

3.   In a bowl, stir together filling ingredients. Spread evenly over dough. Peel and slice peaches; if frozen, thaw and drain. Arrange the peaches on top to completely cover filling.

4.   In a separate bowl, combine sugar and cinnamon. Sprinkle on top of the peaches.

5.   Preheat oven to 350°F. Bake for 30 to 35 minutes until the crust is golden-brown and the filling is set around the edges. Cover with foil the last 10 minutes if the crust looks dark enough at that time.

6.   Remove from oven and cool on wire rack at least 10 minutes before serving.

Small recipe serves 12
Medium recipe serves 18
Large recipe serves 24

BAKE CYCLE: Dough

NUTRITIONAL INFORMATION PER SERVING
Calories 215/Fat 5.8 grams/Carbohydrates 35.6 grams/Protein 5.7 grams/Fiber 1.3 grams/Sodium 139 milligrams/Cholesterol 52.1 milligrams

Savarin

This spectacular French dessert dates back to the seventeenth century. We urge you to try it the next time you have a group of friends in for coffee and dessert. They'll definitely be flattered by your efforts! Incidentally, this is also a great addition to a brunch buffet. Important: *Read through the directions first. This dough will go through only the first kneading cycle in your machine.*

DOUGH

	SMALL LOAF
EGGS	3
MILK	3 tablespoons
SUGAR	2 tablespoons
UNSALTED BUTTER, SOFTENED	½ cup
SALT	½ teaspoon
ALL-PURPOSE FLOUR	2 cups
RED STAR BRAND ACTIVE DRY YEAST	2 teaspoons

I.   Generously butter a 4- or 5-cup ring mold. Place in the refrigerator.

2.   Place dough ingredients in bread pan, select Dough setting, and press Start. You may be tempted to add flour to the bread pan because it's a very gloppy dough. Don't. It should be more like a batter than a bread dough.

3.   After the first kneading cycle (usually 7 to 10 minutes), turn off the machine and allow the dough to rise in the machine for 45 to 60 minutes until doubled in size.

4.   Pour the batter into the prepared ring mold. Cover and let rise in a warm place until the dough is almost to the top of the mold, about 30 to 45 minutes. Preheat the oven to 375°F.

5.   Once dough has risen, bake for 20 to 25 minutes until golden-brown and pulling away from the sides of the pan. Cool in mold 10 minutes, then unmold; cool slightly on a wire rack.

SYRUP

SUGAR	1½ cups
WATER	1½ cups
FINELY GRATED RIND AND JUICE OF 1 LARGE LEMON OR ORANGE	

6. Meanwhile, in a large skillet, stir together the sugar and water for the syrup over low heat until the sugar dissolves. Bring to a boil, reduce heat, and simmer for 2 minutes. Add the lemon or orange juice and rind; remove skillet from the heat. Allow to cool for 5 minutes.

7. Gently place the cake, dark side down, into the syrup in the skillet. (If it's too wide for the skillet, place the cake on the wire rack over a large pan.) With a bulb baster or a large spoon, continually spoon the syrup over the cake until all of the syrup is absorbed into the cake. Have patience—this step takes some time.

8. When all the syrup is absorbed, place a dish over the cake and turn the cake out upside down (dark side up) onto the dish. Then place your serving dish over the cake and repeat the procedure one more time. Now your cake should be right side up (dark side down) on your serving plate. Cover and refrigerate until ready to serve.

FILLING

DARK RUM, BRANDY, KIRSCH, OR GRAND MARNIER (OPTIONAL)	4 tablespoons
FRESH FRUIT, SUCH AS GRAPES, BERRIES, MELON BALLS, ORANGE SLICES, CHERRIES, PINEAPPLE, KIWI, OR PEACHES	
SWEETENED WHIPPED CREAM OR A CUSTARD SUCH AS ZABAGLIONE OR FRANGIPANE	

9. Just before serving, sprinkle the cake with the liqueur of your choice, if desired. Fill the center of the cake with fresh fruit, whipped cream, or a custard.

Serves 10 to 12

BAKE CYCLE: Dough

NUTRITIONAL INFORMATION PER SERVING
Calories 205/Fat 9 grams/Carbohydrates 27.7 grams/Protein 1.9 grams/Fiber .2 grams/Sodium 108 milligrams/Cholesterol 74.1 milligrams

Scottish Baps

*H*ere's a breakfast bun sure to put a smile on the face of any bonny wee lass or laddie!

	SMALL	MEDIUM	LARGE
OLD-FASHIONED OATS	1/3 cup	1/2 cup	2/3 cup
WATER	3/4 cup	1 cup	1 3/8 cups
BUTTER OR MARGARINE	1 1/2 tablespoons	2 tablespoons	3 tablespoons
HONEY	3 tablespoons	1/4 cup	6 tablespoons
SALT	1/4 teaspoon	1/2 teaspoon	1/2 teaspoon
ALL-PURPOSE FLOUR	2/3 cup	1 cup	1 1/3 cups
WHOLE WHEAT FLOUR	2/3 cup	1 cup	1 1/3 cups
MILLER'S BRAN	1/3 cup	1/2 cup	2/3 cup
RAISINS	1/3 cup	1/2 cup	2/3 cup
RED STAR BRAND ACTIVE DRY YEAST	1 1/2 teaspoons	2 teaspoons	2 1/2 teaspoons

1. Place ingredients in bread pan, select Dough setting, and press Start.

2. When the dough has risen long enough, the machine will beep. Turn off bread machine, remove bread pan, and turn out dough onto a lightly floured countertop or cutting board.

3. Grease a large baking sheet.

FOR THE SMALL RECIPE
Gently roll and stretch dough into an 8-inch log. With a sharp knife, divide dough into 8 pieces; roll each into a ball and place on prepared baking sheet.

FOR THE MEDIUM RECIPE
Gently roll and stretch dough into a 12-inch log. With a sharp knife, divide dough into 12 pieces; roll each into a ball and place on prepared baking sheet.

FOR THE LARGE RECIPE
Gently roll and stretch dough into a 16-inch log. With a sharp knife, divide dough into 16 pieces; roll each into a ball and place on prepared baking sheet.

4. Cover and let rise in a warm oven 45 to 60 minutes until doubled in size. (Hint: To warm oven slightly, turn oven on Warm setting for 1 minute, then turn it off, and place covered dough in oven to rise. Remove pan from oven before preheating.)

5. Preheat oven to 350°F. Bake for 20 to 25 minutes until golden-brown.

6. Remove from oven and serve warm.

Small recipe yields 8 rolls
Medium recipe yields 12 rolls
Large recipe yields 16 rolls

BAKE CYCLE: Dough

NUTRITIONAL INFORMATION PER ROLL
Calories 141/Fat 2.1 grams/Carbohydrates 29.1 grams/Protein 3.7 grams/Fiber 3 grams/Sodium 114 milligrams/Cholesterol 0 milligrams

---

Steamed Bread Pudding

When you have a bread machine and love trying one new recipe after another, you invariably end up with quite a few partially finished loaves. Here's one very tasty way to use up those stragglers, and the possible combinations of breads, fruits, and flavorings are endless.

EGGS	3
HALF-AND-HALF	1 pint (2 cups)
SUGAR	⅓ cup
FLAVORED EXTRACT, SUCH AS LEMON, ORANGE, PINEAPPLE, BANANA, ALMOND, RUM, COCONUT, PEPPERMINT, OR VANILLA	1 teaspoon
CUBED, LEFTOVER BREAD OF CHOICE	4 cups (about 3 slices)
CHOPPED FRESH FRUIT OF CHOICE, SUCH AS CHERRIES, APPLES, BERRIES, PINEAPPLE, BANANAS, OR ORANGES	1 cup
OR	
DRIED FRUIT OF CHOICE, SUCH AS CRANBERRIES, BLUEBERRIES, COCONUT, DATES, OR RAISINS	⅓ cup
VANILLA ICE CREAM, FROZEN FAT-FREE VANILLA YOGURT, OR WHIPPED CREAM (OPTIONAL)	

I. Butter a 1½-quart mold or casserole.

2. In a mixing bowl, whisk together eggs, half-and-half, sugar, and extract. Add the bread and fruit and pour mixture into prepared mold. Cover with foil.

3. Place mold inside a steamer or on a rack over boiling water inside a large pan. Cover the pan and steam for 1½ hours until pudding is set, adding more boiling water to pan as needed.

4. Remove from mold and drain on a triple layer of paper towels if excessively moist. Serve warm with vanilla ice cream, yogurt, or whipped cream, as desired.

CREATIVE SUGGESTION: We found the combination of bananas, raisins, coconut, and rum extract well worth waiting for.

Serves 4 to 6

NUTRITIONAL INFORMATION PER SERVING (⅙)
Calories 268/Fat 11.5 grams/Carbohydrates 34.7 grams/Protein 7.6 grams/Fiber 1.2 grams/Sodium 180 milligrams/Cholesterol 134 milligrams

Tropical Bread Pudding

W e offer you this little bit of paradise in a dessert. Enjoy!

EGGS	5
MILK	1½ cups
ORANGE JUICE	½ cup
PINEAPPLE JUICE	½ cup
SUGAR	1 cup
GRATED NUTMEG	1 teaspoon
GRATED ZEST OF 1 LEMON	
SALT	½ teaspoon
CUBED, LEFTOVER BREAD OF CHOICE	6 cups
SWEETENED, SHREDDED COCONUT	½ cup
UNSWEETENED CRUSHED PINEAPPLE, WELL DRAINED	1 (8 ounce) can
MANDARIN ORANGES, WELL DRAINED	1 (11 ounce) can
WHIPPED CREAM (OPTIONAL)	

1. Butter a 3-quart mold or casserole. Preheat oven to 350°F.

2. In a mixing bowl, whisk together eggs, milk, juices, sugar, nutmeg, zest, and salt.

3. In a separate bowl, toss together the bread, coconut, and fruits.

4. Pour the egg mixture into the bread mixture, and gently stir to blend. Pour into prepared casserole.

5. Bake for 50 to 60 minutes until set.

6. Remove from oven and cool on wire rack for 10 minutes. Serve warm with whipped cream, if desired.

CREATIVE SUGGESTION: Substitute ¼ cup Grand Marnier for ¼ of the cup orange juice.

Serves 8

NUTRITIONAL INFORMATION PER SERVING (⅛)
Calories 332/Fat 8.1 grams/Carbohydrates 56.8 grams/Protein 9.2 grams/Fiber 2.3 grams/Sodium 360 milligrams/Cholesterol 136 milligrams

Upside-Down Orange Rolls

We love sweet rolls and coffee cakes that are easy to make but taste great. Here's one that fits that bill.

DOUGH

	SMALL	MEDIUM	LARGE
BUTTERMILK	½ cup	¾ cup	⅞ cup
EGGS	1	1	2
BUTTER OR MARGARINE	3 tablespoons	4 tablespoons	6 tablespoons
SUGAR	3 tablespoons	¼ cup	6 tablespoons
SALT	1 teaspoon	1½ teaspoons	2 teaspoons
ALL-PURPOSE FLOUR	2 cups	3 cups	4 cups
RED STAR BRAND ACTIVE DRY YEAST	1½ teaspoons	1½ teaspoons	2 teaspoons

1. Place dough ingredients in bread pan, select Dough setting, and press Start.

2. When the dough has risen long enough, the machine will beep. Turn off bread machine, remove bread pan, and turn out dough onto a lightly floured countertop or cutting board.

TOPPING

	SMALL	MEDIUM	LARGE
ORANGE MARMALADE	1 cup	1½ cups	2 cups
BUTTER OR MARGARINE MELTED	2 tablespoons	3 tablespoons	4 tablespoons
FLAKED COCONUT OR CHOPPED NUTS	⅓ cup	½ cup	⅔ cup

3. In a bowl, stir together the topping ingredients; set aside.

FOR THE SMALL RECIPE

Butter an 8- or 9-inch square baking pan. Evenly spread the topping mixture in the bottom of the pan. Gently roll and stretch dough into a 9-inch rope. With a sharp knife, divide dough into 9 pieces; roll each into a ball and place in pan.

FOR THE MEDIUM RECIPE

Butter a 9×13×2-inch baking pan. Evenly spread the topping mixture in the bottom of the pan. Gently roll and stretch dough into a 12-inch rope. With a sharp knife, divide dough into 12 pieces; roll each into a ball and place in pan.

FOR THE LARGE RECIPE

Butter two 8- or 9-inch square baking pans. Evenly spread the topping mixture in the bottom of the pans. Gently roll and stretch dough into an 18-inch rope. With a sharp knife, divide dough into 18 pieces; roll each into a ball and place in pans.

4. Cover and let rise in a warm oven 30 to 45 minutes until doubled in size. (Hint: To warm oven slightly, turn oven on Warm setting for 1 minute, then turn it off, and place covered dough in oven to rise. Remove pan from oven before preheating.)

5. Preheat oven to 350°F. Cover pan(s) with foil and bake for 25 minutes. Uncover and bake 8 to 10 minutes more until golden-brown.

6. Remove from oven, invert onto serving dish, and serve warm.

Small recipe yields 9 rolls
Medium recipe yields 12 rolls
Large recipe yields 18 rolls

BAKE CYCLE: Dough

NUTRITIONAL INFORMATION PER ROLL
Calories 306/Fat 6.8 grams/Carbohydrates 58 grams/Protein 4.8 grams/Fiber 1.7 grams/Sodium 388 milligrams/Cholesterol 18.4 milligrams

---

12
Holiday Breads

Challah

This beautiful Jewish bread traditionally served on the Sabbath symbolizes the manna God sent His children in the wilderness. It is usually served as a braided bread on the Sabbath and in other shapes for holidays. For instance, on Rosh Hashannah it is made into a round loaf to symbolize wholeness and the year coming full circle. If you're lucky enough to have leftovers, this bread makes superb French toast.

DOUGH

	SMALL	MEDIUM	LARGE
WATER	¼ cup	⅜ cup	½ cup
EGGS	2	3	4
OIL	3 tablespoons	4½ tablespoons	6 tablespoons
SUGAR	3 tablespoons	¼ cup	6 tablespoons
SALT	¾ teaspoon	1 teaspoon	1½ teaspoons
ALL-PURPOSE FLOUR	2½ cups	3½ cups	5 cups
RED STAR BRAND ACTIVE DRY YEAST	1½ teaspoons	2 teaspoons	2½ teaspoons

1. Place dough ingredients in bread pan, select Dough setting, and press Start.

2. When the dough has risen long enough, the machine will beep. Turn off bread machine, remove bread pan, and turn out dough onto a lightly floured countertop or cutting board.

3. Grease a large baking sheet. You'll need two for the Large recipe.

FOR THE SMALL RECIPE

With a sharp knife, divide the dough into 3 pieces.

FOR THE MEDIUM RECIPE

With a sharp knife, divide the dough into 3 pieces.

FOR THE LARGE RECIPE

With a sharp knife, divide the dough into 6 pieces.

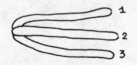  

4. Gently roll and stretch each piece into an 18-inch rope that is slightly thicker in the middle and thinner at the ends. (Hint: Lightly dusting each rope with a little flour before braiding helps to keep them separate and distinct as they rise.) Place the 3 ropes side by side about an inch apart on the prepared baking sheet. Starting from the center, loosely braid the ropes of dough first toward one end and then the other. Pinch to seal and tuck the ends under.

A ROPE BRAID

5. Cover and let rise at room temperature 45 to 60 minutes until almost doubled in size. For this loaf to hold its shape it's important to prevent it from overproofing (letting it rise too long until it's light and airy and then collapses during baking). To test, lightly press dough with finger. It should spring back slightly but not completely.

6. Preheat oven to 350°F during the last 10 minutes of the bread's rising time.

GLAZE

	SMALL	MEDIUM	LARGE
EGG YOLKS	1	1	2
WATER	1 tablespoon	1 tablespoon	2 tablespoons
SALT	1 pinch	1 pinch	⅛ teaspoon
POPPY SEEDS OR SESAME SEEDS (OPTIONAL)			

7. In a small bowl, combine the egg yolk, water, and salt for the glaze. Very gently brush the glaze over the entire loaf. Sprinkle with poppy seeds or sesame seeds, if desired.

8. Bake for 40 to 45 minutes until golden-brown. Cover with foil after 10 to 15 minutes to avoid excessive browning.

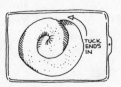

TUCK ENDS IN

TWIST INTO A CIRCLE

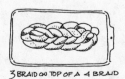

3 BRAID ON TOP OF A 4 BRAID

9. Remove from oven and cool on wire rack.

CREATIVE SUGGESTIONS:

1. Braid the loaf, then shape it into a circle and seal the ends together.

2. Instead of dividing the dough into 3 pieces, roll all of the dough into one long 32-inch rope, twist it, then coil it up in a big circle on a greased baking sheet or pie plate, tucking the ends under. Cover, let rise, glaze, and bake as directed above.

3. For a very large challah, make two batches of the Medium recipe, combine them, and cut the dough into 7 pieces. Braid 4 pieces for the bottom loaf and braid the remaining 3 to be placed on top. Pinch all the ends together and tuck underneath. Cover, let rise, glaze, and bake as directed above.

Small recipe yields 1 loaf
Medium recipe yields 1 loaf
Large recipe yields 2 loaves

BAKE CYCLE: Dough

NUTRITIONAL INFORMATION PER SLICE
Calories 127/Fat 4.2 grams/Carbohydrates 18.5 grams/Protein 3.3 grams/Fiber .6 grams/Sodium 124 milligrams/Cholesterol 45.6 milligrams

---

Cornucopia

*H*ere's a very simple but eye-catching centerpiece for your holiday table. Fill it with fruit, dried flowers, or dinner rolls and you have a useful decoration that will impress your family and guests.

DOUGH

	LARGE
MILK	1⅜ cups
OIL	3 tablespoons
SALT	1½ teaspoons
SUGAR	3 tablespoons
ALL-PURPOSE FLOUR	4 cups
RED STAR BRAND ACTIVE DRY YEAST	2 teaspoons

EGG WASH

EGGS	1
WATER	1 tablespoon

1. Place dough ingredients in bread pan, select Dough setting, and press Start.

2. When the dough has risen long enough, the machine will beep. Turn off bread machine, remove bread pan, and turn out dough onto a lightly floured countertop or cutting board.

3. Cover a cone-shaped object such as an old fruit strainer with foil. If you don't have anything cone-shaped and ovenproof, you can create a cone with crumpled aluminum foil. You'll need something about 10 inches high and 7 inches wide at the base. Spray the cone with a vegetable oil spray.

4. Break off pieces of dough and roll into ropes about 1½ inches in diameter. Set aside 2 ropes that are slightly longer than the circumference of your cone's base. Starting at the tip of the cone, wrap the dough around the cone, pinching the ends of ropes together as you add new ropes.

5. To finish off the opening of the cornucopia, twist together the 2 reserved ropes of dough and attach to the last ropes of dough wrapped around the cone. Set the cornucopia on its side on a lightly greased baking sheet. Preheat oven to 400°F.

6. For the egg wash, combine the egg and water. Brush the entire surface of the cornucopia well with the egg wash.

7. Bake in a 400°F oven for 15 to 20 minutes until golden-brown. Remove from oven and cool on a wire rack. Remove the cone once the cornucopia has cooled. If the interior is soft or damp, you can place the cornucopia back in a warm oven for a few minutes to dry it out.

BAKE CYCLE: Dough

Cranapple Orange Bread

*L*eave a slice of this by the fireplace for St. Nick on Christmas Eve and you're sure to wind up on his list of "Good Little Girls and Boys." This can be a high riser in some machines, so watch it closely the first time you bake it. Don't be tempted to add more flour. This dough is like a batter when it's mixing but it bakes up fine.

	SMALL LOAF	MEDIUM LOAF	LARGE LOAF
ORANGE JUICE	1 to 1⅛ cups	1⅜ to 1½ cups	1⅝ to 1¾ cups
UNSWEETENED APPLESAUCE	2 tablespoons	3 tablespoons	¼ cup
ORANGE OIL OR ORANGE EXTRACT	¾ teaspoon	1 teaspoon	1½ teaspoons
OIL	1 tablespoon	1½ tablespoons	2 tablespoons
HONEY	2 tablespoons	3 tablespoons	4 tablespoons
SALT	½ teaspoon	¾ teaspoon	1 teaspoon
BREAD FLOUR	2⅓ cups	3½ cups	4⅔ cups
NONFAT DRY MILK POWDER	2 tablespoons	3 tablespoons	¼ cup
GRATED ORANGE PEEL	1 tablespoon	1½ tablespoons	2 tablespoons
RED STAR BRAND ACTIVE DRY YEAST	1½ teaspoons	2 teaspoons	2½ teaspoons
DRIED CRANBERRIES	3 tablespoons	¼ cup	6 tablespoons
DRIED APPLE, DICED	3 tablespoons	¼ cup	6 tablespoons
CHOPPED PECANS	3 tablespoons	¼ cup	6 tablespoons

I. Place all ingredients in bread pan except the cranberries, apple, and nuts, using the least amount of liquid listed in the recipe. Select Light Crust setting and Raisin/Nut cycle. Press Start.

2. Observe the dough as it kneads. After 5 to 10 minutes, if it appears dry and stiff or if your machine sounds as if it's straining to knead it, add more liquid 1 tablespoon at a time until dough forms a smooth, soft, pliable ball that is slightly tacky to the touch.

3. At the beep, add the cranberries, apple, and pecans.

4. After the baking cycle ends, remove bread from pan, place on wire rack, and allow to cool 1 hour before slicing.

CRUST: Light

BAKE CYCLE: Raisin/Nut

OPTIONAL BAKE CYCLES: Standard/Whole Wheat/Sweet Bread

NUTRITIONAL INFORMATION PER SLICE

Calories 172/Fat 3.3 grams/Carbohydrates 31.4 grams/Protein 4.1 grams/Fiber 2 grams/Sodium 122 milligrams/Cholesterol .2 milligrams

Eggnog Bread

*D*eck the halls with boughs of holly . . . and loaves of this great eggnog bread. Here's another reason why it's a shame Christmas only comes once a year. It's the only time you can find eggnog in the dairy case. So if this becomes a favorite in your house, start stocking up the freezer now . . . or better yet, find an easy recipe for homemade eggnog.

	SMALL LOAF	MEDIUM LOAF	LARGE LOAF
EGGNOG	¾ to ⅞ cup	1½ to 1⅝ cups	1¾ to 1⅞ cups
OIL	1½ tablespoons	2 tablespoons	3 tablespoons
HONEY	1 tablespoon	1½ tablespoons	2 tablespoons
SALT	½ teaspoon	¾ teaspoon	1 teaspoon
BREAD FLOUR	2 cups	3 cups	4 cups
NUTMEG	1 teaspoon	1½ teaspoons	2 teaspoons
GROUND MACE	¼ teaspoon	½ teaspoon	¾ teaspoon
RED STAR BRAND ACTIVE DRY YEAST	1½ teaspoons	2 teaspoons	2½ teaspoons

1. Place all ingredients in bread pan, using the least amount of liquid listed in the recipe. Select Medium Crust setting and Sweet Bread cycle. Press Start.

2. Observe the dough as it kneads. After 5 to 10 minutes, if it appears dry and stiff or if your machine sounds as if it's straining to knead it, add more liquid 1 tablespoon at a time until dough forms a smooth, soft, pliable ball that is slightly tacky to the touch.

3. After the baking cycle ends, remove bread from pan, place on cake rack, and allow to cool 1 hour before slicing.

CRUST: Medium
BAKE CYCLE: Sweet Bread
OPTIONAL BAKE CYCLES: Standard/Whole Wheat/Rapid Bake

NUTRITIONAL INFORMATION PER SLICE
Calories 161/Fat 4.4 grams/Carbohydrates 26.1 grams/Protein 4 grams/Fiber .8 grams/Sodium 130 milligrams/Cholesterol 16 milligrams

---

Finnish Pulla Bread

T̶his is the traditional Easter bread of Finland. Serve with pride and eat with gusto.

DOUGH

	SMALL	MEDIUM	LARGE
MILK	¼ cup	⅜ cup	½ cup
EGGS	2	3	4
BUTTER, SOFTENED	3 tablespoons	¼ cup	6 tablespoons
SUGAR	3 tablespoons	¼ cup	6 tablespoons
SALT	¼ teaspoon	½ teaspoon	½ teaspoon
ALL-PURPOSE FLOUR	1½ cups	2⅓ cups	3 cups
RYE FLOUR	½ cup	⅔ cup	1 cup
GRATED LEMON PEEL	¾ teaspoon	1 teaspoon	1½ teaspoons
GRATED ORANGE PEEL	¾ teaspoon	1 teaspoon	1½ teaspoons
GROUND CARDAMOM	¾ teaspoon	1 teaspoon	1½ teaspoons
GOLDEN RAISINS	⅓ cup	½ cup	⅔ cup
SLIVERED ALMONDS	⅓ cup	½ cup	⅔ cup
RED STAR BRAND ACTIVE DRY YEAST	2 teaspoons	2½ teaspoons	3 teaspoons

1. Place dough ingredients in bread pan, select Dough setting, and press Start.

2. When the dough has risen long enough, the machine will beep. Turn off bread machine, remove bread pan, and turn out dough onto a lightly floured countertop or cutting board.

3. Grease a large baking sheet. You'll need 2 for the Large recipe.

FOR THE SMALL RECIPE
   With a sharp knife, divide the dough into 3 pieces.

FOR THE MEDIUM RECIPE
   With a sharp knife, divide the dough into 3 pieces.

FOR THE LARGE RECIPE
   With a sharp knife, divide the dough into 6 pieces.

4. Gently roll and stretch each piece into an 18-inch rope. (Hint: Lightly dusting each rope with a little flour before braiding helps to keep them separate and distinct as they rise.) Place the 3 ropes side by side about an inch apart on the prepared baking sheet. Starting from the center, loosely braid the ropes of dough first toward one end and then the other. Pinch to seal and tuck the ends under.

5. Cover and let rise in a warm oven 30 to 45 minutes until almost doubled in size. (Hint: To warm oven slightly, turn oven on Warm setting for 1 minute, then turn it off, and place covered dough in oven to rise. Remove pan from oven before preheating.)

6. Preheat oven to 350°F. Bake for 20 to 25 minutes, covering with foil after 10 minutes to prevent burning.

7. Remove from oven and cool on wire rack(s).

TOPPING

	SMALL	MEDIUM	LARGE
CONFECTIONERS' SUGAR	1 cup	1½ cups	2 cups
MILK	3 to 4 teaspoons	5 to 6 teaspoons	7 to 8 teaspoons
GRATED ORANGE OR LEMON PEEL	½ teaspoon	½ teaspoon	1 teaspoon

8. Combine topping ingredients, stir until smooth. Drizzle over cooled braid(s). Serve.

CREATIVE SUGGESTIONS:

1. Instead of the sugary icing, this braid can be brushed with an egg wash (combine 1 egg and 1 tablespoon of water) and then sprinkled with sliced almonds.

2. You can create a smaller braid to place on top of the larger bottom braid by cutting the dough into 4 pieces instead of 3. Roll 3 pieces into a 12-inch rope, and shape into a braid for the bottom. Cut the remaining piece into 3 pieces and roll each into a 9-inch long strand. Braid together and place on top of the large braid, tucking the ends into the large braid. (See Challah recipe, page 222, for illustration.)

Small recipe yields 1 loaf
Medium recipe yields 1 loaf
Large recipe yields 2 loaves

BAKE CYCLE: Dough

NUTRITIONAL INFORMATION PER SERVING
Calories 207/Fat 7.1 grams/Carbohydrates 31.1 grams/Protein 5.3 grams/Fiber 2.4 grams/Sodium 95 milligrams/Cholesterol 54.8 milligrams

German Stollen

*T*his traditional German Christmas bread, a distant cousin to our fruitcake, is worthy of a place of honor at any holiday party.

DOUGH

	SMALL	MEDIUM	LARGE
RAISINS	1/3 cup	1/2 cup	2/3 cup
MIXED CANDIED FRUIT	1/4 cup	1/3 cup	1/2 cup
GRATED LEMON RIND	2 teaspoons	1 tablespoon	4 teaspoons
RUM OR BRANDY	2 tablespoons	3 tablespoons	1/4 cup
MILK	1/2 cup	3/4 cup	7/8 cup
EGGS	1	2	2
UNSALTED BUTTER, SOFTENED	3 tablespoons	1/4 cup	6 tablespoons
SUGAR	3 tablespoons	1/4 cup	6 tablespoons
SALT	1 teaspoon	1 1/2 teaspoons	2 teaspoons
ALL-PURPOSE FLOUR	2 1/4 cups	3 1/3 cups	4 1/2 cups
CHOPPED, BLANCHED ALMONDS (SEE NOTE, PAGE 242)	1/3 cup	1/2 cup	2/3 cup
RED STAR BRAND ACTIVE DRY YEAST	1 1/2 teaspoons	2 teaspoons	2 1/2 teaspoons

1. Place raisins, candied fruit, and lemon rind in small bowl. Add rum or brandy and let mixture soak for at least 1 hour. Drain well.

2. Place dough ingredients in bread pan, including drained raisin mixture, select Dough setting, and press Start.

3. When the dough has risen long enough, the machine will beep. Turn off bread machine, remove bread pan, and turn out dough onto a lightly floured countertop or cutting board.

4. Grease a large baking sheet.

FOR THE SMALL RECIPE
   Roll or pat dough into an oval about 10×7 inches.

FOR THE MEDIUM RECIPE
   Roll or pat dough into an oval about 11×8 inches.

Roll or pat dough into an oval about 12×9 inches.

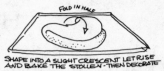

5. Fold the dough in half lengthwise and shape into a slight crescent. With the edge of your hand, press the folded edge lightly to crease. Place dough on prepared baking sheet and cover.

6. Cover and let rise in a warm oven 45 to 60 minutes. (Hint: To warm oven slightly, turn oven on Warm setting for 1 minute, then turn it off, and place covered dough in oven to rise. Remove pan from oven before preheating.)

7. Preheat oven to 350°F. Bake for 35 to 40 minutes until golden-brown.

TOPPING

	SMALL	MEDIUM	LARGE
CONFECTIONERS' SUGAR	1 cup	1 cup	2 cups
MILK	1 tablespoon	1 tablespoon	2 tablespoons
VANILLA	½ teaspoon	½ teaspoon	1 teaspoon
BLANCHED ALMOND HALVES			
CANDIED CHERRY HALVES			

8. In a small bowl, stir together the confectioners' sugar, milk, and vanilla.

9. Remove stollen from oven and, while still warm, frost with icing. Decorate with cherries and almonds in floral designs to resemble poinsettias.

CREATIVE SUGGESTIONS:

1. You can omit the iced topping and sprinkle stollen with a generous amount of powdered sugar instead.

2. Reserve the liquid used for soaking the raisins, candied fruit, and lemon peel and use it in the topping in place of the milk and vanilla.

Yields 1 loaf

BAKE CYCLE: Dough

NUTRITIONAL INFORMATION PER SLICE
Calories 249/Fat 8.1 grams/Carbohydrates 37.8 grams/Protein 5.3 grams/Fiber 1.7 grams/Sodium 244 milligrams/Cholesterol 30.8 milligrams

Hot Cross Buns

*T*hese rolls date back to pagan times in England when the cross symbolized the four seasons and was believed to ward off any evil spirits that might prevent them from rising. From the sixteenth century on, with the cross as a symbol of Christianity, they've been served on Good Friday.

	DOUGH		
	SMALL	MEDIUM	LARGE
MILK	¼ cup	¼ cup	½ cup
WATER	¼ cup	¼ cup	⅜ cup
EGGS	1	2	2
BUTTER OR MARGARINE	2 tablespoons	3 tablespoons	4 tablespoons
LIGHT BROWN SUGAR	3 tablespoons	¼ cup	⅓ cup
SALT	¼ teaspoon	½ teaspoon	½ teaspoon
ALL-PURPOSE FLOUR	2 cups	3 cups	4 cups
GROUND CINNAMON	¼ teaspoon	½ teaspoon	½ teaspoon
GROUND NUTMEG	⅛ teaspoon	¼ teaspoon	¼ teaspoon
GROUND CLOVES	⅛ teaspoon	¼ teaspoon	¼ teaspoon
CURRANTS OR RAISINS	¼ cup	⅓ cup	½ cup
CANDIED ORANGE PEEL (SEE RECIPE, PAGE 247)	3 tablespoons	¼ cup	⅓ cup
RED STAR BRAND ACTIVE DRY YEAST	1½ teaspoons	2 teaspoons	2½ teaspoons

1. Place dough ingredients in bread pan, select Dough setting, and press Start.

2. When the dough has risen long enough, the machine will beep. Turn off bread machine, remove bread pan, and turn out dough onto a heavily floured countertop or cutting board. Grease a large baking sheet.

FOR THE SMALL RECIPE

Gently roll and stretch dough into an 8-inch rope. With a sharp knife, divide dough into 8 pieces; roll each into a ball and place on prepared baking sheet.

FOR THE MEDIUM RECIPE

Gently roll and stretch dough into a 12-inch rope. With a sharp knife, divide dough into 12 pieces; roll each into a ball and place on prepared baking sheet.

Gently roll and stretch dough into a 16-inch rope. With a sharp knife, divide dough into 16 pieces; roll each into a ball and place on prepared baking sheet.

3.   Cover and let rise in a warm oven 30 to 45 minutes until doubled in size. (Hint: To warm oven slightly, turn oven on Warm setting for 1 minute, then turn it off, and place covered dough in oven to rise. Remove pan from oven before preheating.)

4.   Preheat oven to 375°F. Bake for 12 to 15 minutes until golden-brown.

5.   Remove from oven and cool on wire racks.

TOPPING

	SMALL	MEDIUM	LARGE
CONFECTIONERS' SUGAR	½ cup	½ cup	1 cup
LEMON OR ORANGE JUICE	1 to 2 teaspoons	1 to 2 teaspoons	3 to 4 teaspoons

6.   When the buns are cool, combine the topping ingredients to form a rather firm paste. Spoon into a pastry tube or a plastic bag, snip the corner, and squeeze out the topping to form crosses on each bun.

CREATIVE SUGGESTIONS:

1.   Substitute finely diced dried fruits such as apricots for the candied orange peel.

2.   Substitute grated lemon or orange peel for the candied orange peel.

3.   Substitute milk or water for the lemon juice in the topping. You can also add ¼ teaspoon almond or vanilla extract.

4.   Instead of piping the topping, snip crosses into the buns with sharp scissors about 10 minutes before baking.

5.   Glaze the buns before baking with a mixture of 1 egg mixed with 1 tablespoon water.

6.   For a sugar glaze, boil 3 tablespoons milk and 3 tablespoons sugar in a small saucepan. Brush glaze on buns just before baking.

Small recipe yields 8 buns
Medium recipe yields 12 buns
Large recipe yields 16 buns

BAKE CYCLE: Dough

NUTRITIONAL INFORMATION PER BUN
Calories 176/Fat 3.4 grams/Carbohydrates 31.8 grams/Protein 4.5 grams/Fiber 1.2 grams/Sodium 140 milligrams/Cholesterol 35.7 milligrams

Joan's Italian Panettone

*J*oan *Stewart, Linda's supervisor, good naturedly agreed to test this bread time and time again until her Italian tastebuds pronounced it close enough to the real thing to be acceptable. True panettone is much drier than this bread, a texture that is difficult to achieve in the bread machine, but pop a slice of this exquisite bread in your toaster and you'll sweeten your home with the fragrance of anise every morning. Bellissimo!*

	SMALL LOAF	MEDIUM LOAF	LARGE LOAF
WATER	3/8 to 1/2 cup	7/8 to 1 cup	1 to 1 1/8 cups
EGGS	1	1	2
ANISE EXTRACT	1 teaspoon	1 1/2 teaspoons	2 teaspoons
RUM EXTRACT	1 teaspoon	1 1/2 teaspoons	2 teaspoons
VANILLA EXTRACT	2 teaspoons	1 tablespoon	4 teaspoons
UNSALTED BUTTER	1 tablespoon	1 1/2 tablespoons	2 tablespoons
SUGAR	2 tablespoons	3 tablespoons	1/4 cup
SALT	1/2 teaspoon	3/4 teaspoon	1 teaspoon
BREAD FLOUR	2 cups	3 cups	4 cups
NONFAT DRY MILK POWDER	2 tablespoons	3 tablespoons	1/4 cup
ANISE SEEDS	1 teaspoon	1 1/2 teaspoons	2 teaspoons
RED STAR BRAND ACTIVE DRY YEAST	2 teaspoons	3 teaspoons	4 teaspoons
COARSELY CHOPPED PINE NUTS	2 tablespoons	3 tablespoons	1/4 cup
GOLDEN RAISINS	2 tablespoons	3 tablespoons	1/4 cup
CANDIED CITRON	2 tablespoons	3 tablespoons	1/4 cup
CANDIED ORANGE PEEL SEE RECIPE, PAGE 247)	2 tablespoons	3 tablespoons	1/4 cup
BREAD FLOUR	2 teaspoons	1 tablespoon	4 teaspoons

1. Place ingredients in bread pan, except nuts, raisins, citron, candied orange peel, and additional bread flour, using the least amount of liquid listed in the recipe. Select Light Crust setting and Raisin/Nut cycle. Press Start.

2. Observe the dough as it kneads. After 5 to 10 minutes, if it appears dry and stiff or if your machine sounds as if it's straining to knead it, add more liquid 1 tablespoon at a time until dough forms a smooth, soft, pliable ball that is slightly tacky to the touch.

3. In a small bowl, toss together the nuts, raisins, candied fruits, and additional bread flour. Add to the bread pan at the beep.

4. After the baking cycle ends, remove bread from pan, place on cake rack, and allow to cool 1 hour before slicing.

CREATIVE SUGGESTIONS:

1. Substitute dried cranberries for the raisins.

2. Once the loaf has cooled, frost the top with an icing made of ½ cup confectioners' sugar, 1 to 2 teaspoons milk, and ¼ teaspoon vanilla or rum extract.

CRUST: Light
BAKE CYCLE: Raisin/Nut
OPTIONAL BAKE CYCLES: Standard/Whole Wheat/Sweet Bread/Rapid Bake

---

NUTRITIONAL INFORMATION PER SLICE
Calories 181/Fat 4.8 grams/Carbohydrates 30.8 grams/Protein 4 grams/Fiber 1.4 grams/Sodium 126 milligrams/Cholesterol 26.5 milligrams

---

Julekage

Thisisthebread served in Norwegian homes during the Christmas holidays.
Bring a little bit of Norway into your home next yuletide by baking a loaf of
this delicious bread. (In some machines this baked up too light. Switch to the
Medium Crust setting if necessary.)

	SMALL	MEDIUM	LARGE
MILK	⅝ to ¾ cup	1 to 1⅛ cups	1⅛ to 1¼ cups
EGGS	1	1	2
SHORTENING	1½ tablespoons	2 tablespoons	3 tablespoons
SUGAR	3 tablespoons	¼ cup	6 tablespoons
SALT	½ teaspoon	½ teaspoon	1 teaspoon
BREAD FLOUR	2 cups	3 cups	4 cups
GROUND CARDAMOM	½ teaspoon	½ teaspoon	1 teaspoon
RED STAR BRAND ACTIVE DRY YEAST	1½ teaspoons	2 teaspoons	2½ teaspoons
MIXED CANDIED FRUIT	⅓ cup	½ cup	⅔ cup
RAISINS	3 tablespoons	¼ cup	6 tablespoons

1.   Place all ingredients in bread pan except the candied fruit and raisins, using the
least amount of liquid listed in the recipe. Select Light Crust setting and Raisin/Nut
cycle. Press Start.

2.   Observe the dough as it kneads. After 5 to 10 minutes, if it appears dry and stiff
or if your machine sounds as if it's straining to knead it, add more liquid 1 tablespoon at a time until dough forms a smooth, soft, pliable ball that is slightly tacky to
the touch.

3.   At the beep, add the fruit and raisins.

4.   After the baking cycle ends, remove bread from pan, place on cake rack, and
allow to cool 1 hour before slicing.

CREATIVE SUGGESTION: For a festive touch, spread a confectioners' sugar icing
over the top of this loaf and decorate with some candied fruits or colored sugar
sprinkles. To make this icing, combine ½ cup confectioners' sugar, 1 teaspoon milk,
and ½ teaspoon vanilla extract.

CRUST: Light

BAKE CYCLE: Raisin/Nut

OPTIONAL BAKE CYCLES: Standard/Whole Wheat/Sweet Bread

NUTRITIONAL INFORMATION PER SLICE

Calories 149/Fat 2.6 grams/Carbohydrates 27 grams/Protein 4 grams/Fiber 1 gram/Sodium 90.4 milligrams/Cholesterol 15.9 milligrams

Swedish Cardamom Wreath

This eye-catching holiday treat looks and sounds harder to assemble than it really is. Your friends and family will be impressed with your efforts and will thank you for days.

DOUGH

	SMALL	MEDIUM	LARGE
MILK	½ cup	¾ cup	¾ cup
EGGS	1	1	2
HONEY	3 tablespoons	¼ cup	6 tablespoons
BUTTER OR MARGARINE	3 tablespoons	¼ cup	6 tablespoons
SALT	¼ teaspoon	¼ teaspoon	½ teaspoon
ALL-PURPOSE FLOUR	2 cups	3 cups	4 cups
GROUND CARDAMOM	¼ teaspoon	½ teaspoon	½ teaspoon
RED STAR BRAND ACTIVE DRY YEAST	1½ teaspoons	2 teaspoons	2½ teaspoons

I. Place dough ingredients in bread pan, select Dough setting, and press Start.

FILLING

	SMALL	MEDIUM	LARGE
BLANCHED ALMONDS (SEE NOTE)	1⅓ cups (5 ounces)	2 cups (8 ounces)	2⅔ cups (10 ounces)
BROWN SUGAR	⅓ cup	½ cup	⅔ cup
BUTTER OR MARGARINE, SOFTENED	¼ cup	6 tablespoons	½ cup
ALL-PURPOSE FLOUR	2 teaspoons	1 tablespoon	4 teaspoons
EGGS	1	1	2
ALMOND EXTRACT	½ teaspoon	¾ teaspoons	1 teaspoon

2. Place the almonds and sugar for the filling into a food processor and process until finely ground. Add the butter, flour, egg(s), and almond extract. Process until combined into a smooth paste.

3. When the dough has risen long enough, the machine will beep. Turn off bread machine, remove bread pan, and turn out dough onto a lightly floured countertop or cutting board.

4. Grease a large baking sheet. You'll need 2 for the Large recipe.

FOR THE SMALL RECIPE
With a rolling pin, roll dough into a 12×9-inch rectangle.

FOR THE MEDIUM RECIPE
With a rolling pin, roll dough into a 16×9-inch rectangle.

FOR THE LARGE RECIPE
With a rolling pin, roll dough into two 12×9-inch rectangles.

5. Spread dough with filling mixture to within 1 inch of the long edges. Starting with the long edge, roll up the dough; pinch long edge to seal. Place dough on prepared baking sheet(s), sealed-edge down. Shape dough into a circle. Join ends and pinch to seal. With a sharp knife, dough scraper, or scissors, cut two-thirds of the way through the dough at 1-inch intervals. Twist each segment onto its side.

6. Cover and let rise in a warm oven 30 to 45 minutes until doubled in size. (Hint: To warm oven slightly, turn oven on Warm setting for 1 minute, then turn it off, and place covered dough in oven to rise. Remove pan from oven before preheating.)

7. Preheat oven to 350°F. Bake for 15 to 20 minutes until golden-brown.

ICING

	SMALL	MEDIUM	LARGE
CONFECTIONERS' SUGAR	¾ cup	1 cup	1½ cups
MILK	1 tablespoon	1½ tablespoons	2 tablespoons
ALMOND EXTRACT	⅛ teaspoon	⅛ teaspoon	¼ teaspoon

GARNISH

RED AND GREEN CANDIED CHERRIES, CUT TO RESEMBLE FLOWERS OR HOLLY BERRIES AND LEAVES

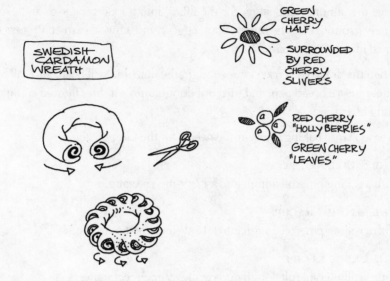

8. Remove from oven and cool on wire rack(s). When cool, drizzle with icing and decorate with 3 flowers or 3 groups of holly berries and leaves made from cut-up candied red and green cherries. To create flowers, cut green cherry in half. Place it on the wreath. Cut slivers of red cherries and place around green cherry in a daisy-like pattern. Repeat twice more. To create holly berries, place 3 red half-cherries in a group. Cut 3 slivers of green cherries and place around red cherries to resemble leaves. Repeat twice more.

Small recipe yields 1 wreath
Medium recipe yields 1 wreath
Large recipe yields 2 wreaths

NOTE: To blanch whole almonds, cover with boiling water for 4 to 5 minutes, drain, and rinse with cold water. Squeeze skins off almonds.

BAKE CYCLE: Dough

NUTRITIONAL INFORMATION PER SERVING
Calories 258/Fat 13.2 grams/Carbohydrates 30.5 grams/Protein 6.1 grams/Fiber 2.2 grams/Sodium 120 milligrams/Cholesterol 26.3 milligrams

---

13
Odds and Ends

ALMOND NUT BUTTER

With an electric mixer or in a food processor, cream together ½ cup softened butter, 1 tablespoon chopped toasted almonds, and ½ teaspoon almond extract.

APRICOT BUTTER

Soften ¼ cup dried apricots in simmering water to cover for 20 minutes. Remove from heat, drain well, and finely chop. In a food processor, cream together ½ cup softened butter, apricots, and ¼ cup apricot preserves.

CHEESE HERB BUTTER

With an electric mixer or in a food processor, mix together ¼ cup freshly grated Parmesan cheese and 2 tablespoons fresh herbs such as basil, oregano, thyme, rosemary, or dill. Add ½ cup softened butter and mix or process until well blended.

Variations:
- Substitute 2 teaspoons dried herbs for the fresh.
- Add 2 cloves minced garlic and ½ teaspoon freshly ground black pepper.
- Add 2 tablespoons minced onion.

CRANBERRY BUTTER

In a food processor, cream together ½ cup softened butter, ¼ cup dried finely chopped cranberries, 2 teaspoons grated orange peel, and 2 tablespoons confectioners' sugar.

Variation:
- Add 2 tablespoons chopped walnuts.

HONEY BUTTER

With an electric mixer or in a food processor, cream together ½ cup softened butter and ½ cup honey.

Variation:
- Add 2 tablespoons chopped pecans.

LEMON BUTTER

With an electric mixer or in a food processor, cream together ½ cup softened butter, 1 tablespoon fresh lemon juice, and 2 teaspoons grated lemon peel.

Maple Butter

With an electric mixer or in a food processor, cream together ½ cup softened butter, ½ cup maple syrup, and ½ teaspoon maple extract.

Mustard Butter

With an electric mixer or in a food processor, cream together ½ cup softened butter and ¼ cup Dijon mustard.

Nut Butter

In a food processor or blender, cream together 1 cup roasted peanuts, pecans, hazelnuts, or cashews and 1½ teaspoons oil until they form a smooth butter.

Variations:

- Add ¼ cup honey for honey nut butter.
- Add ¼ cup maple syrup for maple nut butter.

Kalamata Olive Spread

Place 2 cups of pitted, ripe black olives (preferably Kalamata) and 1 large garlic clove in a food processor and process until finely chopped. Pour into a bowl and stir in 3 tablespoons olive oil until well blended.

Orange Butter

With an electric mixer or in a food processor, cream together ½ cup softened butter and ½ cup orange marmalade.

Parsley Butter

With an electric mixer or in a food processor, cream together ½ cup softened butter, ¼ cup chopped fresh parsley, 1 teaspoon grated lemon peel, and 1 clove minced garlic.

Peach Butter

In a food processor, cream together ½ cup softened butter, ¾ cup peach preserves, ½ teaspoon almond extract, and ⅛ teaspoon nutmeg.

Pesto and Sun-Dried Tomato Spread

With an electric mixer or in a food processor, cream together ½ cup softened butter, 2 tablespoons prepared pesto, and 2 tablespoons chopped sun-dried tomatoes.

Variations:
- Add ½ cup freshly grated Parmesan cheese.
- Substitute 4 ounces of softened cream cheese for the butter.

Praline Butter

We have the great bakers at Toastmaster to thank for this one. It's even better when you use fresh butter made in their Bread and Butter Machine!

With an electric mixer or in a food processor, cream together ½ cup softened butter, 2 tablespoons finely chopped pecans, 2 tablespoons brown sugar, ¼ teaspoon vanilla, and ⅛ teaspoon maple extract.

Rum Butter

With an electric mixer or in a food processor, cream together ½ cup softened butter, 3 tablespoons brown sugar, and 2 tablespoons rum or ½ teaspoon rum extract.

Sesame Butter

With an electric mixer or in a food processor, cream together ½ cup softened butter and 2 tablespoons toasted sesame seeds.

Strawberry Butter

With an electric mixer or in a food processor, cream together ½ cup softened butter and ½ cup strawberry preserves.

Vegetable Herb Spread

In a food processor, cream together 8 ounces softened cream cheese, 2 tablespoons chopped onion, 2 tablespoons chopped carrots, 2 tablespoons chopped celery, 2 tablespoons chopped radishes, ½ teaspoon dried dill, and salt and freshly ground black pepper to taste.

Variation:
- You can substitute any vegetable or herb of choice.

246

Candied Orange Peel

If you've ever wanted to make Panettone in July but couldn't find the candied orange peel, here's a simple recipe to the rescue.

ORANGES	6
WATER	¼ cup
SUGAR	½ cup
EXTRA SUGAR FOR COATING	

1. With a vegetable peeler, peel the outer skin of about 6 oranges into thin strips until you have about 1 cup of orange peel. Cut away any of the white pith underneath; it has a bitter flavor.

2. Place the peel in a heavy saucepan and cover with water. Bring to a boil, then reduce the heat and simmer for 5 minutes. Drain and repeat this process 2 or 3 more times to reduce the bitterness.

3. Rinse out the saucepan then add ¼ cup water, ½ cup sugar, and the orange peel. Heat to boiling and boil until the liquid is completely absorbed and the peels are translucent, about 15 minutes.

4. Place peel in a deep bowl and sprinkle with sugar. Toss until well coated.

5. Place on a rack overnight to dry thoroughly. Store in an airtight container.

Yields about ¾ cup

Cinnamon Crunchies

Y ou'll never have a problem with leftover bread if you turn it into cinnamon crunchies. We like to store these little bite-size pieces of cinnamon toast in a pretty glass jar on the kitchen counter. They're super as an afternoon snack or a quick eat-on-the-run breakfast treat. They also team up well for dessert with a piece of fresh fruit or a bowl of ice cream. By the way, if you store them in an easy-to-reach jar, you might want to add the label "Beware—Addictive" to it.

LEFTOVER WHITE, WHOLE GRAIN, OR SWEET BREAD	6 cups
BUTTER OR MARGARINE, MELTED	½ cup
SUGAR	¾ cup
GROUND CINNAMON	1½ tablespoons

1. Preheat oven to 375°F.

2. Remove crusts from bread and cut into ½-inch cubes. Place bread cubes in a large bowl; drizzle with the melted butter, tossing to coat well. In a small bowl, combine the sugar and cinnamon. Sprinkle the cinnamon mixture over the bread cubes in the bowl, tossing to coat evenly.

3. Place on a rimmed baking sheet. Bake for 15 to 20 minutes, stirring occasionally.

4. Remove from oven and allow to cool completely in pan before storing in an airtight container.

NUTRITIONAL INFORMATION PER ½ CUP SERVING
Calories 123/Fat 6.1 grams/Carbohydrates 17.2 grams/Protein .8 grams/Fiber .4 grams/Sodium 137 milligrams/Cholesterol 0 milligrams

---

Croutons

Here's one of our favorite ways to use up those leftover slices of bread.

LEFTOVER BREAD	6 cups
OLIVE OIL	3 to 4 tablespoons
ITALIAN HERBS	1 tablespoon

1. Preheat oven to 425°F.

2. Cut bread into ½-inch cubes. Place bread in a large bowl; drizzle with olive oil. Sprinkle on herbs and toss to coat.

3. Place on a rimmed baking sheet. Bake for 8 to 10 minutes, stirring occasionally.

4. Store indefinitely in an airtight container.

CREATIVE SUGGESTIONS:

1. If you prefer to trim the crusts from your bread first, use a pizza cutter to make a quick job of it.

2. Add 1 clove garlic cut in half and ⅛ teaspoon crushed red pepper flakes to the olive oil. Heat in a small saucepan, cool, strain, and pour over the bread cubes. Proceed as directed from Step 3.

3. You can also sprinkle ¼ cup freshly grated Parmesan cheese over the bread cubes.

NUTRITIONAL INFORMATION PER ½ CUP SERVING
Calories 52/Fat 3.7 grams/Carbohydrates 4.3 grams/Protein .7 grams/Fiber .2 grams/Sodium 43 milligrams/Cholesterol 0 milligrams

Dog Biscuits

*T*here are some very spoiled dogs by the names of Briscoe, Missy, Susie, Shadow, and Misty who insist on these treats regularly. Thankfully, we're not the only ones this loony about our pets because several specialty cookware stores now carry assorted sizes of dog bone–shaped cookie cutters!

	SMALL	MEDIUM	LARGE
BEEF, CHICKEN, OR VEGETABLE BROTH	½ cup	1⅛ cups	1⅛ cups
EGGS	1	1	2
OIL	2 tablespoons	3 tablespoons	¼ cup
MOLASSES	1 tablespoon	1½ tablespoons	2 tablespoons
ALL-PURPOSE FLOUR	¾ cup	1¼ cups	1½ cups
WHOLE WHEAT FLOUR	¾ cup	1¼ cups	1½ cups
BULGUR	2 tablespoons	3 tablespoons	¼ cup
CORNMEAL	2 tablespoons	¼ cup	¼ cup
MILLER'S BRAN	2 tablespoons	3 tablespoons	¼ cup
WHEAT GERM	2 tablespoons	3 tablespoons	¼ cup
BREWER'S YEAST	2 tablespoons	3 tablespoons	¼ cup
NONFAT DRY MILK POWDER	2 tablespoons	3 tablespoons	4 tablespoons
GARLIC POWDER	⅛ teaspoon	⅛ teaspoon	¼ teaspoon
RED STAR BRAND ACTIVE DRY YEAST	1½ teaspoons	1½ teaspoons	2 teaspoons

1. Place dough ingredients in bread pan, select Dough setting, and press Start.

2. At the beep, turn off bread machine, remove bread pan, and turn out dough onto a lightly floured countertop or cutting board.

3. Roll out dough to ¼ inch thickness. Using small cookie cutters, cut dough into desired shapes. Place on ungreased baking sheets. Continue to reroll the excess dough and cut more biscuits until all the dough is used.

4. Preheat oven to 350°F. Bake for 20 to 25 minutes and cool on wire rack. For crisper biscuits, turn off oven, remove biscuits from oven for 30 minutes, then return to still-warm oven for 3 hours or overnight.

5. Store in an airtight container.

Small recipe yields about two dozen
Medium recipe yields about three dozen
Large recipe yields about four dozen

BAKE CYCLE: Dough

NUTRITIONAL INFORMATION PER BISCUIT
Calories 28/Fat .7 grams/Carbohydrates 4.5 grams/Protein 1 gram/Fiber .6 grams/Sodium 13 milligrams/Cholesterol 3 milligrams

---

Italian Bread Salad

*W*e included a recipe for bread soup (see page 255), so it seems only natural we should come up with a recipe for bread salad, too!

SALAD

CRUSTY ITALIAN OR FRENCH BREAD	8 cups
MIXED GREENS, WASHED AND DRIED	2 cups
RIPE PLUM TOMATOES, DICED	6
SEEDED AND CHOPPED CUCUMBER (OPTIONAL)	½ cup
CHOPPED FRESH BASIL	¼ cup
CHOPPED RED ONION	½ cup
FRESHLY GRATED PARMESAN CHEESE	¼ cup (1 ounce)

DRESSING

EXTRA-VIRGIN OLIVE OIL	6 tablespoons
BALSAMIC VINEGAR	3 tablespoons
STONE-GROUND MUSTARD	¼ teaspoon
LARGE CLOVE GARLIC, CRUSHED	1
SALT	½ teaspoon
FRESHLY GROUND BLACK PEPPER TO TASTE	

1. Tear bread into bite-sized pieces. Place bread cubes on broiler pan and toast in a 475°F oven for 5 minutes until golden-brown.

2. In a small bowl, whisk together the dressing ingredients.

3. In a wooden salad bowl rubbed with a cut clove of garlic, toss together all of the salad ingredients except cheese.

4. Drizzle some or all of the dressing over salad and toss to coat. Set aside for at least 15 minutes to allow bread to absorb the dressing.

5. Toss salad again, sprinkle grated Parmesan on top, and serve.

CREATIVE SUGGESTIONS:

1. You can turn this salad into a meal by adding 3 ounces of diced Italian salami, 3 ounces shredded mozzarella or provolone cheese instead of the Parmesan, and a 15-ounce can of drained garbanzo beans.

2. If you prefer a softer salad, drizzle with dressing and allow salad to stand at room temperature for as long as 1 hour.

Serves 6 to 8

NUTRITIONAL INFORMATION PER SERVING (⅛)
Calories 237/Fat 11.9 grams/Carbohydrates 27.4 grams/Protein 6.1 grams/Fiber 2.5 grams/Sodium 431 milligrams/Cholesterol 2.8 milligrams

---

Lemon Orange Curd

This marvelous spread is so easy to make that it's a shame to spend a small fortune on it in the stores. Serve this with a sweet bread and a plate of fresh fruit for a simple and yummy dessert.

UNSALTED BUTTER	½ cup
SUGAR	1 cup
EGGS	3
FINELY GRATED ZEST OF 1 ORANGE AND 2 LEMONS	
FRESH ORANGE JUICE	½ cup

1. In a microwave-proof bowl, melt butter on HIGH in the microwave for 1 to 2 minutes.

2. In another bowl, combine sugar, eggs, orange and lemon zests, and orange juice; blend with a wire whisk.

3. Slowly whisk in the hot melted butter.

4. Microwave on HIGH 3 to 4 minutes until thickened to a thin pudding consistency, whisking well after each minute.

5. Pour into a clean glass jar and store up to 2 weeks in the refrigerator or pour into sterilized jars and seal.

Yields about 2 cups

Ten Downing Street's Bread Soup

Here's a unique British recipe that comes from a once-popular San Diego restaurant called Ten Downing Street, which unfortunately closed its doors many years ago. The original recipe is quite high in fat, so we've followed it up with a much lighter version that we think is every bit as good. One word of caution: This is a very filling soup, a meal in itself. It's not suitable as a first course, but it sure makes the perfect meal for starving college students—it's cheap, easy to make, very filling, and feeds a gang.

CHICKEN BROTH	10 cups
GOOD LOAF OF BREAD (FRENCH OR ITALIAN)	1
LARGE ONION	1
LARGE CARROTS	2
PARSNIP	1
STALKS CELERY	2
WHITE TURNIP	1
BUTTER	½ cup
FLOUR	¾ cup
HEAVY CREAM	1 cup
MILK	1 cup
SALT AND PEPPER TO TASTE	

I.   Cut or tear the bread into large chunks; place in a large kettle. Add 8 cups of the broth; soak bread until it is very soft.

2.   Meanwhile, wash, peel, and cut the vegetables into small chunks and add to the kettle.

3.   Bring the mixture to a boil and then reduce the heat to low. Simmer for 20 to 30 minutes until the vegetables are tender, adding water if it seems too thick. Stir often as the mixture has a tendency to stick to the bottom of the pan.

4.   Puree the mixture in several batches in a blender or food processor or pass it through a sieve. Return the mixture to the kettle, add the last 2 cups of broth, and bring the mixture back to a boil.

5.   In a small saucepan, combine the butter and flour; cook lightly but do not brown. Add enough of this mixture to the soup to thicken it and give it the creamy texture desired.

6. Add the cream and milk. Season soup to taste with salt and pepper, but do not allow it to return to a boil once the cream has been added.

LOW FAT REVISIONS:

1. Replace the chicken broth with canned or homemade vegetable broth.

2. Omit the butter, flour, cream, and milk.

3. Once the vegetables are tender, puree the soup as directed. Return the mixture to the kettle, add the last 2 cups of broth, and bring to a boil. Serve.

Serves 10 to 12

NUTRITIONAL INFORMATION PER SERVING (¹/₁₂)

ORIGINAL RECIPE:
Calories 403/Fat 22.1 grams/Carbohydrates 38 grams/Protein 12.1 grams/Fiber 2.7 grams/ Sodium 1275 milligrams/Cholesterol 61.8 milligrams

REVISED RECIPE:
Calories 231/Fat 4.5 grams/Carbohydrates 37.4 grams/Protein 9.8 grams/Fiber 2.4 grams/ Sodium 1212 milligrams/Cholesterol 4.8 milligrams

---

Tomato Herb Bruschetta

*I*n the unlikely event that you have a leftover loaf of crusty French or Italian bread, here's one of the best ways to make it disappear. Serve these with a plate of spicy barbecued shrimp for an easy, light summer meal.

PLUM TOMATOES, HALVED, SEEDED, AND CHOPPED	1½ pounds
COARSELY CHOPPED BLACK OLIVES	¼ cup
CHOPPED FRESH BASIL	¼ cup
CHOPPED FRESH OREGANO	1 tablespoon
MINCED GARLIC	1 tablespoon
BALSAMIC VINEGAR	1 tablespoon
OLIVE OIL	1 tablespoon
SALT AND PEPPER TO TASTE	
CRUSTY FRENCH OR ITALIAN BREAD, TOASTED	6 slices

I. In a bowl, combine tomatoes, olives, basil, oregano, garlic, vinegar, and olive oil. Season to taste with salt and pepper. Let sit at room temperature for up to 3 hours to blend the flavors.

2. Mound some tomato mixture on each slice of toast and serve.

CREATIVE SUGGESTION:
Add as desired, sliced green onions, drained capers, fresh lemon juice, freshly grated Parmesan cheese, or crumbled goat cheese.

Serves 6

NUTRITIONAL INFORMATION PER SLICE
Calories 171/Fat 6.2 grams/Carbohydrates 25.1 grams/Protein 4.7 grams/Fiber 3.1 grams/Sodium 332 milligrams/Cholesterol 0 milligrams

Sources

INGREDIENTS

BOB'S RED MILL
Natural Foods, Inc.
5209 S.E. International Way
Milwaukie, OR 97222
1-800/553-2258

A wide variety of specialty grains, cereals, and flours including stone-ground whole wheat bread flour, wheat berries for hand grinding, lecithin, whey, diastatic malt, xanthan gum, and gluten-free flours. (Catalog)

ENER-G FOODS, INC.
P.O. Box 84487
Seattle, WA 98124-5787
1-800/331-5222 (outside WA)

Dietetic specialty foods such as soyquik (replaces instant nonfat dry milk), egg replacer, gluten-free flours, wheat-free and gluten-free bread machine mixes, methocel, xanthan gum, guar gum. (Catalog)

THE GLUTEN-FREE PANTRY
P.O. Box 840
Glastonbury, CT 06033-0840
1-860/633-3826
1-800/291-8386 (orders and catalog requests)
Web site: www.glutenfree.com

Gluten and wheat-free bread mixes for the bread machine and oven baking. Bread machines that work well with gluten-free flours. (Catalog)

JAFFE BROS.
P.O. Box 636-Z
Valley Center, CA 92082-0636
1-619/749-1133

Flours, grains, dried fruits, nuts, seeds, wheat and rye berries, hulled barley. (Catalog)

KING ARTHUR FLOUR
RR2, Box 56
Norwich, VT 05055
1-800/827-6836 (for orders)
1-800/777-4434 (for catalogs)

Various flours, including white whole wheat flour, diastatic malt, xanthan gum, gluten-free flours, plastic bread bags for large loaves and baguettes, caramel coloring for dark rye breads, Lora Brody's Sourdough Bread Enhancer, baking stones and peels, La Cloche, baguette pans, cookbooks. (Catalog)

LORA BRODY'S SOURDOUGH BREAD ENHANCER
Williams-Sonoma
1-800/541-2233

This powder gives a sourdough flavor to any bread.

MISS ROBEN'S DIETARY FOODS
P.O. Box 1434
Frederick, MD 21702
1-800/891-0083

Gluten-free bread mixes. (Catalog)

MONTANA FLOUR AND GRAINS
P.O. Box 517
Ft. Benton, MT 59442
1-406/622-5436

High-quality organic flour and grains. Call for information.

SOURDOUGHS INTERNATIONAL, INC.
P.O. Box 670
Cascade, ID 83611
1-208/382-4828
Web site:
www.cyberhighway.net/
~sourdo/

Sourdough cultures from places such as the Yukon, San Francisco, Russia, France, Austria, Egypt, Bahrain, and Saudi Arabia. They also publish a sourdough newsletter.

UNIVERSAL FOODS CORPORATION
433 East Michigan Street
P.O. Box 737
Milwaukee, WI 53201
1-800/445-4746

Red Star active dry yeast, quick rise yeast, instant yeast in bulk packages, dough conditioner, natural bread fortifier, vital gluten blend, flavor enhancer, quick bread baking powder.

WALNUT ACRES
Penns Creek, PA 17862
1-800/433-3998

Organic flours, grains, cereals, dried fruits, nuts, herbs, and spices. (Catalog)

WICKED GOOD GOURMET
Route 1, Box 402
Bradford, ME 04410
1-207/327-1453
1-800/478-6484 (Visa/MC orders)
Web site:
www.mainemarketplace.com/wgg (online orders)

Haute Stuff Seasoning Samplers for the bread machine, which include 7 days of recipes and seasoning packets such as Sweet Cecily and Orange, Herb, Rye, Lemon Poppyseed, Rosemary Raisin, Tomato Basil, and Vegetable Braid.

Equipment, Accessories, and Miscellaneous Items

APROPOS ENTERPRISES
10464 Clairemont Mesa Boulevard #217
San Diego, CA 92124
1-619/268-7887
Web site:
www.giftbagz.com

BakerBagz specialty gift bags for breads. Clear bags with festive designs for all occasions. Raffia ribbon included.

THE BREAD BAKER'S DIGEST
List owners: Jeff and Reggie Dwork
E-mail: reggie@reggie.com

This mailing list is for discussion and recipe exchange of hand- and machine-made breads. To subscribe, send a message to <bread-bakers-request@lists.best.com>. In the body put these two lines (lowercase, left justified):
subscribe
end

CHEF'S CATALOG
3215 Commercial Avenue
Northbrook, IL 60062-1900
1-800/338-3232

Professional restaurant equipment for the home chef, bread machines, French bread pans, kitchen towels, knives, necklace timer. (Catalog)

DAK GOURMET PRODUCTS
Coast to Coast Distribution
1711 Irvine Ave.
Newport Beach, CA 92660
1-888/921-9557

Replacement parts for DAK bread machines, gourmet kitchen items. (Catalog)

DELTA REHABILITATION, INC.
411 Bryn Mawr Island
Bradenton, FL 34207
Contact: Irwin Franzel

Zojirushi bread machine, the Miracle Mill electric grain mill, replacement parts for Zojirushi machines, SAF instant yeast.

K-TEC
420 North Geneva Road
Lindon, UT 84042
1-800/748-5400
Web site: www.k-tecusa.com

Bread mixes, grain mills, and baking supplies.

MILES KIMBALL
41 West Eighth Avenue
Oshkosh, WI 54906-0002

Personalized paper bread bags and expandable plastic bread boxes. (Catalog)

WANDA'S NATURE FARM FOODS
850 NBC Center
Lincoln, NE 68508
1-800/222-FARM
E-mail: naturefarm@aol.com

Expandable bread boxes, bread machine mixes, including pizza, focaccia, bagel, and pretzel mixes. (Catalog)

Index

264

You can obtain additional copies of this book, or the authors' best-selling cookbooks *Bread Machine Magic* and *The Bread Machine Magic Book of Helpful Hints, Revised and Updated,* at your local bookseller, or by using the coupon below.

ORDER FORM

Please send me the following books:

_____ copies of *More Bread Machine Magic*
(ISBN 0-312-16935-3 $11.95)

_____ copies of *The Bread Machine Magic Book of Helpful Hints,
Revised and Updated*
(ISBN 0-312-13444-4 $11.95)

_____ copies of *Bread Machine Magic*
(ISBN 0-312-06914-6 $11.95)

Enclosed is a check or money order, payable to Publishers Book & Audio, in the amount of $ _____ (please include shipping and handling charges of $3.00 for the first book, and $1.00 for each additional book).

Send books to: Name _____

Address_____

_____

_____

Send this coupon and your payment to: Publishers Book & Audio, P.O. Box 070059, Staten Island, NY 10307. Please allow four to six weeks for delivery.

 For bulk orders (10 or more copies), contact St. Martin's Press, Special Markets Division, 175 Fifth Avenue, New York, NY 10010. Or call, toll free, 1-800/221-7945, extension #645, 636, 628, or 662.